AGENT
TECHNOLOGY
HANDBOOK

THE McGRAW-HILL SERIES ON COMPUTER COMMUNICATIONS (SELECTED TITLES)

To order or receive additional information on these or any other McGraw-Hill titles, in the United States please call 1-800-722-4726. In other countries, contact your local McGraw-Hill representative

Agent Technology Handbook

Dimitris N. Chorafas

McGraw-Hill
New York   San Francisco   Washington, D.C.   Auckland   Bogotá
Caracas   Lisbon   London   Madrid   Mexico City   Milan
Montreal   New Delhi   San Juan   Singapore
Sydney   Tokyo   Toronto

Cataloging-in-Publication Data

N.

ogy handbook / Dimitris N. Chorafas.

Includes index.
ISBN 0-07-011923-6
1. Intelligent agents (Computer software) Handbooks, manuals, etc.
I. Title.
QA76.76.I58C48   1998
006.3'3—dc21   97-15385
                                                                      CIP

McGraw-Hill

A Division of The **McGraw·Hill** Companies

ISBN 0-07-011923-6

*The sponsoring editor for this book was Steven Elliot, the editing supervisor was Paul R.
Sobel, and the production supervisor was Tina Cameron. It was set in Vendome by
Priscilla Beer of McGraw-Hill's Professional Book Group composition unit.*

Printed and bound by Quebecor/Fairfield.

McGraw-Hill books are available at special quantity discounts to use as premi-
ums and sales promotions, or for use in corporate training programs. For more
information, please write to the Director of Special Sales, McGraw-Hill, 11 West
19th Street, New York, NY 10011. Or contact your local bookstore.

*This book is printed on recycled, acid-free paper containing a minimum of
50% recycled de-inked fiber.*

To dean A. R. Frank Wazzan
and the memory of the late
dean L. M. K. Boelter

CONTENTS

Part 2   AGENTS IN NETWORKS, MOBILE
COMPUTING, SECURITY, RELIABILITY,
AND DIAGNOSTICS

Contents

Contents

PREFACE

One of the first concepts taught in a school of journalism is a working definition of *news*. An airplane's taking off and landing on schedule is not news. By contrast, an airplane that explodes after takeoff because of an act of terrorism is *breaking news*, the development of *agents* has not been breaking news yet—but they are making significant inroads with business applications, particularly in telecommunications.

Like all books aiming to provide readers with a competitive edge, this text is written for people who want to be leaders in information technology. Its focus on *agents* is motivated by the fact that their usage increases the performance gap between organizations that know *how to use* information systems effectively and those that don't. Companies that fall behind do so for one of the following reasons:

- They lack appropriate human capital.
- Their culture does not permit them to get off the beaten path.

Precisely for this reason, the target of this book is business professionals: From systems administrators to network specialists and software developers. While telecommunications has been chosen as the implementation area, the text is aimed at all practitioners who want to develop new software paradigms required for advanced applications.

As the careful reader will discover, this book presupposes no knowledge of mathematics or programming practices. Its first objective is that of defining the fundamentals of new information technology. Then it moves quickly to the practical use of agents for real-life problems.

Existing theory is presented to the extent needed to understand the operation and performance of knowledge artifacts and to describe their context. But the main theme is the implementation of agents in a fast-growing information landscape. During the course of this book the reader is prompted to bring up real problems from his or her own work—and more precisely, problems that he or she wishes to solve through novel approaches.

Since technology is now such a basic ingredient of everyday life—not to mention that it serves as the nervous system of any company seeking success in the marketplace—the knowledge and appreciation of the latest technological developments is a "must." Based on these premises, this book addresses in a comprehensive and comprehensible manner three of the key issues in information technology:

- The growing use of interactive agents
- The advantages agents provide in computer applications
- The architectural challenges agents can present and engender

Typically, the reader of this book will be the person who feels the need to update his or her skills and knowhow, and thereby to be a leader in his or her field. But, by its very nature, technological leadership is ephemeral, and this is true not only for persons and companies; it is also true for nations.

At one point in their histories, all the great civilizations—China, Egypt, Greece, and Rome, as well as Britain, France, Germany, Japan, and America—have held the contemporary state of the art in their hands. Always, their worst enemies have been misunderstanding, miscommunication, and inertia. Also a superiority complex has plagued them: "This was not invented here, so it can't be any good."

To survive in the fiercely competitive market that characterizes the global economy, we must always be ready to learn from others. We should never be satisfied with anything but the best. That is why this book is based on worldwide research, bringing to the reader's attention the best solutions and case studies.

The foregoing principles guided the effort leading to the text the reader has in his or her hands. This textbook is divided into three parts, and a total of 13 chapters.

Part 1 focuses on the concepts underpinning the development and practical implementation of *agents*. These intelligent artifacts can be seen as the new generation of expert systems—which are relatively *autonomous* and able to operate interactively from wherever they reside, in workstations, servers, and communications nodes.

The case of the new software paradigm is presented in a convincing manner in Chap. 1. A great deal is demonstrated by means of an advanced research and development project, the "Things That Think" project by the Media Laboratory of the Massachusetts Institute of Technology—and also through the ideas of Alan Kay, John von Neumann, and Alan Turing.

Chapter 2 looks at agents from a different viewpoint: the facts and opportunities they present in connection to knowledge workers. It covers virtual engineering and focuses on a major implementation example: the Mondrian project at MIT. It also examines the practical aspects of the new metaphors, particularly those related to human interfaces.

Following on the steps of these practical examples, the approach taken by Chap. 3 is more generic. The goal is to examine ways and means currently in use for exploiting intelligence and expertise. First, the notion of intelligence is defined: then its impact is analyzed all the way to deciding on the right kind of predicates to be used.

Chapter 4 is practical, providing the reader with what he or she needs to appreciate about the Knowledge Query and Manipulation Language (KQML) and Telescript. It also advises on how to morph expert systems into agents, offering examples as well as outlining the reasons underpinning this transformation.

It has been a deliberate choice in the design of this book to split the more theoretically oriented chapters into two parts and between them to insert a golden horde of practical examples on agents' implementation.

Telecommunications has been chosen as the applications landscape because:

■ It is the fastest-growing field where agents are put to use.

■ It is the most promising implementation domain for the coming years.

The use of agents in networks, mobile computing, security, reliability, and diagnostics is the theme of Part 2. Chapter 5 looks at agents as the new catalyst of telecommunications solutions. The pioneering restructuring of ISO's Open Systems Interconnection (OSI) cannot be done without agents—as the reader will see in this chapter through practical examples.

The use of agents in connection to security is the point of attention of Chap. 6. Examples are taken from the Internet as well as from other public networks and from private communications solutions. Emphasis is placed on mission-critical applications as well as on nonlinear, nontraditional approaches to security.

Because most of the important projects being developed today involve software-hardware codesign, the role of agents in this domain is considered in detail in Chap. 7. One of the subjects that are examined is the support that the Internet Protocol, version 6 (IPv6), can give to security. Another topic included in this chapter is the impact of competitive access providers to the international telecommunications market.

Chapter 8 addresses agents in connection with network reliability, diagnostics, and maintenance. Here again, the emphasis is on practical applications: the benefits agents provide through the exploitation of the intelligence they possess, the fact that they act as vehicles for other functions, and their ability to communicate with other agents and with end users, thereby enhancing system dependability.

Agents represent the true automation of programming products. This is the theme of Part 3. The five chapters of this part examining how the reader can develop his or her own agents, the concepts that will assist him or her in this effort, the more attractive domains regarding business applications, and what he or she must consider to maximize the effect of his or her investment.

Chapter 9 explains through practical examples and quotations the culture that is necessary in developing agents. "The informaiton revolution has changed our perception of wealth. We originally said that land was wealth. Then we thought it was industrial production. Now we realize it's intellectual capital," suggests Walter Wriston, former CEO of Citibank.

Returning to the fundamentals, Chap. 10 focuses on the support to mission-critical applications provided by intelligent software. It considers organizational issues, mathematical notions, and applications requirements. It also explains how and why the knowledge artifacts must be proactive. Marketing operations are taken as an implementation example.

Chapter 11 elaborates on the concepts that enter into the development and use of autonomous agents, demonstrating how they can be used to shrink time-to-market requirements. Examples are taken from a banking environment, specifically loans and investment advice, and merchandizing. Another case study looks at the use of agents in personal communications.

Chapter 12 summarizes the agent story, and at the same time it introduces some other applications in which the use of agents can be of service, such as further uses of morphism and patterning. One of the applications examples is telemedicine; another is value analysis. Chapter 11 also addresses the issues associated with the productization of agents.

The issues connected to a business architecture that can accommodate and make good use of agents and multiagents are the theme of Chap. 12. This text covers primitives and facilitators for the Internet and intranet solutions, reviews the role of Uniform Resource Locators (URLs), and takes the year 2000 and European Monetary Unit (EMU) problems as practical examples of a domain where agent technology can be quite helpful.

Professionals, companies, and nations that over the years declined in their standing did so because they allowed their technological advantage to wither away. As their competitive position slipped from leadership in research, development, and implementation (RD&I), they also surrendered other forms of leadership: Professionals lost their employment, companies dropped behind their competition, and nations were no longer the world players that they used to be.

While high technology will not necessarily guarantee success, lack of it is the best prescription for failure. This is a factual statement, documented through many examples from manufacturing, merchandizing, and banking—as well as from very competitive interdisciplinary sectors such as telecommunications.

This book is intended for anyone who is interested in the use of advanced technology in his or her daily business. Readership includes engineers, managers, marketing people, computer scientists, and those interested in planning, designing, and operating networks.

The book is also addressed to science students and students in information technology. The 13 chapters this book contains provide a preview of the direction software technology will be taking in the next few years.

Let me close by expressing my appreciation to everyone who contributed to the research, and therefore to making this book successful. A complete list of companies, senior executives, and computer specialists is found in the acknowledgments. Particular mention should be made of the advice by Anthony J. Zawilski for his many useful suggestions in restructuring this text, and of the assistance provided by Ulrich Rimensberger in connection to KQML and the Year 2000 Problem. I am indebted to John Wyzalek and Steven Elliot for having seen this book through production, to Paul Sobel for supervising the editing work, and to Eva-Maria Binder for the artwork, the typing of the manuscript, and the index.

DR. DIMITRIS N. CHORAFAS

ACKNOWLEDGMENTS

The following organizations, their senior executives and system specialists, participated in the recent research projects which led to the contents of the present book and its documentation.

United States

FEDERAL RESERVE BANK OF BOSTON

- William N. McDONOUGH, Executive Vice President—Legal
- Richard KOPCKE, Vice President and Economist
- Peter FORTUNE, Senior Economist
- George ALEXAKOS, Examiner
- Katerina SIMONS, Economist
- Joanna STAVINS, Economist
- Jane KATZ, Editor, Regional Review

  600 Atlantic Avenue, Boston, MA 02106-2976

SEATTLE BRANCH, FEDERAL RESERVE BANK OF SAN FRANCISCO

- Jimmy F. KAMADA, Assistant Vice President
- Gale P. ANSELL, Assistant Vice President, Business Development

  1015 2nd Avenue, Seattle, WA 98122-3567

FEDERAL RESERVE BANK OF SAN FRANCISCO

- Matthew FOSS, Manager, Capital Markets

■ Nigel OGILVIE, Banking Supervision and Regulation

101 Market Street, San Francisco, CA 94120 (Teleconferencing from the Seattle Branch of the Federal Reserve Bank of San Francisco)

STATE STREET BANK AND TRUST

■ James J. DARR, Executive Vice President, U.S. Financial Assets Services

225 Franklin Street, Boston, MA 02105-1992

BANKERS TRUST

■ Dr. Carmine VONA, Executive Vice President for Worldwide Technology
■ Shalom BRINSY, Senior Vice President Distributed Networks
■ Dan W. MUECKE, Vice President, Technology Strategic Planning
■ Bob GRAHAM, Vice President, Database Manager

One Bankers Trust Plaza, New York, NY 10006

CITIBANK

■ Colin CROOK, Chairman Corporate Technology Committee
■ Dr. Daniel SCHUTZER, Senior Vice President, Information Technology
■ Jim CALDARELLA, Manager, Business Architecture for Global Finance
■ Nicholas P. RICHARDS, Database Administrator
■ William BRINDLEY, Technology Officer
■ Michael R. VEALE, Network Connectivity
■ Harriet SCHABES, Corporate Standards
■ Leigh REEVE, Technology for Global Finance

399 Park Avenue, New York, NY 10043

MORGAN STANLEY

- Gary T. GOEHRKE, Managing Director, Information Services
- Guy CHIARELLO, Vice President, Databases
- Robert F. DE YOUNG, Principal, Information Technology

1933 Broadway, New York, NY 10019

- Eileen S. WALLACE, Vice President, Treasury Department
- Jacqueline T. BRODY, Treasury Department

  1251 Avenue of the Americas, New York, NY 10020

GOLDMAN SACHS

- Peter T. HOVERSTEN, Vice President, Information Technology
- Leo J. ESPOSITO, Vice President, Information Systems
- David FLAXMAN, Advanced Technology Group
- Malcolm DRAPER, Architect, Communications Systems
- Fred M. KATZ, Applications Architect, Equity Sales and Trading
- Vincent L. AMATULLI, Information Technology, Treasury Department

  85 Broad Street, New York, NY 10004

J.J. KENNY SERVICES INC.

- Thomas E. ZIELINSKI, Chief Information Officer
- Ira KIRSCHNER, Database Administrator, Director of System Programming and of the Data Center

  65 Broadway, New York, NY 10006

MERRILL LYNCH

- Kevin SAWYER, Director of Distributed Computing Services and Executive in Charge of the Mainframe to Client-Server Conversion Process

■ Raymond M. DISCO, Treasury/Bank Relations Manager

World Financial Center, South Tower, New York, NY 10080-6107

TEACHERS INSURANCE AND ANNUITY ASSOCIATION/COLLEGE RETIREMENT EQUITIES FUND (TIAA/CREF)

■ Charles S. DVORKIN, Vice President and Chief Technology Officer
■ Harry D. PERRIN, Assistant Vice President, Information Technology

730 Third Avenue, New York, NY 10017-3206

FINANCIAL ACCOUNTING STANDARDS BOARD

■ Halsey G. BULLEN, Project Manager
■ Jeannot BLANCHET, Project Manager
■ Teri L. LIST, Practice Fellow

401 Merritt 7, Norwalk, CN 06856

TEKNEKRON SOFTWARE SYSTEMS, INC.

■ Vivek RANADIVE, President and CEO
■ Robert RECTOR, Senior Vice President, Client Technical Services
■ Martin LUTHI, Senior Director, Client Technical Services
■ Gerard D. BUGGY, Vice President, Global Financial Sales and Marketing
■ Norman CHEUNG, Director, Quantum Leap Group
■ Bradley C. RHODE, Vice President, Core Technology Engineering
■ Tugrul FIRATLI, Director, Network Consulting Services
■ John E. McDOWALL
■ Tom JASEK, Director, Market Sheet

- Glenn A. McCOMB, Senior Member of Technical Staff, New Technologies
- Murat K. SôNMEZ, Member of Technical Staff
- Murray D. RODE, Member of Technical Staff

    530 Lytton Avenue, Suite 301, Palo Alto, CA 94301

EVANS AND SUTHERLAND

- Les HORWOOD, Director New Business Development
- Mike WALTERMAN, Systems Engineer, Virtual Reality Applications
- Lisa B. HUBER, Software Engineer, 3-Dimensional Programming

    600 Komas Drive, P.O. Box 58700, Salt Lake City, UT 84158

nCUBE

- Michael MEIRER, President and Chief Executive Officer
- Craig D. RAMSEY, Senior Vice President, Worldwide Sales
- Ronald J. BUCK, Vice President, Marketing
- Matthew HALL, Director of Software Development

    919 East Hillside Blvd, Foster City, CA 94404

VISUAL NUMERICS

- Don KAINER, Vice President and General Manager
- Joe WEAVER, Vice President OEM/VAR Sales
- Jim PHILLIPS, Director Product Development
- Dr. Shawn JAVID, Senior Product Manager
- Dan CLARK, Manager, WAVE Family Products
- Thomas L. WELCH, Marketing Product Manager
- Margaret JOURNEY, Director Administration
- John BEE, Technical Sales Engineer

■ Adam ASNES, VDA Sales Executive

■ William POTTS, Sales Manager

6230 Lookout Road, Boulder, CO 80301

MASSACHUSETTS INSTITUTE OF TECHNOLOGY

■ Prof.Dr. Stuart E. MADNICK, Information Technology and Management Science

■ Prof.Dr. Michael SIEGEL, Information Technology, Sloan School of Management

■ Patricia M. McGINNIS, Executive Director, International Financial Services

■ Prof. Peter J. KEMPTHORNE, Project on Non-Traditional Methods in Financial Analysis

■ Dr. Alexander M. SAMAROV, Project on Non-Traditional Methods in Financial Analysis

■ Robert R. HALPERIN, Executive Director, Center for Coordination Science

■ Professor Amar GUPTA, Sloan School of Management

■ Professor Jean-Luc VILA, Finance Dept., Sloan School of Management

■ Professor Bin ZHOU, Management Science, Sloan School of Management

292 Main Street, Cambridge, MA 02139

■ Eric B. SUNDIN, Industrial Liaison Officer

■ David L. VERRILL, Senior Liaison Officer, Industrial Liaison Program

Sloan School of Management, 50 Memorial Drive, Cambridge, MA 02139

■ Henry H. HOUH, Desk Area Network and ViewStation Project, Electrical Engineering and Computer Science

■ Dr. Henry A. LIEBERMAN, Media Laboratory

■ Valerie A. EAMES, Media Laboratory

- Prof.Dr. Kenneth B. HAASE, Media Arts and Sciences
- Dr. David ZELTZER, Virtual Reality Project

  Ames St., Cambridge, MA 02139

UNIVERSITY OF MICHIGAN

- Professor John H. HOLLAND, Electrical Engineering and Computer Science
- Dr. Rick L. RIOLO, Systems Researcher, Department of Psychology

  Ann Arbor, MI 48109-2103

SANTA FE INSTITUTE

- Dr. Edward A. KNAPP, President
- Dr. L. Mike SIMMONS, Jr., Vice President
- Dr. Bruce ABELL, Vice President Finance
- Prof.Dr. Murray GELL-MANN, Theory of Complexity
- Prof.Dr. Stuart KAUFFMAN, Models in Biology
- Dr. Chris LANGTON, Artificial Life
- Dr. John MILLER, Adaptive Computation in Economics
- Dr. Blake LE BARON, Non-Traditional Methods in Economics
- Bruce SAWHILL, Virtual Reality

  1660 Old Pecos Trail, Santa Fe, NM 87501

SCHOOL OF ENGINEERING AND APPLIED SCIENCE, UNIVERSITY OF CALIFORNIA, LOS ANGELES

- Dean A.R. Frank WAZZAN, School of Engineering and Applied Science
- Prof. Richard MUNTZ, Chair, Computer Science Department
- Prof.Dr. Leonard KLEINROCK, Telecommunications and Networks

- Professor Nicolaos G. ALEXOPOULOS, Electrical Engineering
- Prof.Dr. Judea PEARL, Cognitive Systems Laboratory
- Prof.Dr. Walter KARPLUS, Computer Science Department
- Prof.Dr. Michael G. DYER, Artificial Intelligence Laboratory
- Ms. Susan CRUSE, Director of Development and Alumni Affairs
- Joel SHORT, Ph.D. Candidate
- David Chickering, Ph.D. Candidate

  Westwood Village, Los Angeles, CA 90024

SCHOOL OF BUSINESS ADMINISTRATION, UNIVERSITY OF SOUTHERN CALIFORNIA

- Dr. Bert M. STEECE, Dean of Faculty, School of Business Administration
- Dr. Alan ROWE, Professor of Management

  Los Angeles, CA 90089-1421

PREDICTION COMPANY

- Dr. J. Doyne FARMER, Director of Development
- Dr. Norman H. PACKARD, Director of Research
- Jim McGILL, Managing Director

  234 Griffin Street, Santa Fe, NM 87501

NYNEX SCIENCE AND TECHNOLOGY, INC.

- Thomas M. SUPER, Vice President, Research and Development
- Steven CROSS, NYNEX Shuttle Project
- Valerie R. TINGLE, System Analyst
- Melinda CREWS, Public Liaison, NYNEX Labs.

  500 Westchester Avenue, White Plains, NY 10604

- John C. FALCO, Sales Manager, NYNEX Systems Marketing
- David J. ANNINO, Account Executive, NYNEX Systems Marketing
  100 Church Street, New York, NY 10007

MICROSOFT

- Mike McGEEHAN, Database Specialist
- Andrew ELLIOTT, Marketing Manager

  825 8th Avenue, New York, NY

REUTERS AMERICA

- Robert RUSSEL, Senior Vice President
- William A.S. KENNEDY, Vice President
- Buford SMITH, President, Reuters Information Technology
- Richard A. WILLIS, Manager International Systems Design
- M.A. SAYERS, Technical Manager, Central Systems Development
- Alexander FAUST, Manager Financial Products USA (Instantlink and Blend)

  40 E. 52nd Street, New York, NY 10022

ORACLE CORPORATION

- Scott MATTHEWS, National Account Manager
- Robert T. FUNK, Senior Systems Specialist
- Joseph M. DI BARTOLOMEO, Systems Specialist
- Dick DAWSON, Systems Specialist

  885 Third Avenue, New York, NY 10022

DIGITAL EQUIPMENT CORPORATION

- Mike FISHBEIN, Product Manager, Massively Parallel Systems (MAS-PAR Supercomputer)

■ Marco EMRICH, Technology Manager, NAS

■ Robert PASSMORE, Technical Manager, Storage Systems

■ Mark S. DRESDNER, DEC Marketing Operations

146 Main Street, Maynard, MA 01754 (Meeting held at UBS New York)

UNISYS CORPORATION

■ Harvey J. CHIAT, Director Impact Programs

■ Manuel LAVIN, Director, Databases

■ David A. GOIFFON, Software Engineer

P.O. Box 64942, MS 4463, Saint Paul, MN, 55164-0942 (Meeting held at UBS in New York)

HEWLETT-PACKARD

■ Brad WILSON, Product Manager, Commercial Systems

■ Vish KRISHNAN, Manager R+D Laboratory

■ Samir MATHUR, Open ODB Manager

■ Michael GUPTA, Transarc, Tuxedo, Encina Transaction Processing

■ Dave WILLIAMS, Industry Account Manager

1911, Pruneridge Avenue, Cupertino, CA 95014

IBM CORPORATION

■ Terry LIFFICK, Software Strategies, Client-Server Architecture

■ Paula CAPPELLO, Information Warehouse Framework

■ Ed COBBS, Transaction Processing Systems

■ Dr. Paul WILMS, Connectivity and Interoperability

■ Helen ARZU, IBM Santa Teresa Representative

■ Dana L. STETSON, Advisory Marketing IBM New York

Santa Teresa Laboratory, 555 Bailey Avenue, San Jose, CA 95141

UBS SECURITIES

- A. Ramy GOLDSTEIN, Managing Director, Equity Derivative Products

  299 Park Avenue, New York, NY 10171-0026

UNION BANK OF SWITZERLAND

- Dr. H. BAUMANN, Director of Logistics, North American Operations
- Dr. Ch. GABATHULER, Director, Information Technology
- Hossur SRIKANTAN, Vice President Information Technology Department
- Roy M. DARHIN, Assistant Vice President

  299 Park Avenue, New York, NY 10171-0026

United Kingdom

BANK OF ENGLAND

- W.D.R. SWANNEY, C.A., Head of Division, Supervision and Surveillance
- Patricia JACKSON, Special Advisor, Regulatory and Supervisory Policy
- Mark LAYCOCK, Banking Supervision

  Threadneedle Street, London EC2R 8AH

BRITISH BANKERS ASSOCIATION

- Paul CHISNALL, Assistant Director

  Pinners Hall, 105-108 Old Broad Street, London EC2N 1EX

ACCOUNTING STANDARDS BOARD

- A V C COOK, Technical Director
- Sandra THOMPSON, Project Director

  Holborn Hall, 100 Gray's Inn Road, London WC1X 8AL

BARCLAYS BANK

- Alan BROWN, Director Group Credit Policy
- Brandon DAVIES, Treasurer UK Group

  54 Lombard Street, London EC3P 3AH

- Peter GOLDEN, Chief Information Officer, Barclays Capital Markets, Treasury, BZW
- David J. PARSONS, Director Advanced Technology
- Christine E. IRWIN, Group Information Systems Technology

  Murray House, 1 Royal Mint Court, London EC3N 4HH

ABBEY NATIONAL BANK

- Mac MILLINGTON, Director of Information Technology
  Chalkdell Drive, Shenley Wood, Milton Keynes MK6 6LA
- Anthony W. ELLIOTT, Director of Risk and Credit

  Abbey House, Baker Street, London NW1 6XL

NATWEST SECURITIES

- Sam B. GIBB, Director of Information Technology,
- Don F. SIMPSON, Director, Global Technology
- Richard E. GIBBS, Director, Equity Derivatives Derivatives

  135 Bishopsgate, London EC2M 3XT

CREDIT SWISS FINANCIAL PRODUCTS

- Ross SALINGER, Managing Director

  One Cabot Square, London E14 4QJ

CREDIT SWISS FIRST BOSTON

- Geoff J.R. DOUBLEDAY, Executive Director

  One Cabot Square, London E14 4QJ

BANKGESELLSCHAFT BERLIN

- Stephen F. MYERS, Head of Market Risk

  1 Crown Court, Cheapside, London

BRITISH TELECOM

- Dr. Alan RUDGE, Deputy Managing Director

  BT Centre, 81 Newgate Street, London EC1A 7AJ

ASSOCIATION FOR PAYMENT CLEARING SERVICES (APACS)

- J. Michael WILLIAMSON, Deputy Chief Executive

  14 Finsbury Square, London EC2A 1BR

ORACLE CORPORATION

- Mr. Geoffrey W. SQUIRE, Executive Vice President, and Chief Executive

- Mr. Richard BARKER, Senior Vice President and Director British Research Laboratories

■ Mr. Giles GODART-BROWN, Senior Support Manager

■ Mr. Paul A. GOULD, Account Executive

Oracle Park, Bittams Lane, Guildford Rd, Chertsey, Surrey KT16 9RG

E.D. & F. MAN INTERNATIONAL

■ Brian FUDGE, Funds Division

Sugar Quay, Lower Thames Street, London EC3R 6DU

PRUDENTIAL-BACHE SECURITIES

■ Stephen MASSEY, Regional Director—Europe

9 Devonshire Square, London EC2M 4HP

Scandinavia

SVERIGES RIKSBANK

■ Gïran ZETTERGREN, Economics Department

Brunkebergstorg 11, S-103 37 Stockholm

VAERDIPAPIRCENTRALEN (VP)

■ Mr. Jens BACHE, General Manager

■ Mrs. Aase BLUME, Assistant to the General Manager

61 Helgeshoj AllÇ, Postbox 20, 2630 Taastrup-Denmark

SWEDISH BANKERS' ASSOCIATION

■ Mr. Bo GUNNARSSON, Manager, Bank Automation Department

■ Mr. Gïsta FISCHER, Manager, Bank-Owned Financial Companies Department

■ Mr. Gïran AHLBERG, Manager, Credit Market Affairs Department

P.O. Box 7603, 10394 Stockholm-Sweden

SKANDINAVISKA ENSKILDA BANKEN

■ Mr. Lars ISACSSON, Treasurer

■ Mr. Urban JANELD, Executive Vice President Finance and IT

■ Mr. Mats ANDERSSON, Director of Computers and Communications

■ Mr. Gïsta OLAVI, Manager SEB Data/Koncern Data

2 Sergels Torg, 10640 Stockholm-Sweden

SECURUM AB

■ Mr. Anders NYREN, Director of Finance and Accounting

■ Mr. John LUNDGREN, Manager of IT

38 Regeringsg, 5 tr., 10398 Stockholm-Sweden

SVEATORNET AB of the Swedish Savings Banks

■ Mr. Gunar M. CARLSSON, General Manager

(Meeting at Swedish Bankers' Association)

MANDAMUS AB of the Swedish Agricultural Banks

■ Mrs. Marie MARTINSSON, Credit Department

(Meeting at Swedish Bankers' Association)

HANDELSBANKEN

- Mr. Janeric SUNDIN, Manager, Securities Department
- Mr. Jan ARONSON, Assistant Manager, Securities Department

  (Meeting at Swedish Bankers' Association)

GOTA BANKEN

- Mr. JOHANNSSON, Credit Department

(Meeting at Swedish Bankers' Association)

IRDEM AB

- Gian MEDRI, Former Director of Research at Nordbanken

  19 Flintlasvagen, 19154 Sollentuna-Sweden

Austria

BANK AUSTRIA

- Dr. Peter FISCHER, Senior General Manager, Treasury Division
- Peter GABRIEL, Deputy General Manager, Trading
- Konrad SCHCATE, Manager, Financial Engineering

  2 Am Hof, 1010 Vienna

CREDITANSTALT BANKVEREIN

- Dr. Wolfgang G. LICHTL, Director of Foreign Exchange and Money Markets
- Dr. Johann STROBL, Manager, Financial Analysis for Treasury Operations

  3 Julius Tandler-Platz, 1090 Vienna

ASSOCIATION OF AUSTRIAN BANKS AND BANKERS

- Dr. Fritz DIWOK, Secretary General

  11 Boersengasse, 1013 Vienna

WIENER BETRIEBS—UND BAUGESELLSCHAFT mbH

- Dr. Josef Fritz, General Manager

  1 Anschützstrasse, 1153 Vienna

MANAGEMENT DATA of CREDITANSTALT

- Ing. Guenther REINDL, Vice President, International Banking Software
- Ing. Franz NECAS, Project Manager, RICOS
- Mag. Nikolas GOETZ, Product Manager, RICOS

  21-25 Althanstrasse, 1090 Vienna

Germany

DEUTSCHE BUNDESBANK

- Eckhard OECHLER, Director of Bank Supervision and Legal Matters

  14 Wilhelm Epstein Strasse, D-6000 Frankfurt 50

DEUTSCHE BANK

- Peter GERARD, Executive Vice President, Organization and Information Technology

- Hermann SEILER, Senior Vice President, Investment Banking and Foreign Exchange Systems
- Dr. KUHN, Investment Banking and Foreign Exchange Systems
- Dr. Stefan KOLB, Organization and Technological Development

12 Koelner Strasse, D-6236 Eschborn

DRESDNER BANK

- Dr. Karsten WOHLENBERG, Project Leader Risk Management, Simulation and Analytics Task Force Financial Division
- Hans-Peter LEISTEN, Mathematician
- Susanne LOESKEN, Organization and IT Department

43 Mainzer Landstrasse, D-6000 Frankfurt

COMMERZBANK

- Helmut HOPPE, Director Organization and Information Technology
- Hermann LENZ, Director Controllership, Internal Accounting and Management Accounting
- Harald LUX, Manager Organization and Information Technology
- Waldemar NICKEL, Manager Systems Planning

155 Mainzer Landstrasse, D-60261 Frankfurt

DEUTSCHER SPARKASSEN UND GIROVERBAND

- Manfred KRUEGER, Division Manager, Card Strategy

4 Simrockstrasse, D-5300 Bonn 1 (Telephone interview from Frankfurt)

MEDIA SYSTEMS

- Bertram ANDERER, Director

6 Goethestrasse, D-7500 Karlsruhe

FRAUNHOFER INSTITUTE FOR COMPUTER GRAPHICS

- Dr.Ing. Martin GOEBEL
- Wolfgang FELBER

  7 Wilhelminerstrasse, D-6100 Darmstadt

GMD FIRST—RESEARCH INSTITUTE FOR COMPUTER ARCHITECTURE, SOFTWARE TECHNOLOGY AND GRAPHICS

- Prof.Dr.Ing. Wolfgang K. GILOI, General Manager
- Dr. BEHR, Administrative Director
- Dr. Ulrich BRUENING, Chief Designer
- Dr. Joerg NOLTE, Designer of Parallel Operating Systems Software
- Dr. Matthias KESSLER, Parallel Languages and Parallel Compilers
- Dr. Friedrich W. SCHROER, New Programming Paradigms
- Dr. Thomas LUX, Fluid Dynamics, Weather Prediction and Pollution Control Project

  5 Rudower Chaussee, D-1199 Berlin

SIEMENS NIXDORF

- Wolfgang WEISS, Director of Banking Industry Office
- Bert KIRSCHBAUM, Manager, Dresdner Bank Project
- Mark MILLER, Manager Neural Networks Project for UBS and German banks
- Andrea VONERDEN, Business Management Department

  27 Lyoner Strasse, D-6000 Frankfurt 71

UBS GERMANY

- H.-H. v. SCHELIHA, Director, Organization and Information Technology

- Georg SUDHAUS, Manager IT for Trading Systems
- Marco BRACCO, Trader
- Jaap VAN HARTEN, Trader

  52 Bleichstrasse, D-6000 Frankfurt 1, France

France

BANQUE DE FRANCE

- Pierre JAILLET, Director, Monetary Studies and Statistics
- Yvan ODONNAL, Manager, Monetary Analyses and Statistics
- G TOURNEMIRE, Analyst, Monetary Studies

  39 rue Croix des Petits Champs, 75001 Paris

SECRETARIAT GENERAL DE LA COMMISSION BANCAIRE—BANQUE DE FRANCE

- Didier PENY, Head of Supervisory Policy and Research Division
- Michel MARTINO, International Affairs
- Benjamin SAHEL, Market Risk Control

  115 rue de Reaumur, 75002 Paris

MINISTRY OF FINANCE AND THE ECONOMY, Conseil National de la Compatibilite

- Alain LE BARS, Director International Relations and Cooperation

  6 rue Louise WEISS, 75703 Paris Cedex 13

Italy

BANCA D'ITALIA

- Eugenio GAIOTTI, Research Department, Monetary and Financial Division

Banca d'Italia, Rome

ISTITUTO BANCARIO SAN PAOLO DI TORINO

- Dr. Paolo CHIUMENTI, Director of Budgeting
- Roberto COSTA, Director of Private Banking
- Pino RAVELLI, Director Bergamo Region

  via G. Camozzi 27, 24121 Bergamo

Luxembourg

BANQUE GENERALE DU LUXEMBOURG

- Dr. Yves WAGNER, Director of Asset and Risk Management
- Hans-Jörg PARIS, International Risk Manager
- Dirk VAN REETH, Manager Department of Companies and Legal Structures
- Dr. Luc RODESCH, Investment Advisor

  27 avenue Monterey, L-2951 Luxembourg

CEDEL

- André LUSSI, Chief Executive Officer
- Ray SOUDAH, Chief Financial and Investment Officer

  67 Bd Grande-Duchesse Charlotte, L-1010 Luxembourg

Switzerland

SWISS NATIONAL BANK

- Robert FLURI, Assistant Director Statistics Section
- Dr. Werner HERMANN, Risk Management

- Dr. Christian WALTER, Representative to the Basle Committee

  15 Börsenstrasse, 8022 Zürich

BANK FOR INTERNATIONAL SETTLEMENTS

- Claude SIVY, Director, Controllership and Operational Security
- Frederik C. MUSCH, Secretary General, Basel Committee on Banking Supervision

  2 Centralbankplatz, Basel

SWISS BANK CORPORATION

- Dr. Marcel ROHNER, Director, IFD Controlling

  Swiss Bank Center, 8010 Zurich, Switzerland

BZ BANK ZURICH

- Martin EBNER, President
- Peter SJOSTRAND, Finance
- Olivier WILLI, Analyst
- Roger JENNY, Analyst

  50 Sihlstrasse, 8021 Zurich, Switzerland

BZ TRUST AKTIENGESELLSCHAFT

- Dr. Stefan HOLZER, Financial Analyst

  24 Eglirain, 8832 Wilen, Switzerland

CIBA-GEIGY AG

- Stefan JANOVJAK, Divisional Information Manager

- Natalie PAPEZIK, Information Architect

  Ciba-Geigy, R-1045, 5.19, 4002 Basle

ECOLE POLYTECHNIQUE FEDERAL DE LAUSANNE

- Dr. Jean-Daniel NICOUD, Director, Microinformatics Laboratory
- Dr. Boi FALTINGS, Artificial Intelligence
- Dr. Martin J. HASLER, Circuits and Systems
- Dr. Ing. Roman BOULIC, Computer Graphics

  1015 Lausanne, Switzerland

EURODIS

- Albert MUELLER, Director
- Beat ERZER, Marketing Manager
- B. PEDRAZZINI, Systems Engineer
- Reto ALBERTINI, Sales Engineer

  Bahnhofstrasse 58/60, CH-8105 Regensdorf

OLSEN AND ASSOCIATES

- Dr. Richard OLSEN, Chief Executive Officer

  232 Seefeldstrasse, 8008 Zurich, Switzerland

Japan

BANK OF JAPAN

- Harry TOYAMA, Councel and Chief Manager, Credit and Market Management Department

■ Akira IEDA, Credit and Market Management Department

2-1-1 Kongoku-Cho, Nihonbashi, Chuo-ku, Tokyo 103

DAI-ICHI KANGYO BANK

■ Shunsuke NAKASUJI, General Manager and Director, Information Technology Division
■ Seiichi HASEGAWA, Manager International Systems Group
■ Takahiro SEKIZAWA, International Systems Group
■ Yukio HISATOMI, Manager Systems Planning Group
■ Shigeaki TOGAWA, Systems Planning Group

13-3 Shibuya, 2-Chome, Shibuya-ku, Tokyo 150

FUJI BANK

■ Hideo TANAKA, General Manager Systems Planning Division
■ Toshihiko UZAKI, Manager Systems Planning Division
■ Takakazu IMAI, Systems Planning Division

Otemachi Financial Center, 1-5-4 Otemachi, Chiyoda-ku, Tokyo

MITSUBISHI BANK

■ Akira WATANABE, General Manager, Derivative Products
■ Akira TOWATARI, Manager, Strategic Planning and Administration, Derivative Products
■ Takehito NEMOTO, Chief Manager, Systems Development Division
■ Nobuyuki YAMADA, Systems Development Division
■ Haruhiko SUZUKI, Systems Development Division

7-1 Marunouchi, 2-Chome, Chiyoda-ku, Tokyo 100

NOMURA RESEARCH INSTITUTE

■ Tomio ARAI, Director, Systems Science Department

- Tomoyuki OHTA, Director, Financial Engineering Group
- Tomohiko HIRUTA, Manager, I-STAR Systems Services

9-1 Nihonbashi, 1-Chome, Chuo-ku, Tokyo 103

MITSUBISHI TRUST AND BANKING

- Nobuyuki TANAKA, General Manager, Systems Planning Division
- Terufumi KAGE, Consultant Systems Planning Division

9-8 Kohnan, 2-Chome, Minato-ku, Tokyo 108

SAKURA BANK

- Nobuo IHARA, Senior Vice President and General Manager, Systems Development Office VIII
- Hisao KATAYAMA, Senior Vice President and General Manager, System Development Office VII
- Toshihiko EDA, Senior Systems Engineer, Systems Development Division

4-2 Kami-Osahi, 4-Chome, Shinagawa-ku, Tokyo 141

SANYO SECURITIES

- Yuji OZAWA, Director, Systems Planning Department
- K. TOYAMA, Systems Planning Department

1-8-1 Nihonbashi, Kayabacho, Chuo-ku, Tokyo 103

CENTER FOR FINANCIAL INDUSTRY INFORMATION SYSTEM SYSTEMS (FISC)

- Shighehisa HATTORI, Executive Director
- Kiyoshi KUMATA, Manager, Research Division II

16th Floor, Ark Mori Building, 12-32, 1-Chome, Akasaka, Minato-ku, Tokyo 107

LABORATORY FOR INTERNATIONAL FUZZY ENGINEERING RESEARCH (LIFE)

- Dr. Toshiro TERANO, Executive Director
- Dr. Anca L. RALESCU, Assistant Director
- Shunichi TANI, Fuzzy Control Project Leader

  Siber Hegner Building, 89-1 Yamashita-Cho, Naka-ku, Yokohama-shi 231

REAL WORLD COMPUTING PARTNERSHIP (RWC)

- Dr. Junichi SHUMADA, General Manager of RWC
- Hajime IRISAWA, Executive Director

  Tsukuba Mitsui Building, 1-6-1 Takezono, Tsukuba-shi, Ibarahi 305

TOKYO UNIVERSITY

- Dr. Michitaka HIROSE, Dept. of Mechano-Informatics, Faculty of Engineering
- Dr. Kensuke YOKOYAMA, Virtual Reality Project

  3-1 7-Chome, Hongo Bunkyo-ku, Tokyo 113

TOKYO INTERNATIONAL UNIVERSITY

- Dr. Yoshiro KURATANI

  9-1-7-528 Akasaka, Minato-ku, Tokyo 107

JAPAN ELECTRONIC DIRECTORY RESEARCH INSTITUTE

- Dr. Toshio YOKOI, General Manager

  Mita-Kokusai Building—Annex, 4-28 Mita, 1-Chome, Minato-ku, Tokyo 108

MITSUBISHI RESEARCH INSTITUTE (MRI)

- Masayuki FUJITA, Manager, Strategic Information Systems Dept.
- Hideyuki MORITA, Senior Research Associate, Information Science Dept.
- Akio SATO, Research Associate, Information Science Dept.

  ARCO Tower, 8-1 Shimomeguro, 1-Chome, Meguro-ku, Tokyo 153

NTT SOFTWARE

- Dr. Fukuya ISHINO, Senior Vice President

  223-1 Yamashita-Cho, Naka-ku, Yokohama 231

RYOSHIN SYSTEMS (Systems Developer Fully Owned by Mitsubishi Trust)

- Takewo YUWI, Vice President, Technical Research and Development

  9-8 Kohman, 2-Chome, Minato-ku, Tokyo 108

SANYO SOFTWARE SERVICES

- Fumio SATO, General Manager, Sales Department 2

  Kanayama Building, 1-2-12 Shinkawa, Chuo-ku, Tokyo 104

FUJITSU RESEARCH INSTITUTE

- Dr. Masuteru SEKIGUCHI, Member of the Board and Director of R+D
- Takao SAITO, Director of the Parallel Computing Research Center
- Dr. Hiroyasu ITOH, R+D Department
- Katsuto KONDO, R+D Department

■ Satoshi HAMAYA, Information Systems and Economics

9-3 Nakase, 1-Chome, Mihama-ku, Chiba-City 261

NEC

■ Kotaro NAMBA, Senior Researcher, NEC Planning Research
■ Dr. Toshiyuki NAKATA, Manager, Computer System Research Laboratory
■ Asao KANEKO, Computer System Research Laboratory

3-13-12 Mita, Minato-ku, Tokyo 108

TOSHIBA

■ Dr. Makoto IHARA, Manager Workstation Product Planning and Technical Support Dept.
■ Emi NAKAMURA, Analyst Financial Applications Dept.
■ Joshikiyo NAKAMURA, Financial Sales Manager
■ Minami ARAI, Deputy Manager, Workstation Systems Division

1-1 Shibaura, 1-Chome, Minato-ku, Tokyo 105

MICROSOFT

■ James LALONDE, Multinational Account Manager, Large Accounts Sales Dept.

Sasazuka NA Bldg, 50-1 Sasazuka, 1-Chome, Shibuya-ku, Tokyo 151

APPLE TECHNOLOGY

■ Dr. Tsutomu KOBAYASHI, President

25 Mori Bldg, 1-4-30 Roppongi, Minato-ku, Tokyo 106

DIGITAL EQUIPMENT JAPAN

- Roshio ISHII, Account Manager, Financial Sales Unit 1

    2-1 Kamiogi, 1-Chome, Suginamiku, Tokyo 167

UBS JAPAN

- Dr. Peter BRUTSCHE, Executive Vice President and Chief Manager
- Gary P. EIDAM, First Vice President, Regional Head of Technology
- Charles UNDERWOOD, Vice President, Head of Technical Architecture and Strategy
- Masaki UTSUNOMIYA, Manager, IT Production Facilities

    Yurakucho Building 2F, 1-10-1 Yurakucho, Chiyoda-ku, Tokyo 100

Concepts Underpinning the Development and Use of Agents

CHAPTER 1

The New Software Paradigm "Things That Think"

"Come to me for advice, if that's what you want, but don't come to me for a decision," Amadeo P. Giannini, the man who made Bank of America, was saying to his assistants. Suspicious of those who seemed overly eager to agree with him, he would shout: "Are you yessing me?"*

---

*Felice A. Bonadio, *A. P. Giannini, Banker of America*, University of California Press, Berkeley, 1994.

"Yessing" is something that *agents* will not do, though, as we will see in Chap. 3, they may not be able to say no either. *Agents* are a new software paradigm. They are relatively small pieces of autonomous software that act in various roles on behalf of a specific function or user. They could, for instance:

- Route electronic mail and other messages according to given rules
- Traverse the network to mine databases
- Alert their masters to specific events or findings
- Perform corporate tasks such as scheduling meetings
- Execute diagnostics and other routines at network nodes

The agent may reside on the user's machine and be transmitted to distant computers where it carries out its functions. Or it may reside at network nodes. In the one as in the other case, the artifact will move autonomously. This, as we will see through practical examples, is one of the basic characteristics distinguishing an agent from other chunks of software.

To its end user, or *master*, the agent is a personal assistant—its correspondent within the computer's, communications and software landscape in which it works. It is a *proactive* artifact that can perform fairly sophisticated tasks and can also exhibit learning abilities. The agent:

- Knows about the user, his or her wishes and preferred model of operation
- Is informed about other correspondent agents, including their profiles and work patterns
- Is able to collect, handle, and present information to its master's satisfaction
- Can structure system elements as required to tailor solutions to real-time users' needs

Should the agent be enriched with artificial intelligence (AI)? The majority of experts in this field say Yes! Some challenge this argument, however, advancing the hypothesis that agents do not necessarily have to be intelligent to act in an intelligent way. I don't believe this argument is sound.

"Things That Think": The New Mission of MIT's Media Laboratory

Since the early 1980s, tier 1 companies in manufacturing, distribution, telecommunications, and finance, as well as university laboratories, have successfully developed and implemented expert systems.[*]

In the same way that theoretical projects in artificial intelligence have led to expert systems—which constitute the first practical implementation of AI—expert systems have been the forerunner of agents. (See also in Chap. 13 how expert systems can be morphed into agents). It is important to appreciate the evolution from the theoretical aspects of AI to the development and practical applications of expert systems, and from there to networked agents. As this field, whose perspective was opened in the late 1950s, is reaching maturity, today there is a huge body of knowledge about artificial intelligence that we should be using to our competitive advantage. A similar statement can be made about multimedia. "Our multimedia mission is over," said Dr. Nicholas Negreponte, founder and director of MIT's Media Laboratory, at the media lab's tenth anniversary celebration. In its place, a new research consortium called "Things That Think" was set up in October 1995.

At this moment, a significant amount of what the new project suggests is possible seems to come from another planet. But I will stick my neck out and, even at this early stage, say that we can expect this project to bring significant results because Negreponte is a *doer*. When, in the mid-1980s, he started the media lab, he defined far-out objectives and then he proved that he knew how to deliver them. Negreponte's new message is the following:

- The consortium is dedicated to the idea of designing Things That Think, computer intelligence, into everyday products.[†]
- Its aim is to explore ways of moving computation beyond conventional sites into all types of machines and appliances.

By sensing the movements or feelings of their owners or by learning their owners' habits, knowledge artifacts embedded in common devices are projected to perform useful tasks, leading to changes in the way we

---

[*]See D. N. Chorafas, *Knowledge Engineering*, Van Nostrand Reinhold, New York, 1990; and D. N. Chorafas and H. Steinmann, *Expert Systems in Banking*, Macmillan, London, 1991.

[†]The lab has over 100 sponsors. Among them are AT&T, Eastman Kodak, Hewlett-Packard, Hughes Aircraft, IBM, Intel, Microsoft, Motorola, Sony, Procter and Gamble, and Swatch.

TABLE 1-1

Current and
Projected Markets
for Agents in Order
of Importance
(Based on Personal
Research)

Market in 1997
1. Custom-made solutions
2. Information retrieval
3. Telecommunications and messaging
4. Software development

Market in the Year 2000 (Estimated)
1. Telecommunications and messaging*
2. Information retrieval
3. Custom-made solutions
4. Development tools
5. End-user interfaces
6. New desktop and laptop paradigms

This market is expected to be at the U.S. $700 to
$900 million range—out of a total market for
agents at the $3 to $4 billion level. Optimists
think that at 2000 the total market will be well
in excess of $10 billion. I don't believe so.

work and live in our everyday lives. This is consistent with the definition
of agents given in the introduction, even if the goals announced by Dr.
Negreponte seem far-fetched by today's standard applications. For
instance, having eyeglasses that guide us through city streets or wearing
clothing or shoes that relay health information directly to a doctor's database seems the stuff of science fiction.* It should not be forgotten, however, that advances in microelectronics, miniaturization, and experience
in building knowledge-enriched artifacts could make such ideas a reality.

These are basic research projects. Therefore, they represent further-out
applications that will most likely materialize into concrete products after
the year 2000. But agents also have immediate applications that already
give good results. Table 1-1 outlines the market for agents in 1997 and
that projected 4 years down the line: Telecommunications and messaging is seen by far as the Number 1 market in the years ahead. For this
reason, Part 2 is devoted to the use of agents in communications.

---

*See also the discussion on telemedicine in Chap. 11.

No doubt, the further out the solutions are, the more vision and imagination they will require. The researchers who undertook the Things That Think project seem to have plenty of both. Their effort largely rests on interdisciplinary research, involving both development and use of novel:

- Sensor devices
- Expression analysis tools
- Machine intelligence
- Communications protocols
- Programming languages
- Network architectures

For instance, a Tangible Language Workshop is being set up to explore designs associated with *thinking objects*. This will include tools for mechanical, electrical, and electronic design created not only by specialists but also by inventors working in nontraditional ways. The tangible language will be integrated with rapid prototyping tools.

If systems and subsystems can have intelligence, why can't materials have intelligence too? This emphasis on intelligent materials is timely because we are now in the midst of a revolution in materials sciences and in the engineering disciplines that affect them:

- New *superconductors* may have an influence in the next 25 years as great as semiconductors have had in the last 25 years.
- New *photonic* materials are altering communications. Magnetic and structural materials are radically changing vehicles and modes of transport.

Within the new mission MIT's media lab has chosen for itself, some of the contributions by other research projects will be toward smarter instrumentation for flexible manufacturing. This will be supplemented by a new generation of knowledge-enriched computer artifacts.

The November 12, 1996, Meeting at MIT with Professor Michael Hawley

If one asks what impressed me most during the meeting I had with Michael Hawley at the media lab, I would say the breadth of the Things

That Think project and the fact that it addresses everyday objects that can be turned into smart or even intelligent objects. This reference includes lots of things: clothing, watches, furniture, toys, rooms, cars, and appliances. Take the intelligent box by Procter and Gamble (P&G) as an example.

■ Its microprocessor can tell when the content of this soap powder box has reached a minimum level and therefore needs to be reordered.

■ The order would be placed by transmitting it through infrared to the home area network* while the gateway would connect to the P&G computer.

The idea is that next-day replenishment will be achieved. Economies of scale will begin to favor factories strategically located near FedEx hubs, not WalMart, advises Michael Hawley.

At MIT's media lab, P&G also sponsors another project on intelligent diapers. The fiber technology this company has developed is so advanced that NASA addresses itself to Procter and Gamble for advice and assistance. What is missing is the feedback from consumers—from the mother's perception of the usefulness of new fiber technology to herself and her baby, to the diaper's life cycle.

■ An intelligent diaper would provide precious feedback.

■ This would assist both R&D and the marketing people of P&G.

MIT is not the only advanced research center working on intelligent objects. A group of battery and semiconductor manufacturers are collaborating to develop and share ownership in the *smart battery system* (SBS) specification. A smart rechargeable battery contains a microprocessor to accurately report:

■ Its remaining electrical charge

■ Other information that helps increase the battery's life

What distinguishes a smart battery is that it exhibits a level of self-awareness. It knows things such as its chemical composition and what types of controls are needed when charging or discharging. Also it knows when to terminate operation due to low voltage.

By making it feasible for a battery to monitor its own critical parameters, we permit the host system to ask and obtain predictive data on how

---

*See Chap. 9.

long the battery will last at a given load. Using this information, it becomes possible to:

- Control operations
- Inform the user how much more life he or she can expect

Ideally, the smart battery will work with a smart charger, exchanging critical events and service requests. The able use of critical events helps to notify the host of changes in battery status. The host can as well request other crucial data that may interest the controller, the power subsystem, or another device. This communication is assured over a smart bus interface.

As battery technology evolves, discharge characteristics of energy systems become increasingly crucial. Capitalizing on affordable chip technology, the battery will eventually have a database because without factual and documented knowledge of its own history, it is almost impossible to make predictions with any accuracy. The best approach is for the battery to keep track by itself of its critical variables. For this reason, Duracell and Intel have jointly:

- Created a standardized battery—power system interface
- Embedded intelligence into the host-battery interface specification

The way to bet is that smart batteries will populate all portable devices, from notebook computers and personal digital assistants (PDAs) to camcorders and photomachines. The SBS specification can be implemented to increase the attractiveness of products and rejuvenate the market appeal of those that have by now become commonplace. The same is true about the projects currently at the media lab.

Things that think are the way of the future, and there is a need for them. From 1993 to 1996, more than 30 children have been killed in America alone by airbags. As a result, auto executives, insurance industry officials, and safety regulators are now looking into *smart airbags*. These can detect the presence of a child and adjust themselves to deploy at slower speeds, minimizing the risk.[*]

Financial companies, too, are interested in intelligent products, as documented by a project Visa sponsors at MIT. Visa controls about 63 percent of the credit card market, and this market grows at the rate of 20 to 40 percent per year, depending on the country and the year:

---

[*]*USA Today,* November 14, 1996.

- As a market leader, Visa is interested in digital identification including data that describe the person.
- Identification information could be provided through intelligence embedded in the person's wristwatch.

In this connection, the interests of Visa and of Swatch are converging. Visa would like to see eventually that each credit card user could design his or her own type of credit card while continuing to use the network for online connection. Swatch aims to assure that the design of a personalized intelligent watch is at the customer's reach, making, at the same time, the wristwatch the node of an intranet-Internet connection.

Intelligent networks are another way of looking at things that think.* Intelligent networks can be of significant value to watchmakers for their "next product"—as evidenced by the fact that Swatch sponsors such a project at MIT's media labs.

One of the projects that goes far beyond ordinary thinking, even among very futuristic endeavors, is *the programmable brick:* a prototype toy building brick with embedded computational power. The concept is that with programmable bricks, children can learn ideas that were previously taught in engineering courses at the college level. Has this notion been tried before?

Actually, this idea finds its origin in a 70-year-old experience. In the late 1920s the *mecano* was introduced. It allowed kids to learn how to build structures while playing—and for several decades it proved to be a toy that made significant contributions to the education of the young. I see the programmable brick as an intelligent mecano many years down the line.

One of the projects in the orbit of things that think will concentrate on the possibility of a credit card that cannot be stolen because it is smart enough to recognize its owner—increasing security in financial payments significantly.† Another project will focus on developing a type of *magic wand.* As an artifact, the magic wand is projected to be a small, pen-sized object that, in conjunction with voice commands and body gestures, can serve as a remote control for other intelligent and expressive things (objects). Tools of this kind could be used to:

- Explore large information spaces, such as wall-sized multimedia displays
- Paint digital pictures
- Support manipulation of any part that requires intelligent tools

---

*See also Part 2 and Chap. 9 in Part 3.

†See the discussion on security in Chap. 6.

As these examples help demonstrate, significant departures have to be made in terms of new design methods. One of the goals of the consortium is to weave digital media directly into the product fabrication process for sensing and reasoning by things. Let's, however, remember that this is a research project. It will take time to reach a level of practical implementation.

Unstoppable Progress

Things that think targets a cooperative response. This means a response that involves direct and indirect agent-master communications, as well as the ability of artifacts to perceive and understand situations. We will study perception in Chap. 3, but for the moment it is wise to note that perceptual ability of agents changes the notions that have so far guided our hands in expert systems design:

- Through direct response, the agents are able to connect themselves to their master's direct intention(s). There is no gap between intent and response.

- By contrast, indirect responses are derived from knowledge about the action representing the intention. An indirect response may not match the user's intent.

Interfacing between these two classes is found in a whole class of agents' implementations. One of them is said to be actually running in the White House. The Office of Media Affairs at the U.S. president's office receives hundreds of requests each day for information via the Internet.

- White House staff redirects these requests through an agent-based publications server at MIT.[*]

- The server uses a knowledge-based inference to determine which documents the people asking for information should receive.

As applications get more sophisticated, agent-master communications will be built not just by messaging but also by interpreting intentions and associated inference rules.[†] These can be domain independent in the sense that they have unspecified actions such as "know something" or "do

---

[*]*Financial Times*, March 6, 1996.

[†]For predicates, see Chap. 3, and for inference rules, Chap. 10.

something" in their antecedents and consequence. Alternatively they may be domain dependent, which will make them so much simpler to use.

In either case, we are talking of *active things*. Therefore, if the MIT project is successful, and in all likelihood it will be, technology will experience a tremendous evolution from *passive objects* to *active objects* able to:

- Detect
- Manipulate
- Transmit
- Deliver

information about their environment—and to affect the environment in which they live. This is not just a better way of thinking of agents; it is also the only way that makes sense. That is why in the introduction I said that agents are meant to be intelligent. An agent without intelligence will soon become overwhelmed by its environment—and therefore obsolete.

Let's not be nearsighted in terms of goals nor opinionated and inflexible about the great strides that can be achieved in software if we work in earnest to make them happen. After all, who in the early 1970s would have thought of today's huge technological advances? Only 26 years ago, in 1971:

- The 4004 microprocessor was designed by Ted Hoff.
- The first 1K memory chip came off the production line.

As can easily be seen in Fig. 1-1, in the short span of a quarter century, the number of transistors per chip has increased by nearly *four orders of magnitude*—and the size of memory on a chip has made an even greater forward stride.

Our basic understanding of physics has increased to the point where we now can manipulate atoms, an example being IBM's work on argon atoms in the early to mid-1990s. The notion of subatomic particles has been an old dream of the scientific community, and it can be traced to the writing of Greek philosophers Leucippus and Democritus, in the fifth century B.C.:

- Leucippus and Democritus created the atomic theory of matter in response to a nagging philosophical dilemma.
- By contrast, today science and philosophy are (incorrectly) considered to be separate from one another—which is wrong.)*

---

*Hans Christian von Baeyer, The Fermi Solution. *Reflection on the Mechanics of Physics,* Penguin Books, New York and London, 1993.

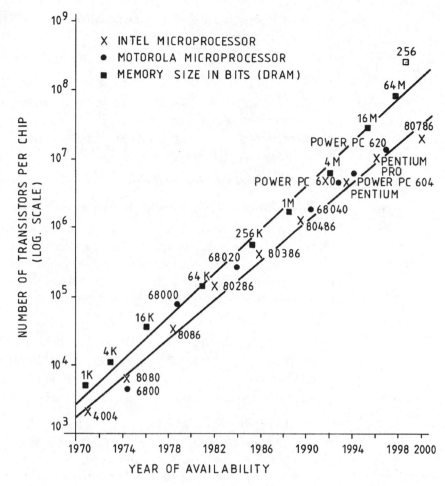

Figure 1-1
Transistor and memory chip densities have increased exponentially: Now Is the time for software advances.

While technology makes things happen, philosophy helps to idealize the real world and therefore conceive new solutions. The bridge between philosophy and technology is predictability*—without it, no major steps forward could be taken.

A good example of this issue is integrated circuitry. Its rate of development has been sustained by the essence of predictability as much as by a succession of increasingly more sophisticated lithography systems used in chip making to project patterns onto wafers.

---

*See also the discussion on the importance of the humanities in Chap. 9.

■ A major contribution to higher densities has also been made by more imaginative engineering design.

■ Such far-out-looking new departures are precisely what has been missing from software developments.

While during the last quarter century hardware led software in forward strides, we should never lose from sight that neither the semiconductor industry nor the software industry is unique. Both are still subject to the principles of economics:

■ The law of supply and demand

■ The value of differentiation provided by research laboratories

Whether their pace of development is rapid or slow, from their birth to maturity and decline, all industries have events and episodes that could act as a way to prognosticate what to expect in the years to come. Railroads, autos, home appliances, and airplanes are references that come easily to mind—all of them having become by now medium-technology industries:

■ It is a reasonable hypothesis that the late 1990s and the first decade of the twenty-first century will be the software years.

■ The time has come when the need for developing sophisticated software for intelligent objects is increasingly felt.

The Internet plays a key role in this connection. As the first incarnation of the information superhighway,* it underlines the need for intelligent artifacts to communicate among themselves and with their masters. This requires higher-level tools able to assure that active objects are aware of, as well as sensitive to, human intentions and emotions.

The greatest challenge that we are facing today is how to incorporate this imaginative software research into new design and manufacturing methods. Another challenge is to perceive and understand the evolving way in which software-hardware artifacts interact with each other and with people. An even more formidable task is to study their role in a broader social context, which leads us to the third computer revolution.

---

*See H. Steinmann and D. N. Chorafas, *An Introduction to the New Wave of Communications and Networks,* Cassell, London, 1996.

The Coming Third Computer Revolution

Dr. Nicholas Negreponte is far from being alone in his predictions about things that think. Among the people who look at autonomous knowledge artifacts as the way to revolutionize the software industry is Dr. Alan Kay, the man who has to his credit the desktop metaphor. Dr. Kay now predicts a third computer revolution. The first took place in the early 1950s with the institutional invasion of mainframes in the corporate business world. We are currently past the midway point of the second revolution, the personal computer and its windows-icons-mouse interface. The late 1990s will see the third wave intimately fusing into a powerful user environment three elements:

- Computers
- Communications
- Knowledge-enriched software

This will be very different from what we are accustomed to today. Instead of using personal computing tools, says Dr. Kay, we will be served by agents in an intimate, interactive multimedia manner—quite different from what we have known so far.

I would add to this projection that, by and large, the new software paradigm will be characterized by *instructable agents*. The incorporation of learning ability will provide truly intelligent assistance to an end user. This may be done for either and both, and it will be driven by a need to improve the inference and the interfacing capabilities of agents.

In practical implementation terms, instructable agents will act as entities or processes with *goal*-inducing reasoning. Other agents will be intelligent toolboxes able to provide active assistance to their masters, as we discussed earlier. Figure 1-2 suggests that the use of intelligent artifacts has become a necessity because 70 percent or more of the jobs important to managers and professionals are still *not* computer supported. This is not only because current software policies and practices are retrograde and lack imagination but also because computer interfaces are becoming more complex and increasingly heterogeneous.

As they currently stand, human-machine interfaces cannot continue grouping all the operations we want them to handle, on the screen. Slowly they come to the point where the multitude of menus and icons

Figure 1-2
Further strides in
computers and com-
munications depend
on intelligent soft-
ware.

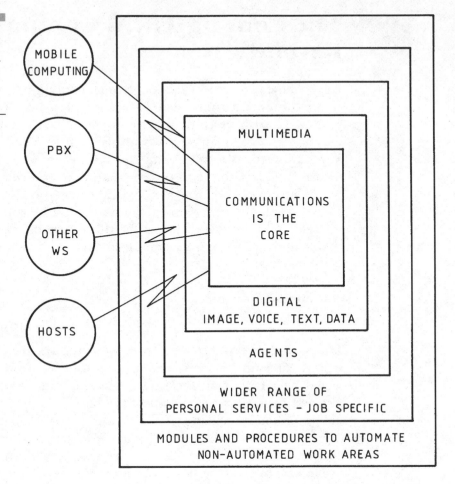

70% OF WORK AREAS
ARE STILL NOT AUTOMATED

are rejected by their users, and this rejection risks becoming massive. To be accepted:

- Human-machine interfaces should be subject to personalization.
- Instructable agents should be used as they are the best way to achieve effective customization results.

According to the Kay hypothesis, a key difference between currently available tools and agents is that an agent looks and talks to the user while a tool, as a passive object, is something the *user* looks at and manipulates. To reach the needed level of intimacy, agents must:

- Learn a great deal about their master
- Be able to interpret correctly what he or she wants

An obvious and important query is, how long will it take for active objects to become part of our everyday life? While exact dates cannot be stated, it is sure that it will not take over 100 years as has happened with other technologies. Facsimile technology, for instance, was developed in 1842 by Alexander Bain, a Scottish clock maker, but only in the 1980s did Sharp, Canon, Ricoh, and Toshiba popularize digital fax with fast, low-cost machines.

The evolution of fax is a good lesson. Admittedly, there had been intermediate developments, but no mass market. In the early 1920s, German inventors improved the process, permitting photographs to be sent overseas. Then AT&T, RCA, and Western Union developed systems that transmitted pictures for newspapers and weather maps. The market for such applications, however, was, at best, restricted, and therefore stagnant.

By contrast, the Japanese addressed the mass market—and that's what agents try to do. Not only have the first agents already appeared but they are also functioning in growing numbers of implementation domains.* Over the next few years we will see a progression toward increasingly smarter, more capable agents—not only from things that think, but also in a myriad of other projects.

Ovum of London forecasts that the combined American and European market for agents will grow to $2.6 billion by the year 2000. Their functions will include messaging and information retrieval—two domains projected to account for more than half of the agents' market. I personally think that instructable agents will be the hottest-selling class.

Another projection is that, before the year 2000, agents will not be constructed but will develop themselves using the tools made available through high technology. After all, the concept of agents is a direct descendent of Turing's machine, von Neumann's automata theory, and McCulloch's artificial intelligence (as we will see in a later section), all of which support the notion of self-adaptive, self-perpetuating artifacts.

The Role of Autonomous Agents

Dr. Pattie Maes, who manages the Media Lab's autonomous agents group at MIT, defines a software agent as "a process that lives in the world of

---

*Many implementation examples will be given in this text. Part 2 focuses on the domain of telecommunications.

computers and networks and that can operate *autonomously* to fulfill a set of tasks." Her definition distinguishes software agents on the basis of:

- Their affiliation
- The role they play
- The nature of their intelligence

A *userbot,* Maes says, works for one user, knows that user's interests, habits, and preferences, and acts on the user's behalf. Examples of this type of an agent are a personal news editor and an electronic shopper that may, for instance, operate on the Internet.

By contrast, a *taskbot* performs more generally useful tasks for a group of users or for all the users on a network. For instance, a taskbot might index the World Wide Web, do network load balancing, or perform diagnostics. We will see plenty of examples of taskbots in Part 3.

This distinction is useful, but to avoid dichotomies that some time down the line may prove to be irrational, I prefer to use the terms *agent* and *knowledge robot* (or *knowbot*) interchangeably. Dr. Maes's work is important in that it is:

- Oriented toward *learning agents*
- Stresses the development of collaboration among knowledge artifacts

As we saw earlier, the notion of instructable agents is fundamental. It underpins the new software paradigm, which should not be procedural, hence algorithmic, but rather heuristic. An agent can learn not only from its master but also from its peers by:

- Querying other agents via a bulletin board
- Asking peers what they would do in the present situation

Agents should also be able to learn, over time, which peer agents are good sources for particular types of information. Far from being theoretical, these concepts have a very practical applications domain that we should be willing and able to exploit.

Several software agents have been implemented at the media lab, among other organizations. *Maxims,* for example, is an e-mail-handling agent that works with personal computers.* It can assign priorities to

---

*See also in Chap. 2 the discussion on Mondrian.

messages based on the sender and decide which messages to archive and which to forward or delete:

- Maxims watches its master's patterns.
- Once trained, it is able to suggest a viable action.

Maes's definition of agents is influenced by her work, which focuses on these two scenarios for software artifacts: agents that watch over one's shoulder and learn how to do things and agents that learn from their peers who provide recommendations. Either and both kinds can act as memory helpers. They can schedule meetings or serve as guides for the World Wide Web. They can also act as filters and critics—which would require a somewhat higher level of intelligence.

One of the new agents under development is *Yenta*. Its job is to introduce the user to people with similar interests. Similar agents could match patients with doctors treating rare diseases, or they could bring together generalist doctors with specialists.

Some years ago doctors at a Los Angeles hospital had teamed up with rocket scientists and developed an agent that brought specialist doctors' help to the generalist. The artifact ran on a PC equipped with an optical disk. It accepted laboratory input on a patient, and subsequently:

- Presented to the generalist the options that existed in a diagnosis
- Visualized results from other similar cases
- Suggested a specialist doctor that the generalist might wish to contact

One important characteristic these implementations of intelligent artifacts have in common is that they are autonomous agents. The ability to be autonomous is vital because they operate in a dynamic environment. They must not only sense but also act within the applications landscape for which they are designed, based on:

- Knowledge
- Learning
- Reasoning
- Adaptation

Quite significantly, the autonomous nature of the agents requires that there is no central reasoner or control. The artifacts interface with one another through simple message passing. Each can be directly connected to sensors and effectors. All are adaptive to changes, and they are proactive.

New Bottles for New Wine: Reinventing the "Eins"

A study I conducted in the mid- 1990s among American and European companies documented that 35 percent of the origin of new software products comes from direct client demands. As Fig. 1-3 shows, taken together, market studies conducted by software companies and internal research and development projects account for another 38 percent. Agents can be seen as having originated within this 38 percent share.

Agents, however, are not monolithic constructs as, for instance, is the case with Cobol programs. They can take many different forms, depending on the nature of the system whose requirements they serve. It is also possible to build agents that work in simulated environments. Because they are active objects, both in a physical and in a logical setting agents can perform:

- Control missions
- Surveillance
- Exploration

In connection to World Wide Web navigators and browsers, for instance, agents are being developed to support a rather rigorous form of search-

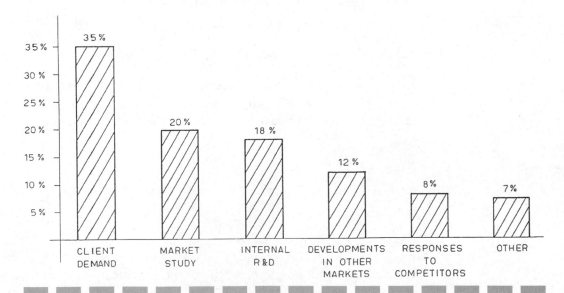

Figure 1-3 Origin of new products in the software business.

ing. It is being forecast that these will evolve into itinerant intelligent artifacts able to provide significant services to their masters—and to the network.

Artifacts differ among themselves because of their inference engine. A major difference between heuristic and algorithmic agents is that the former have a *lifelike* behavior that is nonmechanical and can be spontaneous. Typically, instructable agents are modeled as distributed artifacts:

- They consist of small competence modules.

- Each is an expert at achieving a given task.

Those of us who worked as programmers in the 1950s, quite often in straight machine language, knew how to build small competence modules—the "subroutines," as they were called at the time.* But this knowhow got lost in the mammoth software constructs built in the 1960s, 1970s, and 1980s by the bureaucracy of EDPers—in Fortran, Cobol, and other languages which are awkward by today's standards.

There are also other concepts of the last 60 years that played a major role in the development of computing but somehow got lost only to be reinvented. Alan Turing is best known for the metaphor of the machine that bears his name. But he has also made two major contributions to the way we use agents:

- The concept of *eins*

- Simultaneous scanning

Simultaneous scanning is a knowledge engineering process that used clone machines to test 26 hypotheses (letters) at each position of the German Enigma cryptography engine. The clones were manufactured in England by copying an Enigma machine found in a captured German submarine.† This can today be very effectively done in real time by agents. Agents can be replicated and used to test hypotheses in parallel to solve a single problem.

The same is true of the test of the *eins* (German for "one"). To break the German secret code, Alan Turing, Peter Twinn, and Joan Murray conceived the idea of a specialized machine that could be used to encrypt the 4-letter word *eins*—at all positions of the larger Enigma. This was done with the day's wheel order and plugging—and it proved

---

*A term coined by Dr. John von Neumann.

†F. H. Hinsley and Alan Stripp (eds.), *Code Breakers. The Inside Story of Bletchley Park*, Oxford University Press, Oxford, 1993.

instrumental in unlocking the German secret code. Something similar can now be done by agents regarding:

- Data streams on the network
- The mining of database contents[*]

One can argue that *genetic algorithms* (GA) are a combination of simultaneous scanning and *eins,* plus some added features.[†] Mathematically, as well as in a business sense, convergence to multiple optima emulates the way natural systems behave.

- With GA, descriptions, states, values, and connecting links evolve genetically.
- This evolution is accomplished through crossovers and mutations, which have a significant effect on how future descriptions are encoded.

In a genetic algorithm, the notions of niches, species, and constraints are mapped through modifications made to the selection scheme. This is a kind of extensibility via natural selection processes, a notion underlying the heuristic GA procedure.

My thesis is that *search heuristics* underpin Alan Turing's *eins* and simultaneous scanning, as well as John Holland's genetic algorithms. These and similar approaches produce a computing perspective with an efficiently focused search. Problem-specific information can be built into the operators or the problem's coding. The great merit of GA is that it makes apparent the potential of search heuristics and recombinations. An increasing number of mission-critical applications are being approached with this perspective—from telecommunications problems (see Part 2) to computer-aided design financial engineering.[‡]

In more than one sense, agents are a continuation of the work done by computer pioneers in the 1940s and 1950s—which lapsed into oblivion. If the late Dr. John von Neumann was still around, he might well have said that agents constitute practical applications of *automata.* But agent technology also has other prerequisites, which reflect the new concepts of the 1990s. Today, software solutions that are worth their salt find themselves in the quarter space defined by Fig. 1-4. They must feature low personnel requirements, a high level of sophistication, and high

---

[*]See Chaps. 9 and 12; also D. N. Chorafas and H. Steinmann, *Database Mining. Exploiting Marketing Databases in the Financial Industry,* Lafferty, London and Dublin, 1994.

[†]See D. N. Chorafas, *Rocket Scientists in Banking,* Lafferty, London and Dublin, 1996.

[‡]See D. N. Chorafas, *Chaos Theory in the Financial Markets,* Probus/Irwin, Chicago, 1994.

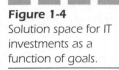

Figure 1-4
Solution space for IT
investments as a
function of goals.

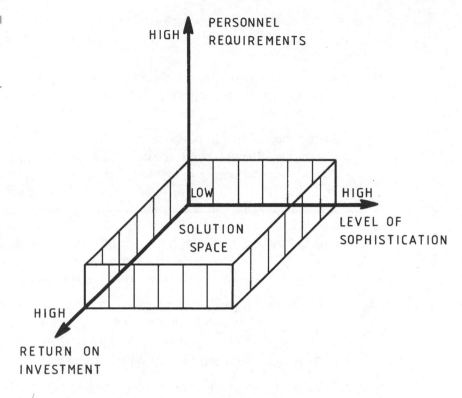

return on investment (ROI). I was impressed by the attention paid to
ROI at Comdex, Fall 1996, Las Vegas, Nevada.

von Neumann's Automata, McCulloch's AI, and Agents

The best way to appreciate what might happen in the future is to study
what has taken place in the past, and from there to make inferences and
extrapolations. There is always much to be gained by considering the
lessons learned from developments connected to scientific efforts versus
the alternative of ignoring them or looking at them lightly.

One of the issues that strikes me in connection to agents, at least at the
current state of the art, is what Dr. John von Neumann said about *automata*. His opinion has been that, in spite of its prima facie quantitative character, the concept of automata may in fact stand for something *qualitative*.
This conflicted with the prevailing hypothesis in the early 1950s:

- When an automaton performs certain operations, these must be expected to be of a lower degree of complexity than the automaton itself.

- If an automaton has the ability to construct another one, there must be a decrease in complexity as we go from the parent to the filial (child) or, offspring, frame.

At the root of this hypothesis was the notion that in order to make this generation effective, there must be various arrangements in the parent automaton that see to it that a functional description is interpreted—and that the constructive.operations that it calls for are carried out. From there came the deduction that the filial's complexity or sophistication must be diminished compared to that of the parent. Von Neumann, however, pointed out that not everything needs to fit into this model. His thesis has been that although the foregoing notion has some plausibility, it is essentially in contradiction to some natural phenomena:

- Organisms reproduce themselves—or, more precisely, they produce new organisms—with no decrease in complexity.

- There are also long periods of evolution during which complexity increases, which can happen with automata.

Progressing by analogy in the context of agents, we should not expect a decrease in sophistication as one agent makes another agent. The production (or reproduction) of agents by agents is still a theory in its infancy, but von Neumann's remarks are most valid and should not be lost from view.

Von Neumann speculated that, because natural organisms are directly derived from others of lower complexity, in terms of human-made systems, there exists an apparent conflict of plausibility and evidence. To a significant extent, this plausibility is based on our hypotheses which themselves derive from Dr. Alan Turing's theory of computational automata. Another major contributor has been Dr. Warren S. McCulloch.

In the Hixon Symposium, which took place in Pasadena on September 20, 1948, Dr. McCulloch explained how he came to be interested in the connectionist problem and those issues that later became known as *artificial intelligence*. He said that his initial interest was in philosophy and mathematics, and that he had come from that background to the study of psychology.

The problem that excited McCulloch's imagination was how a science like mathematics could ever arise. To find an answer, he gradually shifted into psychology and from there into neurophysiology. "The attempt to construct a theory in a field like this, so that it can be put to any verification, is tough," McCulloch suggested. "Humorously enough, I started at the wrong angle, about 1919, trying to construct a logic for transitive verbs."*

According to McCulloch's own account, his work in 1919 was mainly a problem in modal logic, and it was not until he saw Turing's paper that he began to head in the right direction. Then, with Walter Pitts's help, he formulated the required logical calculus, treating the brain as a Turing machine:

- We should look at the brain as an information processing device that performs a great variety of functions in logic and intuition.

- McCulloch wanted an artificial intelligence construct able to address the kind of functions a brain must perform.

This could be, for instance, an artifact capable of taking a logical proposition and manipulating it—whether at the time of its occurrence or afterward. Something was needed to construct a theory able to state how a nervous system could do anything.

Neural networks were born out of this simple set of assumptions. Agents, particularly instructable agents, could be constructed by following similar principles. However, though connectionism helps in learning tasks, few agents are neural networks, and the two concepts should not be confused.

Other crucial questions also come to mind. When we say that "we emulate the brain," to which functions are we indeed referring? Are we talking more of the right brain or of the left brain? If of the right brain, is our artifact more conceptual or more behavioral? If of the left brain, is it analytical or directive?

Figure 1-5 explains in a snapshot what underlies this analogy. Applied experimental psychology has addressed all four quadrants. Research on agents has not yet done so. The dominant concepts and processes are along causal, rather than teleological, lines—which means that agents tend to be analytical rather than conceptual, and hence, left brain rather than right brain. But the die is not yet cast. New work on agents may change this direction.

*F. Brody and T. Vamos (eds.), *The Neumann Compendium*, World Scientific, Singapore, 1995.

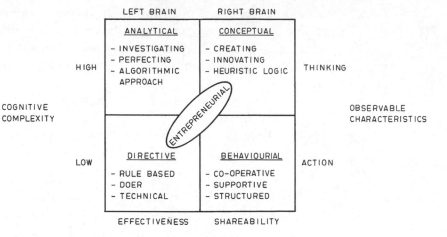

Causality, Teleology, and Mathematical Models

The first task in dealing with any problem is to formulate it unambiguously, expressing it in a rigorous sense whether in words or mathematically. Both in the case of natural and of artificial systems, any formulation of how to create or reproduce new entities with improved behavior must explain the facts of *evolution* of behavior as well as the *regulation* of the process. This means the mechanism will turn out the same or an essentially similar product after time t. This can be done through:

- Causality
- Teleology

The notion underpinning a process of *causality* is that if we know the state of the system now, then we can use this knowledge to predict its state immediately thereafter, and maybe for a short time after that. The shorter the duration of the forecast period, the more accurate the prediction should be—and, in many cases, could be.

In scientific prognosis, it does not really matter that greatly whether the forecast occurs well before the fact or just before the fact—as long as the prediction period is within the required tolerances or limits. Therefore, mathematical modeling presupposes the ability to describe correctly along a causal or teleological pathway—in other terms, whatever pathway has been chosen.

A *teleological* approach takes a whole view of the history of the system between two moments that are separated. Through a finite stretch of the artifact's or system's behavior, teleology asserts that the historical process under study must satisfy certain criteria, usually stated in terms of a function that is either *maximizing* or *minimizing*.

Teleology is the study of final causes. It is as well the fact or quality of being directed toward a definite end or of having an ultimate purpose. This is particularly attributed to natural processes. Teleology is contrasted to mechanism. In teleology, a single event does not determine the next event, but the process must somehow be viewed as a unity that is subordinate to a general law. The whole can be understood only in reference to this general law, whose formulation must be made very carefully.

With agents we have not reached that state. What we have is *ontology*: the specification of a domain of discourse among agents, in the form of definitions of shared vocabulary, including classes, relations, functions, and object constants. An agent ontology:

■ Specifies a domain-specific language for agent interaction

■ Describes agent behavior in terms of time-varying parameters

In certain cases, causal and teleological characteristics are complementary. In other cases, they substitute for one another. Both approaches—causality and teleology—essentially describe the same thing, the choice being a matter of method. For instance, Newton's approach is causal, while d'Alembert's is teleological:

■ Finite differences provide a causal description of events.

■ The description given by transition probabilities (Markov chains) is teleological.*

Essentially, what divides the two methods is the choice of a process of mathematical transformation. Causality follows sequential steps, which may be stochastic or deterministic, while with teleology the system's history is not determined by anything happening at one moment but through a holistic view. This calls for much more sophisticated models.

No matter how simple or complex are our agents, they must have a structure that relates to the process being emulated. If this is not done for each of the agent's distinct internal steps or processes, it should at least be done in reference to the whole agent. This we often try to do

---

*See D. N. Chorafas, *Statistical Processes and Reliability Engineering*, Van Nostrand, Princeton, N.J., 1960.

through abstraction, but abstraction may lead to a restricted class of behavior because of the number of assumptions about the behavior that the technique refers. A model, von Neumann said, is a mathematical artifact which, with the addition of certain verbal interpretations, describes observed phenomena. Its justification is that it is expected to work. To be comprehensible, this model must be rather simple—a statement that fully applies to agents. Mathematics, however, can be simple or complex depending on where our knowledge lies at a given moment. What we know is simple. What we don't know is complex. Figure 1-6 makes this

Figure 1-6
As with mathematical models, so with agents: simplicity and complexity are relative.

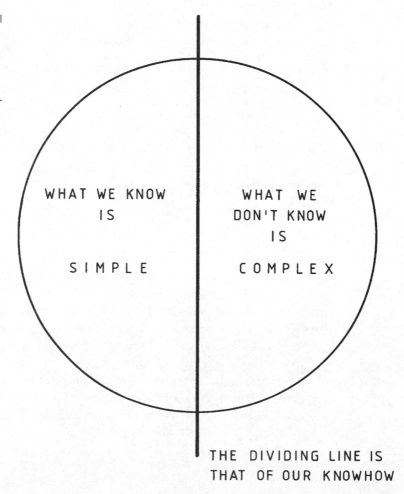

WHAT WE KNOW
IS

SIMPLE

WHAT WE
DON'T KNOW
IS

COMPLEX

THE DIVIDING LINE IS
THAT OF OUR KNOWHOW

distinction, which can be extended to characterize the knowledge bank of agents.

In terms of software development, for instance, for people accustomed to Cobol or Fortran programs, with no experience in knowledge engineering, the concept of agents, and their development and usage, is very complex. Agent behavior overwhelms them because it is not unambiguously explained. Minds working in the linear fashion of software centralization and batch processing find even the concept of autonomous, instructable agents overwhelming because it is alien to their programming culture.

Computer-Mediated and Computer-Participative Applications

Another issue that is alien to many people's cultures, including information technology specialists, one that is relevant to agents, is the fairly significant difference that exists between computer-participative and computer-mediated applications. This distinction provides a dichotomy between the simple and the complex as well as between the new and the old.

Computer-mediated applications are generally those classified under data processing and, by extension, also under the term *multimedia*. Multimedia conveniently covers the evolution that has taken place from data-related computation to the handling of voice, video, text, and graphics.

It is important to appreciate that as long as we talk of the more classical software, the process remains fundamentally machine centered. Therefore, it covers the earlier wave of applications in which the computer acts as mediator. In such role, the machine supports the capture, storage, retrieval, and presentation of media information:

- While filtering and editing may also be needed in a *computer-mediated* environment, the machine does not actively participate in creating that process. It simply executes commands.

- By contrast, in *computer-participative* applications, the software analyzes the audio and video data input, taking actions based on the result of this analysis.

In other terms, the computer becomes an *active* participant in media processing. For instance, it stores, filters, and maintains an online database of financial news or other issues such as those involved in a corporate memory facility.[*]

To perform this mission in an able manner, the artifacts running on the machine must comprehend and analyze the content of multimedia digital streams and of databased information elements. As explained earlier, they must be *active objects* rather than traditional passive objects, or, more precisely, they must be *thinking objects*.

The thinking objects are agents, implemented through intelligent software. Not only should such software be designed to ride the technology curve, but also its underlying environment must be conveniently portable to higher performance platforms as they become available.

- Increasing the sophistication of media processing calls for computer-participative approaches.

- The media processing must be dynamic, steadily incorporating new software-based improvements.

Object-oriented disciplines contribute to the creation of computer-participative architectures. Because the *object,* not the *record,* is the basic unit of reference, a number of computers can act as servers—with objects' autonomous agents moving freely around the network. In this way, the agents bring themselves closer to the end user and to the end user's problems.

Additional flexibility is provided by the knowledge engineering artifacts embedded in the network nodes, which Dr. Maes calls *taskbots.* *Metarules*[†] help in handling a number of logically distinct databases, each of these designated as shared or personal information elements. The latter I prefer to call *microfiles* to avoid misinterpretations about their ownership.

- Microfiles are typically stored locally for higher-speed access, but they are part of the more general database resources.

- Locally storing microfiles avoids the overhead of object locking and other operations for managing shared data and supports processing even when the server or network is not available.

---

[*]See also D. N. Chorafas, *Risk Management in Financial Institutions,* Butterworth, London, 1989.

[†]See also Chap. 10.

Agents can see to it that groups of objects are transferred to and from servers and microfiles through check-in and check-out procedures. These can be supported by other agents that uphold data integrity and privacy—or that assist in database-wide passthrough while providing security.*

The chosen discipline defined by the metarules must see to it that programs are divided into two dynamically defined partitions, organized along *in-band* and *out-of-band* axes of reference. In a multimedia environment, for example, audio, video, and other temporally sensitive information flow through the media-driven partition along the in-band axis.

In-band processing consumes most of the system resources and also conforms to the timing constraints of *perceptual time*. Agents enforce timeliness policies. Out-of-band processing performs event-handling functions, such as:

- Event-driven code known from interactive applications
- In those situations in which agents wait for their master's inputs and other events before taking action

In some of the more advanced projects, software modules communicate through the exchange of payloads that are passed by procedural calls. The flow of media between modules is structured as a sequence of payloads, each of which is labeled with a type identifier time stamp. This approach can support heterogeneous media streams including uncompressed video-audio, compressed video, and sequence control indicators.

---

*See also Chap. 6.

CHAPTER 2

Agents: Facts and Opportunities for Knowledge Workers

The new departures in machine intelligence that were introduced in Chap. 1 can be better appreciated if we keep in mind one of the main themes in modern organizations. Today, the new generation of knowledge workers has changed the demands placed upon the technological supports required to do a neat job. Because knowledge workers represent society's most valuable asset, *brainpower*, they have gained the upper hand in industrial and business life, and they have provided themselves with the opportunity to shop around for the best offer.

In the past, many senior people would argue that managers should possess generalized skills which could be applied to any industry. Today, the leading notion is that it is rather a specific culture and knowhow that enable professionals and managers to make appropriate decisions. However, both schools of thought are wrong:

■ Knowledge workers can perform best if they are specialists and generalists at the same time.

■ This is, however, a demanding job that cannot be sustained over long periods without sophisticated assistance.

Modern technology sees to it that this assistance can be effectively supplied through interactive intelligent artifacts—the agents, or knowledge robots, that Chap. 1 introduced. Companies develop and implement them in conjunction with their computers and communications systems.

Agents have been described as a new type of software acting as autonomous vehicles that communicate with their peers and with humans by exchanging messages. They can be as simple as small subroutines, but, as often, they can be somewhat larger programming entities:

■ Dedicated to specific process(es) on a personal workstation, server, or network

■ Featuring distinct control threads within a single address space

■ Capable of interconnecting separate processes on different machines, using communications language(s)

As we will see in Chap. 9, when we talk about how to construct an agent, this new type of software engineering has many elements in common with object-oriented programming.[*] Like an object, an agent provides a message-based interface independent of its internal data structure, heuristics, or algorithms. Differences lie in the language of the interface and proactive stance taken by agents, as opposed to passive objects.

---

[*]See also D. N. Chorafas and H. Steinmann, *Object-Oriented Databases,* Prentice-Hall, Englewood Cliffs, N.J., 1993.

Knowledge Workers and Advanced Projects in Information Technology

Advanced projects in information technology are made by and for knowledge workers. The resulting new software artifacts may be employed by financial institutions, manufacturing companies, merchandising firms, or universities. Some software development laboratories currently envision millions of interactive knowledge artifacts resident in:

- Intelligent networks
- Distributed databases
- High-performance computers
- Personal workstations

Agents will make the difference in moving from telephony and the current relatively limited *multimedia* approaches to the intelligence-enriched broadband solutions projected for the year 2000 and beyond. Figure 2-1 provides a visual presentation of this transition, which is expected to start before the end of the 1990s and will probably require a whole decade to complete.

These knowledge agents will be actuators, advisors, and assistants. The integration of human knowhow and machine agents is projected to be seamless, often making it difficult to appreciate which is which. Most

Figure 2-1
Evolution in telecommunications and intelligent artifacts.

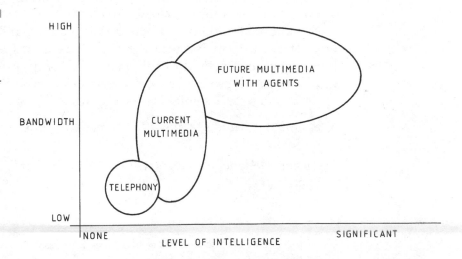

importantly, this transition will change the socioeconomic character of work and a good part of our social life. Therefore, some of the projects in high technology, which are well launched at the present time, concern themselves not only with advanced software but also with the effects of social change—for instance, a world in which people actively publish electronic knowledge and get paid each time it is used. This can be accomplished by:

■ Instrumentally expanding knowledge systems

■ Making the contents of knowledge systems widely available on high-bandwidth communications networks

■ Providing format and language translation as automatic services on those networks

■ Assuring that future applications capitalize on these assets, assisted by knowledge robots

Innovative companies are already regularly capturing and reapplying their knowledge in *research, development, and implementation* (RD&I)—from product design to manufacturing and sales, or alternatively, in financial forms and structures all the way to the development and delivery of banking services. We will talk about how knowledge can be captured in Chap. 3.

Knowledge is being built into all kinds of products, from banking, like derivative instruments,* to automobiles, microwave ovens, and photo machines. This process is accelerating due to the advent of interactive electronic systems, personal digital assistants (PDAs), and integrated computing and communications devices. All these advances make it feasible to exploit diverse knowledge-based solutions.

The knowledge industry sees to it that products and processes are in a wave of change. For instance, the financial systems of the twenty-first century will make current banking practices seem primitive by comparison. The entire process of design, marketing, and distribution will be enabled by a seamless online *knowledge web*:

■ Knowledge-based systems will interactively construct new financial vehicles.

■ Custom-designed products will be built using artifacts already in operation.

---

*See also D. N. Chorafas, *Advanced Financial Analysis*, Euromoney, London, 1994.

Products can be personalized cost-effectively with single, customized units—which is the ultimate objective of the current progression toward more advanced systems. Agents are important tools for this type of solution and are necessary to gain and sustain market competitiveness.

Knowledge robots will assure that customization ends will be reached interactively online. At the bottom line the process will be enriched from highly automated reasoning artifacts that control the design, production, sale, and delivery steps characterizing a product. The top layer will require the expertise of knowledge workers.

Figure 2-2 suggests a line of reasoning along this path, applicable to the financial industry. Abstracted from a project I have recently con-

Figure 2-2
Technology-assisted operations in the financial industry for business competitiveness and risk management.

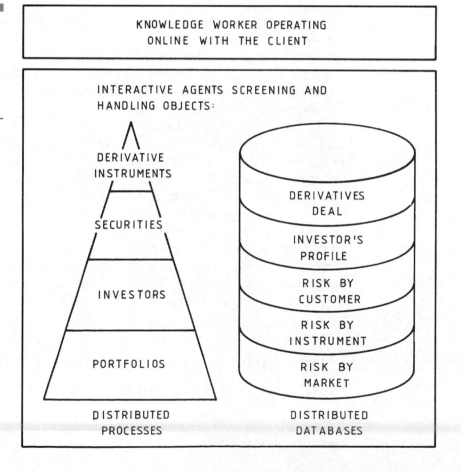

ducted, it demonstrates how the knowledge worker is still online but is greatly assisted by means of interactive agents that:

- Specialize in different types of derivatives
- Assist in personalizing hedging policies
- Help in the control of risk

The careful reader will appreciate that this solution requires rethinking our products and processes. This job is not that easy, but it is doable. It is, as well, a fact that many industrial products and financial instruments are long overdue for a complete overhaul. Autonomous learning agents could revolutionize products and services enabling us to attain both:

- Increased quality
- Lower costs

Computer-assisted banking, for example, has been around for about 30 years since the beginning of real-time applications. But it existed in an environment that inhibited its full development. Only in the mid- to late 1980s did accelerating global competition force banks to build more advanced tools and methods such as expert systems, and to model dynamically a comprehensive financial environment.

Knowledge-engineered software can do the job for which it is built quite effectively. In the years to come, agents will increasingly address critical issues because, whether in the manufacturing industry or in banking, the most important challenge in making technology more effective is to transform our systems from the islands of automation that have existed into an intelligent, enterprise-wide nervous system.

The new design should assure that the interaction of managers and professionals with their knowledge agents is transparent and natural. The target of advanced projects in information technology targeted for knowledge workers is to permit an interactive appreciation of the *scope of competition* and the *mode of competition* in the quadrants illustrated in Fig. 2-3. The knowledge worker's ability to compete when assisted by agents is the main theme of this chapter.

Virtual Engineering: A Landscape for the Implementation of Agents

The realization of faster product development cycles through interactive prototypes is a worthwhile objective. Quick looks at design concepts,

Figure 2-3
Scope of competition
and its expanding
landscape.

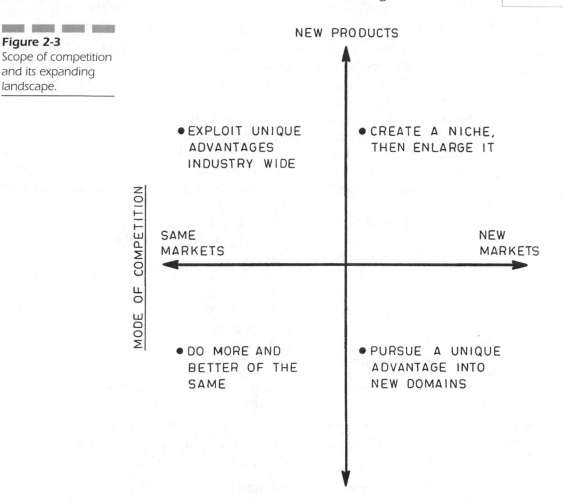

what-if studies, and fast layout sketches permit research or investigation to be done through simulation—saving time and money. A number of terms are currently used to describe this process:

- Virtual engineering
- Virtual reality*
- Design synthesis
- Real-time simulation
- Rapid prototyping

---

*See D. N. Chorafas and H. Steinmann, *Virtual Reality: Practical Applications in Business and Industry*, Prentice-Hall, Princeton, N.J., 1995.

In the way it is used in this book, the term *virtual engineering* goes all the way from research, development, analysis, and design to manufacturing. It incorporates the advantage of simulation with ease and speed but also supports interactivity, which permits subsecond response both from the agent and from the knowledge worker.

Virtual engineering rests on the time-tested concept of real-time simulation. Since the early 1960s digital simulation proved to be a very helpful procedure. Simulation is a *working analogy* that rests on the mathematical model of a known situation, process, or business environment.

In essence, agents are real-time simulators of knowledge, operating through a working analogy.* *Analogy* means a similarity of properties without identity. When we are able to construct analogous systems, measurements or other observations made on one of them can be used to predict the reaction of the others.

Alternatively, when analogous physical and logical systems are found to exist, we can emulate the physical entity and its behavior through the use of the logical artifact. We will return to this concept in Chap. 8 when we talk of metaphors. This is exactly what agents do—and, in fact, this is more or less what has been practiced since the 1950s with the first software programs ever written:

- The difference between today and yesterday is that now we work by means of *real-time simulations,* not offline in a batch or delayed time mode.

- Real-time response is a prerequisite for agents, as it is with virtual banking and virtual engineering.

With all knowledge workers, simulation is an iterative process through which we improve upon a model, decide upon a scenario, run the experiment, analyze the results, develop an alternative scenario, and consult in real time with other domain experts. We can then improve the model again and repeat the cycle.

- Because of perceived benefits, tier 1 companies are active in converting offline software into online, interactive solutions operating within an integrated business environment.

- Virtual numerical control, for instance, is accomplished through the emulation of the machine tool and its controller in a simulated workcell.

---

*See also the discussion in Chap. 12 on analogical reasoning.

Figure 2-4
Relation between
velocity and error in
an actuator system.

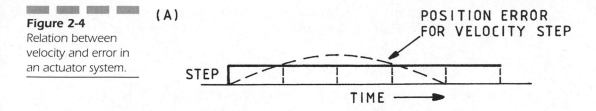

(A)

POSITION ERROR
FOR VELOCITY STEP

STEP

TIME ⟶

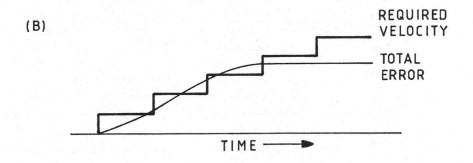

(B)

REQUIRED
VELOCITY

TOTAL
ERROR

TIME ⟶

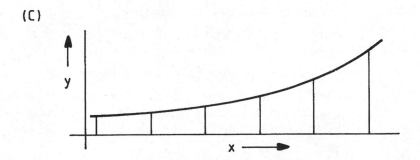

(C)

An example from modeling in a numerical control environment is
given in Fig. 2-4. Its objective is to control within a prescribed tolerance
the relationship between velocity and position in an actuator system.
Numerical control is nearly a 40-year-old art, but today agents can be
instrumental in improving its quality.

One of the important benefits of numerical control simulation is the
ability to optimize processes and resolve design problems before they
occur on the production floor. For this reason, engineering schools are

in the process of incorporating a broad range of the new graphical analysis tools into their curricula:

- Analysis, synthesis, simulation, optimization techniques, and computer graphics have become a "must."
- The design engineer is programming in the large.* Whatever tactical adjustments might be necessary are actuated through agents. This is an example of the knowledge worker—agent relationship illustrated in Fig. 2-2.

As we will see through a wealth of practical examples, a variety of knowledge workers are today using the new graphical tools. Processes and procedures that exploit the power of the computer to model products and processes are actively sought after by the most competitive organizations.

It is precisely these same organizations that are now developing and implementing agents. Experiences in virtual engineering have demonstrated that while necessary in its strictest sense, real-time simulation is not enough. The same is true of the older generation of computer-aided design (CAD). Object orientation and knowledge agents are means, not goals. They are the means for the renewal of existing processes. There exist similarities and differences between these two subjects:

- In object-oriented programming, the perceived meaning of a message can vary from one object to another.
- In agent-based software engineering, artifacts use a common language with agent-independent semantics.

The imaging business provides a good application example where both object orientation and agent technology can make significant contributions. It enriches computer-aided design of manufactured parts with machine vision, desktop publishing, virtual reality, and other graphic arts.

Most image processing companies use commodity computers, along with a little bit of specialized hardware and a lot of mathematical software—both commercial off-the-shelf and custom software. There is a

*D. N. Chorafas, *Visual Programming Technology*, McGraw-Hill, New York, 1996.

stream of imaginative projects, pushing the frontiers of computerized imagery in areas such as:

- Visualization
- Manipulation
- Pattern recognition*

A steady flow of innovation sees to it that what is hot today may be swept aside in a year or so by emerging competitors with better technologies. Therefore, as the chapter will go on to explain, the foremost engineering companies are quick to develop and implement new, agent-assisted methods.

A Practical Use of Agents with the New Generation of Computer-Aided Design

A combination of image technology and knowledge artifacts can locate objects, read labels, and inscriptions, measure dimensions, and precisely position components for mounting or assembly. With the gift of sight artifacts, automated manufacturing machines can often work faster than fingers and can deal with objects:

- Too small to see well with the naked eye
- Too massive to precisely position by hand

In Chap. 12 we will define this process as *visibilization*. Other knowledge artifacts help to manipulate graphic images, preview printed photos, examine 3D views, and handle blueprints. These have been used to advantage in publishing, the graphic arts, engineering, and architectural design—and they are now entering finance.

Based on a project currently under way, Fig. 2-5 illustrates the uses of agents at the workstation level to provide a flexible choice of tools necessary for database mining and number-crunching computational chores. The application is computer-aided design—where knowledge artifacts, among other things, choose and optimize the *bill of materials* (BOM).

*See Chap. 12.

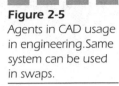

Figure 2-5
Agents in CAD usage
in engineering. Same
system can be used
in swaps.

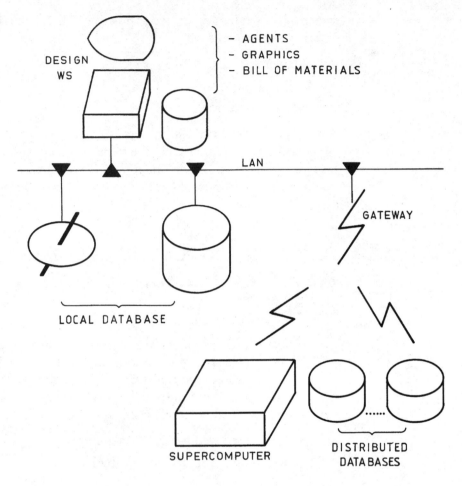

A new technology of high-level, *editable representations* (EReps) is being introduced into CAD and may prove to be a major extension to what has so far been achieved in solid modeling or feature-based design. Conceptually, EReps are analogous to a high-level programming language in the same way that command streams on existing CAD systems compare to executable machine language.

Each editable representation command or gesture would require many low-level operations from existing CAD modules. The agent that interprets the editable representation satisfies the role of a geometry compiler, or interpreter.*

---

*See D. N. Chorafas, *Programming Systems for Electronic Computers*, Butterworths, London, 1962.

- First, it translates the editable shape representation through a sequence of geometric operations.

- Then, using an underlying modeler, the geometric operations are translated into a more traditional *boundary representation* (BRep).

Assisted by knowledge artifacts, EReps aim to fulfill design feature definitions that extend solid modeling technology to serve downstream applications in analysis and manufacturing. This is supposed to be independent of the specific modeler employed to create the BRep.

A higher level of abstraction provides editable archiving to leverage valuable design assets as families of future designs. EReps *store the rules* that specify how to construct geometry as a function of parameters and constraints, rather than storing the geometry itself. This solution:

- Captures design intent*

- Fulfills the prerequisites for the creation of design knowledge banks

Through the use of intelligent interactive artifacts, EReps also support the interoperability requirements to optimize the design and manufacturing process. They help in providing a standardized approach to communicate nongeometric attributes to capture design intent as well as geometric information from different commercial modelers.

While this example comes from engineering, it is just as applicable in finance. Nikko Securities, one of the top three brokers in Japan, is actively using computer-aided design software in projecting and managing new swaps† instruments. This is done with a client-server solution similar to the one shown in Fig. 2-5, accessing remote databases and supercomputers for a variety of tasks.

Whether in engineering or in banking, a number of factors point to the need for using agents to enrich the solutions currently available through computer-aided design. For instance, everybody with experience in industry appreciates the importance of integrating technical studies and plans—from research and development to engineering, manufacturing, and field support.

- Assisted by agents, designers can use computer programs that simulate product performance.

---

*See also D. N. Chorafas, *Engineering Productivity Through CAD/CAM*, Butterworths, London and Boston, 1987.

†A *swap* is a transaction in which one financial instrument is exchanged, or swapped, for another. Typically, two parties are exchanging forward obligations.

■ Agents interpret the results of online experimentation and help in making decisions through rapid prototyping.

This is of strategic significance as companies begin to reengineer their product development processes. It is precisely for this reason that serious users of computers have instituted interactive intelligent environments that integrate the activities required for a product's life cycle.

Simulated output analyses have been conducted for some years with the assistance of expert systems that serve as advisors to the designer, industrial engineer, or salesperson. But while every engineer and salesperson needs to understand the simulation technology and tools that can be used to better the products and processes with which he or she works, it is just as important to appreciate the contributions made by agents.

The Mondrian Project at MIT: Agents for Human Interfaces*

Whether in engineering, manufacturing, or finance, many computer applications have been hampered by the lack of attention to human interfaces. Projects typically place emphasis on the mechanics of algorithms, rather than on issues such as graphical representation, interpretation of direct manipulation actions, and interactive user feedback.

To correct this deficiency, MIT developed *Mondrian,* an object-oriented graphics editor that can learn new graphical procedures through programming by example. This project constitutes a first-class example of the effective use of agents:

■ The user demonstrates a sequence of graphical editing commands illustrating how the new procedure should work.

■ An interface agent records the steps of the procedure, tracking relationships between graphical objects and dependencies among interface operations.

Using heuristics, the agent generalizes a program that can then be used on analogous examples. The artifact represents all operations using pic-

---

*See also the discussion on human interfaces in Chap. 10; also, in the same chapter, see the reference to Jacaranda.

torial storyboards of examples. It also employs synthesized speech to narrate its interpretations of the user's actions.

The Mondrian project uses *instructable agents,* as defined in Chap. 1. As a memory refresher, these are pieces of software that provide intelligent assistance to a user but that also learn from acquired experience. Such agents are used to attain:

- More efficient interfacing
- Better inference capability[*]

In practical implementation terms, agents have been incorporated into Mondrian entities or processes that have *goals-inducing* reasoning. Note that this is not necessarily a universal practice. As we will see in subsequent chapters, other researchers see agents as intelligent toolboxes with a primary purpose of providing active assistance to their users.

The MIT researchers have suggested that the use of intelligent artifacts has become necessary because computer interfaces are today more complex and increasingly heterogeneous. Human-machine interfaces cannot continue grouping the number of operations on the screen into complex menus or large groupings of icons. Such interfaces will be massively rejected by their end users. By contrast, what is needed is a simple interface that can be subject to personalizing itself, learning from the end user's habits. On the premise that an intelligent artifact must be able to provide personalized assistance, the Media Laboratory of MIT has developed a design of interactive *domino icons* able to show their user *before* and *after* images. A block diagram of the interface and its commands are shown in Fig. 2-6:

- The system writes a code transparent to the user.
- It translates the code and executes.
- As a feedback, it responds in English to explain what it did.

Mondrian and other similar MIT projects have been instrumental in applying artificial intelligence techniques to human-machine interaction. Independent solutions developed in the area of autonomous agents and commonsense representation are now being combined to implement more sophisticated *interface agents*.

The examples that we saw earlier in this chapter with virtual engineering and with EReps help demonstrate the need for such intelligent

---

[*]The sense of inference is discussed in Chap. 10.

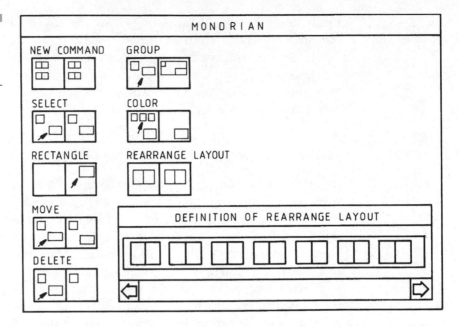

interfaces. The more complex our systems become, the more we need to provide expert assistance to the knowledge worker engaged in practical computer applications.

Knowledge artifacts of Mondrian variety differ from current-day interfaces in that they act autonomously. They perform many of the time-consuming, more mundane tasks the user normally would have to do manually:

- The agent is able to learn from the user it serves, by observation and querying its master.

- The agent can be self-customizing according to the user's goals, preferences, habits, and history of interaction with his or her workstation.

Mondrian incorporates a software agent that records the user's actions. Such actions are unlike conventional macros. Rather, they work interactively actuated by events, messages, positions, clicks, and keystrokes. The agent generalizes the recorded actions to extend a procedure in storage by analogous examples. It does this by:

- Comprehending input arguments

- Storing dependencies among graphical operations

- Recognizing significant relationships and their aftermaths

The chosen solution provides both visual and audio feedback to the user, by means of an interactive natural language narration. An example can be taken from layout tasks where it would be useful to capture notions of a personalized presentation style. For instance, a set of visual regularities in design that carry semantic meaning could be recognized by the interface as a template. We will see a practical example in the following section.

Domino Icons: The Able Use of Before and After Panels

Capitalizing on the knowledge embedded in the agent, the user can teach Mondrian a simple procedure—for instance, rearranging the articles on the front page of a newspaper, restructuring multimedia files in a management report, or manipulating layout drawings. All these are practical, everyday examples.

User-friendly, human-machine communication is assisted by the system's interface, which is based on *domino icons*. These represent visual examples of the use of each operation, with each domino icon having two parts:

- A *before panel,* showing a representation of state of the screen before the invocation of an operation

- An *after panel* that presents the state of the screen after the operation is completed

In the Mondrian layout, the left side of the domino is the *before panel*; the right side is the *after panel.* Some of the set of operations which were shown on screen in Fig. 2-6 are built in; others are user defined.

Unlike traditional icons, where a single picture represents a single operation and vice versa, a Mondrian operation can be represented by a possibly infinite number of pictures. They are all related since they are all instances of the use of the object representing that operation:

- This finer granularity opens significant opportunities to the knowledge worker in interacting with the machine.

- It acts as a microscope in the investigation of problems, whether these are in engineering or in management.

Mondrian supplies built-in icons for operations such as creation of graphic objects, their movement in a given landscape, or their deletion from memory. But the system can also help the user to construct icons dynamically that represent operations that are important *to him or her.* It does so through the presentation of examples that have intrinsic properties.

Video annotations are represented graphically to enhance visualization and enable logs to be shared among users. Palettes of commonly employed sets of iconic annotations connect to the facilities of a memory-based representation, and their use is mediated by knowledge artifacts.

An applications example, for instance, is a New Command operation that prompts the user for the name for a new command. After naming, the agent creates a new domino icon labeled with that name:

- The *before* picture of the newly created domino represents a schematic sketch of the current arrangement of, say, a compound electronic document screen.

- Initially the *after* picture is left empty, but it will be filled in at the conclusion of the definition, with a sketch representing the final state.

A key problem in recording user-demonstrated procedures is how to give feedback about the abstractions that the system considers significant. The visual feedback takes the form of a visual storyboard, inspired by storyboards that are employed as a visualization technique in applications such as animation and multimedia design. The idea is to supply a static visualization of the events that occur in a dynamic process. The individual frames of the storyboard can be thought of as a succession of overlapping dominos. Each pair of frames is labeled by the name of one of the artifact's operations.

Another kind of feedback is auditory—synthesized speech. The system narrates the user's actions in real time, employing a software speech generator. Templates are attached to each expression in the Lisp code generated by Mondrian, and a simple natural language processor reads the code to the user.

What I like about this project is that it can be used not only to express graphically ideas underpinning a learning process but also to incorporate the *mechanics of learning* into the process:

- The user influences program behavior by interacting with software in a teacher-student mode.

- This benefits the agent that is equipped with a knowledge acquisition facility.

Machine learning is approached as an issue of interaction by means of an intelligence-enriched language that the human teacher finds easy to use. This is the best means to convey notions to the artifact, which are in turn absorbed by the agent. The user-friendliness of the interaction is as important as the logical power of the inference method, hence leading to tradeoffs: The use of more powerful inference mechanisms will allow the teacher to present ideas of greater complexity with less input. The price to be paid is that it may be harder for the teacher to understand just how to convey a specific knowledge, or for the artifact to represent effectively what it has learned.

The MIT project has optimized the issue of tradeoffs by means of direct manipulation of graphical interfaces. As the Mondrian project manager was to comment, the time has come to couple advances in machine learning with modern, direct manipulation of graphical interfaces. Mondrian has been an avant-garde project. The lessons learned from it have a general applicability for future software engineering.

Using Agents for Better Adaptation to Complex Problem-Solving Situations

One of the objectives sought after with agents is a cooperative response that might integrate direct or indirect inputs and outputs. A *direct output* is the result of a reference to a direct intention (literal meaning) of a question. An *indirect output* is the result of a reaction to an indirect intention or to a precondition of an intention.

These types of responses can be significant for retrieval reasons. Their appropriate analysis permits the development of cooperative response generation mechanisms, whose usefulness can be extended to other domains other than interactive database retrieval. In the general case, such action will require the assistance of agents.

For this particular reason, researchers at MIT are currently working on an approach that goes beyond case retrieval to incorporate adaptation necessary for problem solving. A parameter-driven design technique makes the problem of adaptation simpler to address through agents. *Case-based design* involves:*

---

*See also the discussion on analogical reasoning in Chap. 12.

- Compilation of a lexicon of terms to describe problem features
- Selection of appropriate features for indexing cases
- Specification of database schemata
- Definition of case-based authoring standards

As the MIT researchers suggested, case-based approaches are most relevant because a key problem in applying knowledge engineering techniques to visual design domains is that much of the knowhow possessed by experts is best expressible in terms of visual examples or metaphors. We will talk of metaphors in a later section.

The incorporation of visual examples greatly improves the more traditional expert systems methodology. A still better method is supported by capturing design knowledge more directly through an interactive graphical interface. Learning agents can see to it that the design expert manipulates concrete examples assisted by a graphical editor:

- The editor is equipped with an interface agent that records and interprets the user's actions.
- It then produces a generalized description of the procedure, which becomes interactively available.

Once learned, the design procedure can subsequently be applied to examples that are similar but not identical to those on which the artifact was originally trained. AT MIT, this approach has been investigated with Mondrian, which uses programming by example to capture interface actions that represent an expert's problem-solving behavior.

A different way of making this statement is to say that a better alternative to trying to extract the knowledge verbally from the expert, as it has been the practice with expert systems, is to acquire such knowhow by letting the expert interact directly with a learning agent. This is achieved through the use of a graphical interface to collect pertinent knowledge.

The user interacts with the system to perform problem-solving procedures, and the artifact employs the recorded sequence of actions to compile a textual description in the form of rules, frames, and/or heuristics. Visual design approaches have a significant advantage over the traditional verbal and textual methods for knowledge acquisition:

- The emergence of example-based and case-based knowledge acquisition changes the role of the knowledge engineer.
- From transcoding knowledge for computer consumption, the knowl-

edge engineer now advises the visual design expert on how best to choose salient examples.

Though computer-literate users may routinely employ the services of a knowledge engineer, online consulting by agents can add value as the knowledge engineer's role shifts from one of trying to force the expert's knowledge into rule representation, to one of helping a domain expert to modularize knowhow.

The MIT project also explored how modern computer graphic imagery can be used as a tool to help programmers visualize software. Other leading projects—for instance, one at the University of Tokyo—implement a range of experimental debugging systems for programming in the large and for programming in the small:

■ *Programming in the large* is the grand design, which can be significantly assisted through agents and iconic representation.*

■ *Programming in the small* refers to coding and debugging—being made both simpler and more user-friendly by means of visual approaches and agents.

Visual programming opens new avenues for automation in what is now a largely manual coding job. Both for coding and for debugging, advanced solutions use color, animated typography, and three-dimensional visual representation of programs.

Few people really appreciate the very significant benefits to be obtained from visual programming and visualization. Typically visualization is seen as the translation of numbers into graphics, but in reality it represents more than that. Seen as a problem-solving procedure:

■ Visualization is the study of software mechanisms that allow computer users to perceive, employ, and communicate visual information *interactively.*

■ This is more a problem in cognition† than a programming issue because it involves image synthesis, transmission, storage, and understanding.

Therefore, it is not surprising that visualization spans many scientific fields, academic disciplines, and domains of research. Neither is it surprising that the visualization process can be assisted, indeed enriched,

---

*D. N. Chorafas, *Visual Programming Technology,* McGraw-Hill, New York, 1996.

†See Chap. 3.

through the use of agents. There is synergy between agent technology and visualization which we will be well advised to explore.

Taking Advantage of the Practical Aspects of Metaphors

One demonstration of the potential of Mondrian concerns the personalization of a reporting scheme designed to convey results from financial analysis. This application integrates knowledge from different sources with the user's idiosyncratic ways of looking at information. The agent acts as an assistant to the user in:

- Establishing the procedure for retrieving information
- Personalizing the presentation of results

The Number 1 lesson learned from this experience is that the employment of agents is a far more preferable approach than reprogramming to customize an interface. The agent strategy presented significant advantages both from the user's viewpoint and from that of the developer.

Classical programming is error prone and takes time to accomplish; furthermore, its dependence on manually performed systems analysis often results in deviations between the user's requirements and the computer software. *Computer-assisted software engineering* (CASE) improves upon this process but does not revolutionize it. By contrast, agents support a seamless transition from new requirements to new applications.

Visualization is greatly assisted by classification. Whether in finance or in manufacturing, knowledge workers often communicate important information by drawing and labeling diagrams that fit certain conceptual classes. Agent technology now makes it possible:

- To communicate knowledge to a machine by using graphical indications of parts and of an overall structure
- To communicate by employing graphical metaphors rather than using textual databases or procedural programming languages

A *metaphor* is a paraphrase, an allegory—something that both knowledge workers and machines can understand. In a metaphor, one thing is linked to another *as if* it were that other thing. If we change the metaphor, the meaning communicated between human and machine will also change. This makes the process as a whole both flexible and adaptable. We will see practical examples with input/output in Chap. 10.

In some cases, this flexibility can go to extremes because the notion of a metaphor may mean different things to different people. According to one definition, a metaphor is constituted by a principle of resemblance over time through symbolism. Therefore, it is expressed by repetition despite disparity. In this sense, the conditions enabling a metaphor to function are fundamentally of a cyclic nature, and largely historical. This is the sense of recursion in language. Poetry, for instance, is rife with metaphor.

Expressionist writers, however, disagree with the historical hypothesis. Carl Einstein, for instance, says: "Metaphor and metaphoricity refer to more than one literary process; they characterize a general mood and attitude. In the metaphor one avoids repeating facts and weakens contact with reality. Metaphoricity is justified by the illusion of arbitrarily creating something new every moment."[*]

Following Einstein's hypothesis, to generate new propositions by recursion means to determine the new term from the old terms. The next term in the sequence may also be new, hence needs to be defined; while according to the alternative hypothesis it should be one of the preceding terms.

While contradicting one another in regard to recursion, both definitions converge in the sense that the poetic world is composed of metaphors taken from the real and perceptible world. This is also the etymological sense of the term *metaphor,* which in Greek, means bringing to a higher, or *meta,* level.[†]

In another way, however, *meta* might be a peer level but of a different nature. Einstein says: "The literati lost a sense of factual events and trusted in the empty power of their worlds." A metaphoric process is here seen as a translation from the real state to a verbal expression:

- A metaphor has a notion of metamorphosis, which converts a word having a quasi-natural identity to one having the character of a unique consciousness.

- In turn, this concept of a metamorphosis underpins the process of *morphism*—which is a seamless, real-time transformation through artifacts, as we will see in Chaps. 4 and 12.

Metaphors are very helpful in expression as well as in understanding. Wolfgang Goethe once remarked that man knows himself in so far as he

---

[*]Sibylle Penkert (ed.), *Die Fabrikation der Fiktionen,* Rowohlt, Hamburg, 1973.
[†]See also Chaps. 9 and 10, the discussion on the construction of agents.

knows the world, which he becomes aware of only in himself and sees himself only in it.* Goethe's aphorism comes pretty close in characterizing intelligent artifacts.

The metaphorical meaning must be defined not as an aspect of the syntactic and pragmatic features of the sentence but rather as a kind of utterance. This utterance creates a communications situation that must be judged under the criterion of whether or not it is meant to be metaphorical.

Based on these fundamental notions, we might look at the computer-readable graphical annotation of images as metaphors to be directly manipulated by an editor. This editor must be able to communicate relationships that tell the system how to interpret and generalize certain actions:

- Other machine-understandable metaphors can explore voice input.
- In this way, the user can explain actions to agents as they are being performed.

Using "for-instance" metaphors, the system can compare various real-world cases to find differences that help in their classification. Alternatively, the user can provide explicit guidance in the form of decision criteria expressed in a sense of metaphoricity—which can easily be extended by a user conversant in programming.

The reference to the classification facility to be supported by the agent is important because taxonomy lies at the heart of every scientific and business field. Classification is instrumental in structuring the domains of systematic inquiry. A taxonomy provides basic concepts, assists in elaborating theories, and permits the search for outlayers or anomalies. Therefore, classification can be instrumental in prediction.

---

*Goethes Werke, *Bedeutende Fördernis durch ein einziges geistreiches Wort*, Christian Wegner, Hamburg, 1960.

CHAPTER 3

Thinking Machines: The Search for Exploiting Intelligence and Expertise

"*Thinking* is those mental processes we don't understand," said Dr. Alan Turing. Dr. Niels Bohr teased his students and his assistants by saying: "You are not thinking. You are just being logical." Many experts believe that thinking may not be the result of a small set of profound rules. Rather, it comes from a variety of things that somehow we know but find it difficult to express how we know them or what they are.

One of the basic kinds of thinking, advises MIT's announcement of goals for the Things That Think project (of which we spoke in Chap. 1), is *perception*. A good part of the importance of focusing on perception results from the fact that we have drifted from being a society of participants into a society of observers. Our universe of creations comes from a much smaller group of people than it once did. At the same time we appreciate that:

- Human-made devices can span the range from passive reception to active control.
- It may be possible to reengage people in creatively shaping the world around them.

Perception is vital because it is not possible to understand people without understanding their emotions. Agents can be of much greater assistance to their masters if they learn to perceive, respond to, and communicate empirical and emotional states—which is another of the goals of the Things That Think project.

In explaining why it is important to put perception capability into things, Dr. Seymour Papert takes the example of an intelligent tennis ball that makes noises to tell how the player's toss was wrong and how to correct it. "Until now," says Papert, "children have learned by working with inanimate objects and with animate people. But this is a barrier that we are about to jump over. I believe we will now see a radical change in the way children learn."

The hitch is that we cannot endow human-made artifacts with perception if we first don't understand how perception works with humans and other animals. The lack of a *process understanding* for perception will put us at a disadvantage because we will not be able to connect our implementations of machine intelligence to reality.

Therefore, prior to going into issues concerning the practical implementation of agents in the telecommunications industry and in networks—which is done in Part 2—we will examine the processes of thinking and of perception. We will do so in a matter-of-fact fashion, leaving some of the more theoretical subjects to be discussed in Chaps. 8, 9, and 10, which deal with the construction of agents.

Questions Pertaining to Awareness and Expertise

As we have seen in Chaps. 1 and 2, there are many types of agents, and all of them have in common the notion of *expertise*. In real life, some-

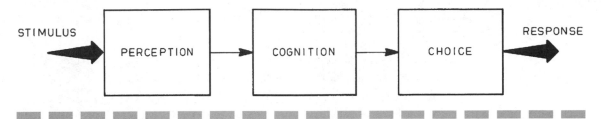

Figure 3-1   A very simple chain of events: perception, cognition, and choice.

body is considered an expert if he or she has a large knowledge domain in the form of facts and rules. An expert will also have the necessary knowhow to find missing information through access to libraries, by browsing or through a discovery process that permits him or her to comprehend, filter, and integrate massive quantities of references. The simplest way this can happen is in concrete steps from *stimulus* to *response*. Figure 3-1 shows, in block diagram form, the needed sequence of actions that involve perception, cognition, and choice.

The ability to perform these functions is critical because both the human expert and the expert artifact will often be required to demonstrate an individual experience generally not found in the literature of the domain. Alternatively, the expert's knowhow must go beyond what is generally available. This, incidentally, is also what it means to be a known specialist in a given field.

Knowledge is the trademark of the expert. This knowledge enables the expert not only to recognize and formulate problems but also to choose promising problem-solving strategies. Some of them will be successful; others will not. If they turn out to be unsuccessful, the expert goes back to the point from where the scenario he or she followed failed, or even to the very beginning of the exercise. In addition, he or she tries another alternative course, using an algorithmic approach or trial and error. In discovery, heuristics are more likely to succeed than algorithms.*

As we will see later in this chapter, the interplay that takes place between rules and memory underpins the process of intelligence. This is confirmed by a number of studies that have analyzed the characteristics

---

*See D. N. Chorafas, *The New Information Technologies—A Practitioner's Guide*, Van Nostrand Reinhold, New York, 1992.

that experts have in common. The studies report that among the foremost characteristics are:

- The facility to conceptualize changes in sequence and interdependencies, getting an integrated picture of what takes place
- A highly developed perceptual ability to understand facts and figures, along with the ability to recall them correctly
- The knowhow needed to estimate properly the accuracy of inputs, filtering out noise but examining outliers*

Many researchers treat these points as basic notions underpinning intelligence and expertise, and they are correct in doing so. The goal is to match these abilities through knowledge-enriched software in its modern form: *agents*.

Following this line of reasoning, Dr. Neil Gershenfeld is investigating at MIT how to make the objects around us "aware." He is also studying how to develop efficient ways for agents to communicate with us—both as a matter of course and by exception. A good deal can be learned from the way people behave in terms of perception and recognition. Some people avoid eye contact with people around them, just not to have to communicate with them.

There is also the need to learn how to communicate with inanimate things. The hypothesis is that communicating, for instance, with your refrigerator, would involve using *smart materials*. For instance, in clothing, Gershenfeld suggests by "placing computing in our shoes, we can quite literally `boot up' every morning." The researcher also suggests that people may exchange virtual business cards by shaking hands.

But not everybody is convinced that these processes have intrinsic worth. "Maybe these guys' brains need booting up," said someone who heard this argument. "It always amuses me to see scientists desperately trying to create the need for something that definitely is not needed—so that the poor guy from cloud 9 can continue to justify his existence."

This remark is contrarian, but being contrarian gives perspective. The remark matches another one made in France, that the reason why no cure can be found for cancer is that more people live from cancer than die from it. This, too, is a matter of perception.

---

*Dimitris N. Chorafas, *How to Understand and Use Mathematics for Derivatives*, vol. 2, Euromoney, London, 1995.

Dr. Alex Pentland, head of MIT's Perceptual Computing section, is also working on giving computers perceptual capability, but he follows a different path. With his group, he is developing ways for computers to:

- Recognize people
- Understand their actions

He is, for example, studying how to endow machines with the ability to differentiate among human faces and to recognize facial expressions. Other projects look into the ways and means through which objects could perform a number of useful tasks. For instance, toasters, chairs, or lamps that sense the movements or feelings of their owner and learn their owner's habits to improve their own performance.

The common thread in these ideas is that for them to become reality, not only computational capabilities but also intelligence must be embedded into things. Making this happen will involve challenging the obvious and providing new support tools, such as intelligent sensors. It will also require novel design methods that weave digital media directly into the fabrication process.

Once these goals are reached, newer, even more far-fetched goals will surface. There will always be still higher levels of expertise to be considered, which the current state of the art in software cannot match. The principle is that in order to go from "here" to "there," we must:

- Pay rigorous attention to detail
- Simplify complex problems
- Be able to deal with tradeoffs or conflicting goals

All these are signs of an intelligent conduct. Other indicators of intelligence are knowing when to avoid inappropriate strategies* and how to prioritize alternatives. These are some of the jobs done by experts.

Experts usually have a strong degree of responsiveness and adaptability, and they do show a high tolerance to stress. However, while necessary, this is not sufficient to define experts. They must also use their *intelligence*. But do we know what this word means?

---

*See the section on the importance of negation later in this chapter.

Do We Know What Constitutes the Notion of Intelligence?

George Bernard Shaw is rumored to have said: "People think that I am intelligent because I use my brain a couple of times per week." Statistically he was right. Many people don't like to use their brains,* or simply they have not been trained to do so. Can we conclude that they have intelligence that they do not exploit?

It would be preposterous to think that intelligence can exist only in a shell of bone—and not in metal casting or in a plastic shell. However, to have a meaningful discussion on this subject, it is wise to start with the fundamentals so that a common ground can be established:

- Is there anything that could be called "intelligence" in the first place?

- If there is, what might constitute a process of *natural intelligence?*

Dr. Tibor Vamos believes that the notion of intelligence is human-made. Thinking of intelligence, he says, began first of all because of a need to justify the supremacy in the relations characterizing humans and animals. As such, the whole concept lies in the very origins of human species discrimination.†

This hypothesis, which is iconoclastic and therefore has its own merits, considers the concepts of *intelligence* and *knowledge* as being self-reflexive and related to the issues of complexity, as well as to noncomputability. Let's, however, for the time being, regard intelligence and knowledge *as if* they were two separate subjects. At a later time we can discuss whether or not such separation makes sense.

One of the hypotheses, hence tentative statements, formulated by Dr. Vamos is that thinking about intelligence starts with the problem of understanding. That much has been said in the introduction and in the first part of this chapter in discussing perception. But other experts think that this definition falls short of espousing the concept that intelligence is the ability to recognize the causes of logical relations of phenomena.

Since no two researchers addressing the issue of intelligence proceed in the same manner, or target the same ends, it is wise to first try to identify and analyze the process and fundamental components under-

---

*See also Dr. Bohr's dictum in the introduction.

†T. Vamos, *Minds and Minds, and Machine,* Computer Automation Institute of the Hungarian Academy of Sciences, Budapest, 1994.

pinning intelligence. Once this has been achieved, we can start building a factual and documented model.

The underlying process can be explained in a simple way capitalizing on the notions that have been presented in Fig. 3-1. As Fig. 3-2 demonstrates, this earlier model can be brought one notch further by substituting choice with conceptual modeling, logical representation, and the ability to store the outcome for retrieval later on. This we will call *memory.*

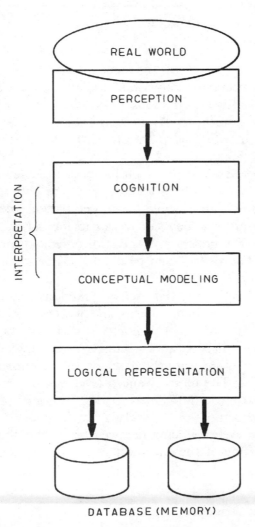

Figure 3-2
Memory and interpretation: Key elements of intelligence.

REAL WORLD

PERCEPTION

COGNITION

CONCEPTUAL MODELING

LOGICAL REPRESENTATION

INTERPRETATION

DATABASE (MEMORY)

An answer can now be given regarding the manner in which the fundamental component parts contribute to the process of intelligence. Figure 3-2 can help as a guide to describe the functionality represented by these component parts. Seven steps characterize an increasingly intelligent behavior:

1. Memory

2. Calculation

3. Learning

4. Inference, speculation

5. Abstract thinking

6. Concretization of thoughts

7. Integration

The top three items in this list focus on *knowledge*—a reason that I suggested the concepts of knowledge and intelligence, and their processes are not necessarily synonymous. Knowledge is the result of *learning* and retaining what we learn. We need *calculating* ability to understand the quantitative and qualitative aspects of the world around us and of our own actions.

Plato once suggested that a philosopher must have a good *memory.* It is fundamental to thinking, and it enables the pulling together of events from past time into a whole for contemplation. Absence of reflection does not permit us to be aware of our former selves. Yet, the mapping of the past into the present and the future depends on all conduct being directed by knowledge—and to a significant extent by *virtue,* which is knowledge that cannot be taught.

Nobody in his or her right senses would say that items 1, 2, and 3 are widespread among Homo sapiens, and we know precious little of what is the case with the other characteristics. For instance, issue 4 is even more exclusive. Inference and speculation come by levels that help in discriminating a more primitive layer of intelligence from one which is more advanced. The most advanced level will be abstract thinking in a mathematical sense. This leads to the discovery of new laws and its antithesis: the demolition of old laws.

The lower level of intelligence, well below the discovery of new laws, is the borderline of the current state of the art characterizing agents.*

---

*There exists an exception: In the early 1980s an expert system, AM, did come close to discovering a couple of mathematical laws.

Autonomous knowledge artifacts have memory and calculation ability. They also can learn, as Chap. 1 explained. They are endowed with an inference engine, but only at the more elementary layers—though this will change with time and with experience.

Based on these premises, MIT's Things That Think project seeks to bring out the artifacts' latent intelligence by way of community interaction. This interaction will involve many entities—some animate and others inanimate. To help in meeting such objectives, MIT's Media Group will focus on *sensing things:*

- Developing materials and devices to enable formerly passive objects to become active
- Exploring *thinking links,* that is, the software and hardware needed for intelligent things to communicate among themselves and with their users

The infrastructure of thinking things is *communications.* "Between things and thinking lies everything that links them into systems," advises MIT's announcement about the new project. It also adds that it is absurd that cellular phones, laptops, and other appliances are barely on speaking terms—either with each other or with paper records. Therefore, the project suggests that its *BodyNet* will become one of the most important linkages in the networks domain.

The BodyNet targets the devices around one's body, using intrabody signaling as well as more conventional links.* Protocols to be developed will define the shared architecture—eventually leading to better personal information—in an intelligence-enriched net.

"Here at the [Media] Laboratory we have started to believe that this is an absolutely pivotal era," says Dr. Michael Hawley. "We are moving from a world where none of our everyday things communicate, to one where all of them will"—or at least might.

As far as smart machines are concerned, the areas that have already been harnessed include memory, learning ability, and the lower layers of inference. Therefore, laboratory work will be able rather quickly to implement the suggested communications capability. But what about the higher intelligence strata?

---

*See also the discussion in Chap. 12 on telemedicine.

Negation as an Intelligence Test

Dr. Fritz Zwicky, one of the best astronomers of the twentieth century, was a great believer in the method of *negation* and subsequent reconstruction. The first step of his approach was to look for statements, theories, or systems of thought that pretend to absolute truth, and *deny them.* "You are almost certain to be correct in this," Zwicky maintained, "because it is extremely unlikely that anyone knows the absolute truth about anything."*

Great scientists will challenge the obvious and take nothing for granted. But the ability to proceed with factual and documented negation is something we have not yet achieved with models; though the test of hypotheses can be thought of as coming close to it. Typically in scientific investigation, when we accept a finding or a theory, we do so tentatively because we have no evidence for its rejection. By contrast, we are much surer when we reject a finding or theory since there is evidence for doing so.

Rejection however happens as a result of natural intelligence, after much abstract thinking and subsequent concretization of thoughts through testing and experimentation. Human-made artifacts have not yet achieved that level of intelligence—though one day they might.

By extension, at the current state of the art, I don't consider agents as being able to fulfill the prerequisites of intelligence described in the preceding section under items 5, 6, and 7: abstract thinking, concretization of thoughts, and integration. Let me explain what I mean by this through an example.

Say that a rocket scientist working in the banking industry[†] has been given the mission to develop agents in collaboration with computer-literate users. The artifacts are meant to be interactively employed throughout the bank. This type of knowledge construct was developed in early 1987 to map and analyze mutual funds in terms of:

- Assets
- Return on assets
- Type of investment
- New subscriptions
- Redemptions

---

[*]Wallace and Karen Tucker, *The Dark Matter,* William Morrow, New York, 1988.

[†]See D. N. Chorafas, *Rocket Scientists in Banking,* Lafferty Publications, London and Dublin, 1995.

The environment that was developed supported the visual navigation across each fund, calculated risk and return, and easily changed reference years or other characteristics in framing the graphical presentation to the user. Each step was assisted through a knowledge artifact, whose rules reflected the way financial analysts worked at that time.

This solution extended the benefits that had been previously obtained through graphics editors used in connection with analytical results from spreadsheets, knowledgeable action acquired through earlier expert systems, and messaging by means of electronic mail. The role of the agents was essentially that of:

- Providing the knowledge worker with value differentiation
- Making more sophisticated interface by means of visualization

As this project, which addressed the crucial variables of mutual funds, got more sophisticated, reporting was done by means of a three-dimensional representation of spatial data. This was way ahead of the state of the art at the time of our reference. The background design resembled what we would call today "virtual reality modeling," with abstractions of real-world entities. This approach permitted the developers to structure and revamp an *information landscape* in *time* and *space* with 2D and 3D dynamic visualization. A project done in parallel, in the same bank, investigated case-based learning, using as a source of information ticker data as well as speech input.

In fact, a small-vocabulary, speaker-dependent device was used, and it was thought to suffice for input choices among a fixed set of relations. This could enable the user to interactively control priorities and determine a sequence scheme, but not to make major changes to the artifact's behavior.

It would have been difficult, indeed, to find a better project in the banking industry—except for one detail. The artifact got its knowhow from traders and mapped into itself the then-prevailing investment rules. But a few months down the line, in October 1987, the market crashed.

Investment rules radically changed, but the learning artifact had no capability for massive rejection of its knowledge bank's contents. In short, it could not say no. What it could do successfully was to ride on the X landscape in Fig. 3-3. But when it reached the precipice, it got lost. It could not fly to the Y landscape and still function.

Let's keep this example in mind when we talk of agents, with all due respect to leading laboratories who put brainpower, time, and money into the development of increasingly more sophisticated artifacts. Smaller changes and linear transitions can be perceived and handled by lower-level intelligence, but:

Figure 3-3
The beginning of understanding how to handle nonlinearities in financial systems.

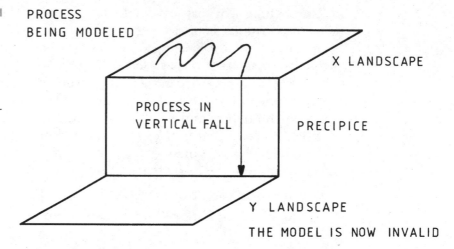

Figure 3-3

- Modeling abstract thinking and the concretization of thoughts are huge jumps required to address *complexity*.

- Complexity is that ill-defined area that lies in the transition between *stability* and *chaos*, and we don't yet know how to model it very well.[*]

An environment changing in a nonlinear fashion assures us of many new aspects coming into this transition. Therefore, there are many unknowns and surprises that we cannot yet teach our agents to handle in a rigorous and robust manner.

Let me add this as a conclusion: To keep the system in which our mind operates under control, it is necessary to possess an integrating ability—which is the highest level of intelligence. Such integration goes well beyond perception and conception. It involves the issues underpinning complexity, by which new details are added, boundaries are extended, and frames of reference may be radically changed.

Analyzing and Exploiting the Concept of Intelligence

We must admit that beyond the identification of the main ingredients that contribute to a concept of intelligence, we don't really know what precisely constitutes intelligence in human beings—though we think of

[*]See D. N. Chorafas, *Chaos Theory in the Financial Markets*, Probus/Irwin, Chicago, 1994.

humans as being the most intelligent in the animal world *on Earth*. Capitalizing on what we have discussed so far in this chapter, we can say that:

■ The more we are able to develop hypotheses and test them, the more we are capable of addressing and manipulating a complex logical structure.

That statement is based on two pillars. On the one side is the networking of minor judgments, through which the expert can reach a major judgment. This is the algorithmic or heuristic component. On the other are the facts that largely rest on our observations and are stored in memory as *episodes*.

The reference to the animal world on Earth has been made because we don't know whether there are intelligent beings on other planets, though we tend to think that since it is likely there is life on other planets, there might also be some kind of intelligence. Could this be a higher intelligence than ours? It certainly could—but it could also be totally different. Intelligence is always a relative issue; it cannot be expressed in absolute terms. It is a reflection of the environment, the situation, and the subject that we consider.

The human mind is a mystery. The irony is that the more we attempt to learn about it, the more mysterious it becomes. A major obstacle in resolving this mind puzzle is that we have only finite brains and limited lifespans for attacking this most challenging and vast question. We have a mystery trying to resolve another mystery.

How does the mind function? What is extrasensory perception, and how does it work? What's the limit of memory capacity? Is it all in the brain, or all over the body, as Dr. John von Neumann speculated? What is the limit of intelligence? How do human brains unite to accomplish great feats, such as:

■ Designing and flying airplanes

■ Landing human beings on the moon

■ Splitting the atom

■ Designing computers

■ Inventing radar

■ Integrating complex systems

It would be silly to pretend that we know the answers. Yet, we try to construct intelligent artifacts such as agents. The apparent paradox is due to the fact that the word *intelligence* is quite often used to denote the most sophisticated tasks that we listed earlier. This is wrong.

As explained earlier, at the current state of the art, *agents* address the lower levels of intelligence. From the experience we have gained from the practical use of expert systems, we know that this is indeed doable. By lowering our sights, we can expand the implementation horizon of human-machine intelligence.

It may be rewarding to speculate where this might lead in terms of human-made artifacts. In his paper to which reference was made earlier, Tibor Vamos makes a provocative statement: "Let us suppose that mankind gets extinct, and only those machines remain which will be results of further developments of technology. Will they be equally intelligent as their natural predecessors, or more, or less?"

Whether "more" or "less" depends on the time an answer is given. Today it will probably be "less," but 10 or 15 years down the line it might well be "more." The basic issue is cultural; precisely what was said earlier, that it is preposterous to think intelligence can exist only in a shell of bone. Intelligence can as well develop and be implemented in other than carbon life, and this other sort of intelligence might well be more advanced than the natural systems that we know.

The three-dimensional frame of reference in Fig. 3-4 aims to provide a bridge between what we don't know about how intelligence works. The kernel is semantics, a bias coming from the fact that as Homo sapiens, we attach meaning to practically everything. The object is cognitive views with visual interaction.

As the reader will appreciate, Fig. 3-4 is fairly simple. There are two reasons why this and similar figures have been included in the text. First, it is always wise to try to present complex issues in simple forms. Second, I am convinced that this is the best way to acquaint the reader to the three-dimensional presentation—and by extension to 3D thinking.

Returning to the seven basic ingredients of intelligence that we discussed earlier, and supposing they are valid, the next question becomes: "How does imagination work?" This can be analyzed into subqueries:

- How can so many ideas be formulated in the psychological realm?
- How is what we call the "mind" composed in a structural, physical, and logical sense?
- What are the limits to the unknown powers of the mind?*

Factual and documented answers to these queries are not forthcoming. At the current state of the art—based on expert systems experience—we can say that the more sophisticated software becomes, the more it is emulating a process of intelligence and mapping it into the machine. As

---

*The powers of the mind may be unknown, but we know from experience that there exist always limits.

Figure 3-4
Cognitive views with
visual interaction.

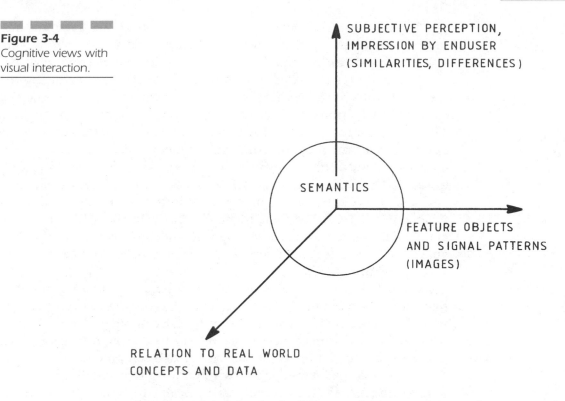

SUBJECTIVE PERCEPTION,
IMPRESSION BY ENDUSER
(SIMILARITIES, DIFFERENCES)

SEMANTICS

FEATURE OBJECTS
AND SIGNAL PATTERNS
(IMAGES)

RELATION TO REAL WORLD
CONCEPTS AND DATA

already explained, a basic difference between agents and expert systems is that agents are proactive knowledge robots, activating themselves through message passing or other means. By contrast, expert systems have primarily been user-activated artifacts which, however, were instrumental in opening up new software frontiers.

Every year in the dozen years that have elapsed since expert systems started becoming popular has seen an evolution in their design and usage. But advancement across a knowledge frontier brings up the need to explore a number of philosophical questions to avoid working in a vacuum.

Thinking by Analogy and the Evolution of Human-Made Systems*

As we discussed earlier, there is no way of answering in a definite manner the query: Will human-made systems be more intelligent than peo-

---

*See also Chap. 12 on data analysis, analogical reasoning, and pattern recognition.

ple? But we can make some hypotheses based on known facts and figures, which necessarily involve some deliberate choices.

We will need to be helped in this task by inferences from what has been learned over the years from human-made systems. In tracing the history of software abstraction, we can approximate a process whereby embedded functionality is crystallized from an original rough idea. This has a counterpart with natural systems, as experts are to some extent aware of the notions behind an abstraction. Not only is the emergence of an abstraction significant in itself but it also propels a process to address the need for turning that abstraction into coherent thought.

Those of us old enough to have worked in the beginning of the computer era can remember some interesting facts. In the 1950s when programs were written in machine language, and later on in assembly language, they were thought of simply as ways of making computers behave as the programmer desired.

Early software's main goal was to turn general-purpose computers into special-purpose machines. It was mainly economic reasons that prevented job-specific, special-purpose physical computers from actually being built every time a new problem had to be solved—even if such practice was followed up to a point with analog computers.

Slowly, programs developed into something that could be called a *behavioral harness* of digital computers. It became the job of the programmer to write routines that would lead human-made machines to exhibit the desired problem-level behavior.* However, it was not that easy to translate problem-connected information into computer-level instructions of the program. By the time this was done, the intent of the instructions with respect to the problem was no longer visible—and sometimes it got distorted.

This amounted to a lack of visibility in connection to the problem, and eventually it led to programs that were virtually impossible to understand on their own. The aftermath was the rather general belief that computer programming is essentially a routine job about which not too many questions should be asked.

This belief is wrong. But naive languages by today's standards—such as Cobol, Fortran, and SQL—tend to perpetuate this lack of appreciation of what machines can do in the intelligence domain. To put it bluntly, legacy-type programs have never been recognized as intelligent artifacts, and the large majority of computer specialists still consider them to be dumb.

---

*See also in Chap. 2 the example with numerical control of machine tools.

Like what became known as *microcode,* routines written in a naive language have classically been seen as little more than what the machine language term has implied. They are soft-wired procedures making a computer play the tune that the programmer wanted it to play. It took nearly a quarter century of programming effort enriched by knowledge engineering—since the university-led artificial intelligence (AI) projects of the 1950s and 1960s—to appreciate that machines can be endowed with some special skills.[*] For instance:

- They can use their knowledge bank[†] for prioritizing which analogies to consider first.
- They can employ brain parallelism to good advantage in situations involving cognition, like robotics and machine vision.

It is indeed fundamental to properly understand the role *analogies* play in perception. Thomas Edison once suggested that most of his inventions started out as *analogs.* The breadboard model of the motion picture camera looked like a phonographic black box and gradually evolved from there.

Other inventors spoke about their reliance on *metaphors* coming from their own introspections—a concept discussed in Chap. 2. This too is a characteristic of intelligence and the way we use it in order to reach a fruitful end. We employ metaphors to:

- Cope with complex situations
- Solve problems
- Make decisions

Usually in human intelligence these metaphors are not very deep. We get power from them because of the immense breadth of knowledge from which we can choose them—yet, by so doing, we often fail to appreciate that almost all of our thinking is metaphorical.

Solving problems by analogizing to far-flung specific knowledge is something agents one day will try to do. For the time being, they can employ a rather comprehensive skeleton of general knowledge to directly use elements from a growing body of specific knowledge from which to draw analogies:

---

[*]See also in Chap. 11 how an agent can perform skill-level work in connection to a financial application.

[†]See also D. N. Chorafas, *Knowledge Engineering,* Van Nostrand Reinhold, New York, 1990.

- In terms of exploiting knowledge, artifacts can become independent of their programmer by learning.
- We know from personal experience that the more we know, the more we can learn. Agents might do the same.

However, it is fairly difficult to learn without starting from a well-established initial foundation. The best learners have a broad body of knowledge. This underlines the role of memory—which, as we have seen, is the starting point of a process of intelligence.

Let me close this section with the following thought in regard to agents. *If* their knowledge bank is large and representative enough, *then* adding a new piece of knowledge ought to be doable just by connecting to it other existing pieces. Among all available hypotheses, this seems to be the way humans learn how to learn. Computers can do just as well in terms of analogical reasoning*—and eventually they might be able to do better than natural systems.

That Little-Known Process We Call "Knowledge"

Knowledge is the expression of *relations* among facts or episodes, as well as between these facts and their values. Defining such relations, establishing causality, mapping the relations through signs and rules, and manipulating them to obtain a result—are all signs of knowledge.

One of the fundamental characteristics of knowledge is that within the *domain* to which it pertains, it can serve multiple purposes. Superior knowledge is flexible, and the relations it brings to bear are dynamically adjustable to the situation we confront, as well as through time.

Many people in industry tend to use the term *skills* to denote a somewhat lower level of knowledge. Skills are more narrowly focused, and more specific. But what particularly distinguishes skills from knowledge is that their flexibility is of a significantly lesser degree. The current generation of agents has skills, not knowledge in the wider definition we have seen. Agents, however, can be expected to evolve and show knowledge characteristics in the years ahead.

---

*See Chap. 12.

Knowledge can be taught or acquired from experience. The same is true of skills. Contrasting to this is *virtue*. Socrates described virtue as knowledge that cannot be taught. Applied experimental psychology distinguishes different types of knowledge:

■ *World knowledge* is the information acquired through formal education and day-to-day experience.

This type of knowledge ranges from the perception and remembrance of facts to crystallized intelligence and fluid intelligence. Notice that since the beginning of this chapter we have maintained that the process of perception can be handled through agents.

■ *Crystallized intelligence* is our ability to use an accumulated body of general information to make judgments and solve problems.

Psychologists think that crystallized intelligence comes into play in understanding problems and issues. It is also called upon in dealing with problems for which there are no clear answers but only better and worse options.

■ *Fluid intelligence* is the ability involved in seeing and using abstract relationships and patterns, which is a higher-level intelligence than the level we called "crystallized."

Psychologists and medical doctors suggest that fluid intelligence remains high for people who are logically and physically active into their eighties. The process of ascertaining that knowledge and intelligence do not decay is defined by *staying involved,* as contrasted to withdrawing from life.

Being mentally active means continuing intellectual interests. This increases intelligence through old age. Another key factor is having a flexible personality. People most able to tolerate ambiguity and enjoy new experiences maintain their mental alertness in the best possible manner till they turn into minerals.

The human characteristics of knowledge and intelligence can be fairly well explained in these terms. Once this is done, they could be used as a background to elaborate on the development and use of agents—and of knowledge artifacts in general. One way for doing so is to restructure what we just said in terms that fit human-made systems.

First the constructive view: As I will never tire of repeating, one of the best domains of implementation for simulators and models at large—and therefore for agents—is as *trainers*. Trainers are crucial contributors to knowledge. Not every person or every company understands the impact of this proposition. Yet, interactively operated real-time models and knowledge artifacts can be instrumental teachers. As such, they contribute to preventing that most unforgivable offense: Doing something one does not understand.

Another major contribution is rapid product development to get early control of the market. In finance, for example, there is no more plain vanilla banking. In the 1980s, a bank had 6 to 9 months for new product development, and a few months more to skim the cream from the market. Now if it has a new product, it will end up on its competitor's desk within a fortnight.

Derivatives are a new product in banking. However, derivatives dealers report that margins on complex transactions have fallen from about 25 basis points to 2 basis points within the past 2 years. In more competitive markets many bankers suggest that margins have been absolutely crushed.

Agents, models, and worst-case scenarios can be instrumental in minimizing the deadly sin of overconfidence and inadequate monitoring procedures. In many deals those sins can quickly mean that small losses balloon out of control. For instance, the Barings debacle, where defective internal controls and speculation in equity index led the venerable British bank into bankruptcy.

Agents are not going to perform miracles, but since skills and knowledge are acquired, artifacts enriched with intelligence can perform knowledge acquisition. A knowledge acquisition interface would evolve into a component of perception. As shown in Fig. 3-5, like people, artifacts also require:

- Practice on knowledge acquisition
- The ability to develop a descriptive, updatable model of expertise

Dr. Daniel Bricklin, the man who designed the first spreadsheet, once suggested: "People think a new piece of hardware is inherently more capable, but it all depends on the software you are using." Intelligence augmented by computers typically follows that principle as reflected in Fig. 3-5.

We can better appreciate the successive steps shown in Fig. 3-5 if we recall that there have been two types of orientation in artificial intelligence work so far. The one is *theoretical* and tends to stay on the main track of brain research. The other focuses on *applications development*.

For both approaches, the guideline is: *If we understand the problem, we know how to solve it.* Both aim at opening the gates of the unknown; the second, however, follows the added goal of providing practical results. Agents are the products we obtain from this second line of effort.

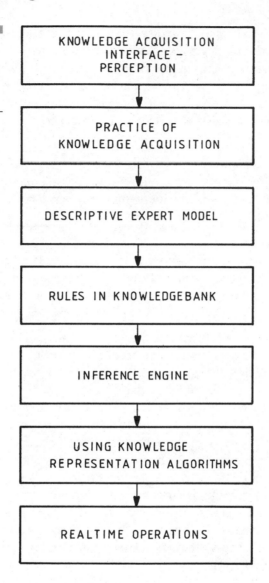

Figure 3-5
Development and usage of skills and knowhow by an agent.

KNOWLEDGE ACQUISITION INTERFACE – PERCEPTION

PRACTICE OF KNOWLEDGE ACQUISITION

DESCRIPTIVE EXPERT MODEL

RULES IN KNOWLEDGEBANK

INFERENCE ENGINE

USING KNOWLEDGE REPRESENTATION ALGORITHMS

REALTIME OPERATIONS

Mapping the Expert's Knowledge into Interactive Agents

In the early 1980s, talking of artificial intelligence constructs, Dr. Ted Hoff, the inventor of the microprocessor, was to comment: "We need to develop algorithms that make computers more reasonable. Computers that have more of a personality than just the operating system." A few years down the line agents provided the response.

An important phase in the development of an agent is the construction of rules that, as we saw in Fig. 3-5, constitute the knowledge bank and permit the activation of the inference engine.* Three types of knowledge can be distinguished: declarative, procedural, and metaknowledge.

■ *Declarative knowledge*

This is a knowledge structure resembling a statement of facts, relations, and objects. Or it is a statement of events and rules in the context of heuristic mathematical expressions.

■ *Procedural knowledge*

This construct is akin to an algorithmic structure. It is expressed as a sequence of commands for action(s), leading from variable input data to an output characterized by specific, fairly well expressed results.

■ *Metaknowledge*

Metaknowledge is control knowledge; the construct contains knowledge about knowledge. This is a most vital component of the knowledge bank because it tells us how to use available knowhow. In Chap. 10 we will talk of metarules and metadata.

This approach creates a frame of reference defining the domain in which an agent can act. Figure 3-6 illustrates the constraints that are imposed by considering how the variables associated with each axis in the framework interact with one another to create a *reasoning* mechanism. This may be *deterministic* or *stochastic*. Whether the approach taken in their design is stochastic or deterministic, the software constructs we call "agents" must be enriched by the knowledge of experts in specific domains. By distilling their expertise into a set of laws, entering them into the system, an expert contributes to the production of application programs that:

■ Help nonexperts solve problems in the expert's domain, which they do as expert systems by responding to queries

■ Take the initiative in addressing situations as they develop, alerting their master or *asking* questions, which is the behavior of interactive agents

---

*See Chap. 12.

Figure 3-6
A frame of reference of intelligent action by an agent and associated constraints.

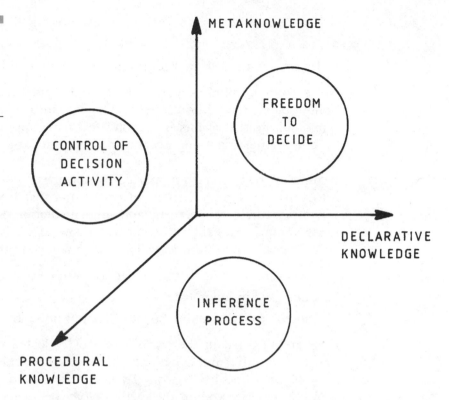

This makes the new generation of knowledge-enriched artifacts much more agile than the old; their service goes beyond a mere contribution to a decision-making process. We must also appreciate that the development of agents is a *steady process.* As we saw earlier, the available knowledge changes, and so do the user's interactive needs.

Finally, another distinction worth making in connection with human-made artifacts of a certain intelligence level is between those following quantitative approaches and the others that are qualitatively oriented. Classically, computers are number crunchers. This, however, may be changing.

At the current state of the art, models have been quantitative rather than qualitative, the latter requiring a more complex approach and involving approximate reasoning. Qualitative or approximate reasoning relies on linguistic variables, qualifiers, and plausibility concepts—all of which can be expressed through fuzzy engineering.*

---

*See D. N. Chorafas, *Chaos Theory in the Financial Markets,* Probus/Irwin, Chicago, 1994.

- *Cost, pleasure, distance,* and *volume* are examples of linguistic variables.
- *Low, high,* and *reasonable* are qualifiers.
- *Very, quite,* and *about* are hedges that can be used with qualifiers.

Noise words are phrases such as *should be* that impact the readability of policy statements without affecting logical meaning. Current projections indicate that agents will evolve featuring approximate reasoning by employing fuzzy engineering components and *genetic algorithms* (GA).*

Some of the inferences supported by nonlinear processes reveal a new horizon in reasoning. Others reflect results that have been obtained already. Research, development, and implementation (RD&I) of human-made systems that exploit the expert's knowledge has shown that, in a generic sense, expert knowledge has three main components:

1. Facts, such as those that might be listed in a book
2. Rules used in judgment
3. Procedural issues telling how to go about doing things

Facts are reflected in the organization of collected references that are based on training and experience. Many of these episodes would typically be of a heuristic nature. By contrast, procedural knowledge is based on practice and on the methodology being adopted in regard to analogies and associations. Hypotheses, testing, and reasoning are part of procedural knowledge. The same is true of the intelligence necessary for negation.

The Very Important Issue of Choosing the Right Kind of Predicates

One of the lessons learned in the 1980s with the design and use of expert systems is that their development should reflect whether we want the artifact to have *assistant knowledge* or *examiner knowledge.* This choice

---

*See D. N. Chorafas, *Rocket Scientists in Banking,* Lafferty Publications, London and Dublin, 1995.

influences the features to be built, as well as the actual implementation. The two different types of agents

- Assistant to
- Examiner or analyzer

pose different requirements and design perspectives. The "assistant-to" artifact has essentially secretarial and administrative duties. It helps with time management, in the exchange and classification of electronic mail, in bringing up reminders on things that are due, or in locating a missing reference.

The "examiner's, or analyzer's," functions are different. This artifact uses reasoning for referral, research, presentation of analytical results, and user overrides. Based on database mining or on the filtering of data streams, an analyzer agent decides on the next initiative and takes responsibility in terms of:

- Evaluation
- Explanation
- Discourse

More complex agents can integrate the two functions as shown in Fig. 3-7. Generally, however, agents should be designed rather simply, addressing either the one function or the other. Whichever the choice may be, there is a need for observing prerequisites that sustain the knowledge-oriented functions. Such sustenance is provided by means of *predicates*, which constitute the inference engine.

The meaning of the word *predicate* is to proclaim, declare, or affirm. Precisely, it means to *affirm* a quality, attribute, or property, based on arguments, conditions, or facts—hence, on the logical structure underpinning the agent's general behavior and specific actions. We will look into the use of predicates in Chap. 8 when we talk of inference.

Etymologically, the verb *to predicate* means to involve as a connotation, make an affirmation or statement, or use words that make a statement. As this definition suggests, predicates can be of different sorts—such as a verb of complete meaning, a verb and its adverbial modifier, a transitive verb and its object, a linking verb and its complement, or an algorithm describing any of the above in mathematical form.

The interest in predicates in connection to agents centers on their use as reasoning mechanisms, specifically, in terms of semantic reasoning. As we have seen earlier, declarative knowledge and procedural knowledge are reflected through predicates, but they should be supplemented

Figure 3-7
Block diagram of
component parts of a
complex agent.

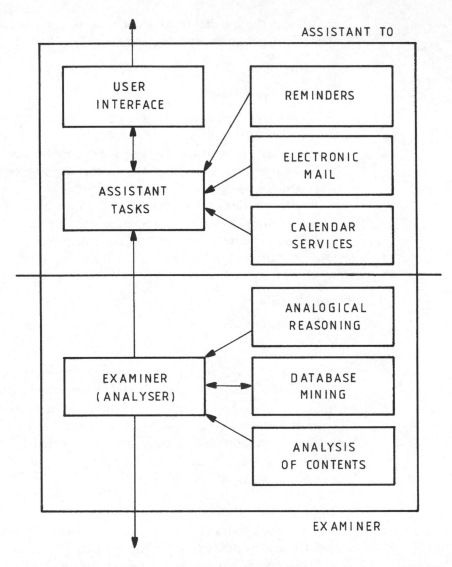

by a metaknowledge component. Metapredicates help in structuring a
generic system characterized by:

- *Consistency,* hence a system without contradictions
- *Generality,* whereby any fact or rule can be encoded
- *Flexibility,* where facts, stages, and values can be used in more than one
  way

The use of agents is not alien to this concept. In fact, the development
of agents is a manifestation of this fact. Equally basic is the observance

of the principle that new experiences should always be integrated with existing knowhow expressed by the rules in the knowledge bank and by episodes.

There are as well two other important characteristics that must be supported through metaknowledge. One of them is *additivity,* which means the agent can evolve easily with new facts and rules being added or old ones deleted. This enhances the artifact's flexibility.

The other vital characteristic is *explanation facility.* The agent's line of reasoning would need from time to time to be displayed, with justification provided for a given response. This is also true with expert systems, but the interactivity characterizing agents can augment the justification requirements.

Let's keep in mind that predicates and metapredicates are the building blocks in the development of all sorts of mathematical models. Typically in physics, engineering, finance, and many other domains, we construct conceptual models in order to

- Simplify
- Idealize
- Conceive

a certain situation that may be too difficult to understand without abstraction. As we have discussed since Chap. 1, models permit their developers and their users to gain insight, exercise foresight, and take action.

Modelling needing a language, and it is so much more efficient if the language is Knowledge enriched. Chapter 4 presents the Knowledge Query and Manipulation Language (KQML), as well as telescripts. It also discusses morphony and gives some practical examples.

Part 2 will capitalize on the concepts outlined in this chapter and in Chap. 4. The issues we have discussed in connection to thinking machines will help to focus on the implementation of agents in communications and in networks. This is why these chapters addressing conceptual subjects had to precede those of practical applications.

It has been a deliberate choice to split the more theoretical background into two sets: Part 1 has presented the fundamentals. Following the discussion on applications, Part 3 explains how agents can be constructed. Blending the practical and the theoretical aspects permits the reader to gain the best of both worlds—and therefore learn how agents can be effectively implemented.

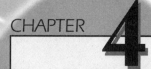

KQML, Morphism, Telescript, and Software Development

To help the reader in better appreciating the evolution of languages for networked agents, this chapter begins with a brief history of communications. Programming languages in the telecommunications domain can be seen as a continuation of communications processes oriented toward human-machine interaction—and indirectly toward human-to-human communications.

The Homeric (809 to 750 B.C.) poems are said to have been passed from mouth to mouth, surviving as a recital legend and being transcribed quite late in ancient Greek history. There are as well tribes, like the Polynesians, who never used the written word until western civilization was forced upon them by the explorers.

The invention of writing did not provide all by itself the means of wider distribution and popularization of scripts in regard to identical copies of specific texts or utterances. The first consistent effort to do this was made at the time of the Ptolemies in Egypt, where, in the famous Library of Alexandria important scripts were dictated to a two-digit number of scribes, thus developing clone copies on papyrus.

The wider distribution of scripts did not come until the perfection of movable type for printing by Gutenberg in A.D. 1450. A couple of centuries later, books, magazines, newspapers, and other leaflets became part of everyday life, embedded into the fabric of society. But information could not be transmitted fast over wide distance until:

- The invention of the telegraph in 1836
- The advent of telephony in 1874
- The development of radio broadcasting in the 1920s

While the exact date of the invention of computers is uncertain because so many nations and people dispute the parenthood, I will put it around 1936 with scale models and analog computers coming somewhat earlier—and digital differential analyzers as well as digital computers right after.

The earliest way to communicate with computers, and therefore instruct them in a procedural way, was through *machine language* (ML). That was also my first programming experience at UCLA in 1953 with the standard western automatic calculator (SWAC) originally designed by Dr. John von Neumann.

In 1954, Dr. Grace Hopper, one of the best computer scientists on record, designed Flowmatic—the first *symbolic assembly language*. Assembly-level languages are usually referred today as *second generation*—the first generation being ML.

Compiler- and interpreter-level languages were developed in the 1955 to 1958 time frame,* starting with a timid departure: SAP for the IBM 704, this time frame saw the internal translator (IT) by Dr. Alan Perlis, Fortran by Dr. Jim Bachus (based on IT), and Cobol by the Codasyl Committee. These are generally known as *third-generation languages* (3GL).

---

*See D. N. Chorafas, *Programming Systems for Electronic Computers*, Butterworths, London, 1962.

There is what might be called a "$3^{1}/_{2}$-generation language" like Simula (in 1968), which eventually led to object-oriented systems. Also the language C was designed at Bell Telephone Laboratories in connection to Unix, in the same time frame. C++ can be seen as the merger of concepts that were brought forward by C and Simula.

The term *fourth-generation language* (4GL) is usually reserved for *computer-assisted software engineering* (CASE) tools, which largely work through precompilation. There is a myriad of them, and in general they are incompatible among themselves. There are as well many unfulfilled claims about the support CASE tools can provide.

Another level of reference are knowledge engineering languages like Lisp, Prolog, and the CASE tools of the early 1980s connected to them such as KEE and ART. I would be tempted to classify them as a $4^{1}/_{2}$-generation languages. After all, they add up to the same process, that of instructing computers.

It is, however, wise to note another direction in software development that has broken down the barrier between computer users and the effort of communicating with the machine. Until *natural language* programming can be effectively implemented through voice, *visual programming* is carrying the day. Visual programming solutions are way ahead of the large majority of CASE tools. They constitute a new direction in software development and usage based on interactive visualization.

I classify visual programming as well as the Internet programming constructs as *fifth-generation languages* (5GL). At the Web site, this includes HTTP and HTML at the base and Virtual Reality Modeling Language (VRML),* Knowledge Query and Manipulation Language (KQML), Telescript, Active X, and Java at the upper layer.

The Internet programming tools provide environments for truly distributed constructs, going beyond client-server tools. They support the base on which agents can be developed, as well as the structures in which they can operate.

The Knowledge Query and Manipulation Language

The Knowledge Query and Manipulation Language is a high-level communications construct that also features a protocol for exchanging infor-

---

*D. N. Chorafas, *Visual Programming Technology*, McGraw-Hill, New York, 1997.

mation independent of content syntax and ontology. KQML makes it feasible to wrap information and commands, offering a uniform view of an agent as a knowledge bank.

- In the context of knowledge sharing, the conceptualization is specified by means of *ontology.*
- Like formal specification of a program, a description is provided of concepts and relationships that can exist for an agent.

A similar reference is valid for a group of agents. Emphasis on multiagent approaches is consistent with the use of ontology as a set of concepts. Notice that this is a different sense of the word *ontology* from its typical use in philosophy.

KQML is used as a language for application programs that collaborate among themselves or interact with one or more intelligent systems. This is done by means of an extensible set of *performatives* expressing beliefs and attitudes toward some information element(s). The goal is one of sharing knowledge and of supporting cooperative problem solving.

KQML's extensible set of performatives help in defining the permissible operations that agents may attempt on each other's knowledge and goals. Among themselves, these performatives comprise a substrate supporting the development of higher-level models of interagent interaction. Examples are:

- Contract nets
- Negotiations

Networkwide solutions can be provided through HTTP and KQML interfaces. Figure 4-1 shows a network with *N* workstations—*N* being a 2-digit

Figure 4-1

Network interfaces through HTTP and KQML to relational and object DBMS, WAIS servers, and Gopher servers.

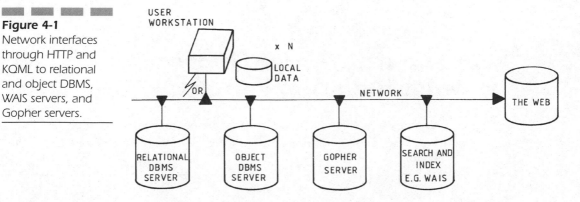

number. To the network are attached relational and object-oriented servers. There is as well access to a Gopher server, a WAIS server, and the Web.

One of the facilities offered by KQML is its ability to develop a basic architecture for knowledge sharing through a special class of agent(s).* These are known as *communication facilitators*. Their job is to coordinate the interaction of other agents:

■ The set of KQML performatives defines the permissible operations that agents may attempt on each other's knowledge and goals.

■ KQML enhances architectural possibilities for knowledge sharing through communication facilitators.

Current applications domains of KQML can be found in concurrent engineering, intelligence-enriched planning and scheduling, diagnostics and maintenance, and interactive design for a faster time to market. Interactive computational finance is another domain where KQML may be of assistance.

The common need underpinning all these domains is the use of knowledge robots (knowbots). KQML is seen by many as a language and protocol structure suitable for the development and use of agents in a groupware environment:

■ Helping in the implementation of knowledge-enriched software architectures

■ Assisting interactive design procedures involving small, intelligent applications modules

The development of KQML is part of a larger project known as the *Advanced Research Projects Agency* (ARPA) *Knowledge Sharing Initiative*. This has been aimed at the development of a methodology and techniques for building knowledge banks that are sharable and reusable. Such aims have led to the need to include in KQML both:

■ A message format

■ A message-handling protocol

to support runtime knowledge sharing among agents. Message sharing and message passing are of vital importance in agent interactions within an intelligent system, as well as in sharing knowledge in cooperative problem solving.

---

*See also Chap. 13.

Mention should be made of a special project known as *KQML 95*. This, too, has been promoted by the Advanced Research Projects Agency to develop the next version of KQML, as well as to expand the new language's coverage for unexpected situations.

The KQML effort was seeded with government funding and promoted largely through private initiative. Thus it lacks central control, and therefore many of the current KQML implementations are different from one another. As a result, there exist a number of KQML dialects. The KQML 95 project is intended:

■ To reduce the expanding set of dialects

■ To provide coordination among the different standards-setting bodies

Among the approaches being used to address these issues is a revision of the KQML syntax, which is being undertaken to create a convergence of the existing dialects, while keeping in perspective the need for additional performatives. The latter are necessary to assure the security of transactions, enhance the implementation in different applications domains, and promote wider adoption of KQML. Another goal is to explore the development of a standard ontology:

■ For communications networks

■ For mediator services

Other needs currently noted are to extend the current KQML to deal with results from cooperative problem solving, as well as to enhance the user's ability to work with several standard content languages. These ends are pursued through state transition diagrams, codes of error and defaults, and knowledge-enriched semantics and syntactics. Concomitant with this effort is one aimed to support a variety of distributed architectural platforms—a subject that is addressed in Chap. 12.

Extending the ARPA Knowledge-Sharing Effort

The ARPA Knowledge Sharing Initiative includes a broader community than the Advanced Research Projects Agency itself. There is, for example, the ARPA/Rome Laboratory Planning and Scheduling project, which uses the *Knowledge Representation Specification Language* (KRSL) for specifying shared ontologies. It also includes built-in ontologies for:

- Time measurement
- Resource management
- Other mission-critical factors

The Air Force Office of Scientific Research contributes to this effort. Other projects relating to KQML are currently promoted by the National Science Foundation (NSF) and the Corporation for National Research Initiative (CNRI), as well as by different companies and universities interested in promoting knowledge engineering applications.

Apart from KRSL, which partly complements and partly competes with KQML, other projects targeting interlanguage knowledge sharing and communication among heterogeneous agents. One of them is supported by the *Knowledge Interchange Format* (KIF). KIF focuses on the interchange of knowledge among disparate programming artifacts:

- It has declarative semantics.

These semantics address the meaning of expressions in the representation without appealing to an interpreter for manipulation reasons.

- It is logically comprehensive.

Hence it provides for the expression of arbitrary sentences in the first-order predicate calculus.

- It makes uncertain knowledge representation feasible through non-montonic reasoning rules.

KIF is also instrumental in the definition of objects, functions, and relations, which can be very helpful in building shared ontologies. This is an extension to ARPA's Knowledge Sharing Initiative to help in solving the problems of the late 1990s and beyond.

As we saw earlier in this chapter, one of the aspects critical in the development of communicating agents is a common syntax with common semantics. This has not escaped the attention of ongoing research projects and working groups. In the context of KQML and similar efforts, *common syntax* is supported by the:

- Interlingua Working Group
- Common Knowledge Representation Systems Specification (KRSS) Working Group

There is as well an effort on *common pragmatics* carried out by the:

- Interfaces and Architectures Working Group

A common denominator among all these efforts, largely characterized by the output of the working groups, is the development of tools and of an infrastructure that may be able to support rapid access to information by end users:

■ At the appropriate level of detail
■ From the most economical sources
■ At any time, anywhere in the world

The fulfillment of these objectives requires a fairly sophisticated interaction among many information agents, as well as the existence of artifacts that can:

■ Compose new custom documents from databases and other agents
■ Forward the query to domain expert librarians, as necessary
■ Find related information when the document is read, bringing this information to the user's attention

The ARPA Knowledge Sharing Initiative also has other aspects—for instance, the ability to recognize whether a link is current or out of date, whether the document is really dynamic or is a static snapshot of dynamic data, and whether the link(s) miss(es) some important new references.

These goals are worth pursuing on their own merits, as well as within the implementation perspectives of the Internet. Many enhancements are sought in the World Wide Web domain such as embedding queries in the document originated by the author or the reader. Also:

■ Developing new protocols such as an HTTP + KQML joint that supports links as queries
■ Providing agile network interfaces to servers under different relational and object DBMS, Gopher servers, and search servers

General queries may need to be answered cross network and cross server. They can be embedded into custom-assembled report(s) with data and text extracted from other sources with summaries, but may also incorporate commands, figures, moving images, custom-analyzed information, and live news. All should be supported by agents whose mission is to find, access, recognize, and/or massage the information elements.

Universally Acceptable Knowledge Languages and KQML Preformatives

Is there purpose for a universally acceptable knowledge language on the Web? A vague way of answering this question is: Maybe. A more crisp answer will be: No!—though there is an Interlingua Working Group that developed the Knowledge Interchange Format and there are as well other working group efforts, as we saw earlier in this chapter.

In tackling the issue of a universally acceptable Web knowledge language, many people usually say that in a fast-expanding implementation domain, "a standardized programming language will soon become a straitjacket." This is an argument that I have heard since the early to mid-1950s with the first symbolic languages, and it is valid to a significant extent.

But those specialists who maintain that there is plenty of scope for common semantics also have a point. We can gain a great deal from a common vocabulary and agreed-upon common meanings to describe the subject domain. Even on this issue, however, there is dissent because programming is too vast a field for just one ontology. The alternative concept is that there should be many domain-specific ontologies published, though some will be sharable.

But is it not true that KQML has at least some basic characteristics that can be considered as *common* with other knowledge languages and object-oriented approaches? This too is an argument that makes sense. Such characteristics, and the notions underpinning them, can be expressed in three bullets:

- KQML's current syntax is Lisp based.
- It has embedded in it many elements of C++.
- It features important provisions for binary data and structures.

As shown in Fig. 4-2, KQML is a layered language with each level having an embedded functionality. A KQML message is a content expression typically enclosed in a speech act inside a communication envelope. The outer envelope in this schema addresses the mechanics of communication. The logic of communication is mapped in the message. The kernel is the content of communication expressed in an agreed-upon language, such as KRSL or KIF.

Figure 4-2
KQML: A layered language or, more precisely, an embedded structure.

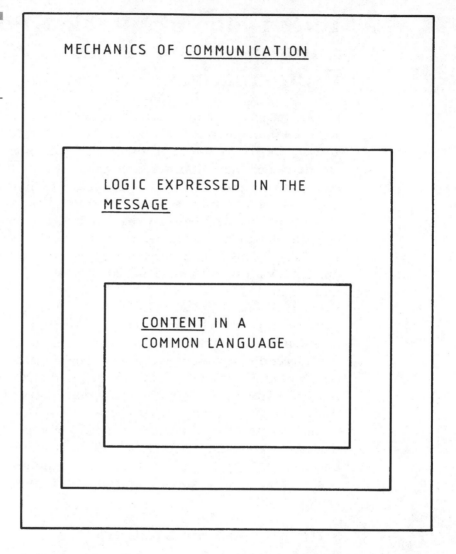

- Through the content layer of a message, two parties can communicate in any language they agree on.
- KQML features reduce the importance of universality and communality in linguistic constructs.

At the other end of the structure shown in Fig. 4-2, the communication layer is packet oriented and low level. In KQML, it is currently served through TCP/IP—but it could be built on other protocols or electronic-mail solutions. This increases the flexibility of the language.

One of the characteristics of KQML is that the subject of protocols is seen from a fairly broad perspective. Supported communications protocols handle simple synchronous transactions such as query and reply and ack and nack, characteristics of multiresponse messages, and monitoring chores, as well as other communications services like forwarding and broadcasting.

At the message layer, each KQML expression is a speech act described by a *performative*. Examples of performatives are Subscribe, Ask, Tell, Untell, Achieve, and Unachieve. Performatives are classified into three groups:

- Core

- Standard

- Extended

Core performatives are at the kernel and consist of a small set of formally defined primitives used to define others. The job of *standard performatives* is to reserve names for others, particularly those that most agents will want to handle. *Extended performatives* consist of groups of agents that are able to define and use extensions.

Examples of basic query performatives are Evaluate, Ask-if, Ask-in, Ask-one, and Ask-all. Multiresponse query performatives are Stream-in and Stream-all. Reply and Sorry are response performatives. Generic informational performatives are:

- Tell, which means add content to the information store

- Untell, which means remove content from the information store

- Achieve, which means add content to the goal store

- Unachieve, which means remove content from the goal store

Other KQML performatives are known as Generators. Examples are Standby, Ready, Next, Rest, and Discard. Still others are capability definition performatives, such as Advertise, Subscribe, Monitor, Import, and Export. There exist as well networking performatives, for instance, Register, Unregister, Route, Forward, and Broadcast.

In conclusion, the need for intelligent information networks supported by agents brought forward the specifications of KQML as the language that supports agent architectures. KQML primitives and performatives can be used for efficient communication purposes. As we will see in Chap. 12, developing architectural characteristics, steady experimentation, and daily experience gained from real life will all help in the evolution of the KQML language.

Morphing Expert Systems into Agents

It should not have escaped the attention of the knowledgeable reader that much of what we have said about agents in Chaps. 1, 2, and 3 is not that different from the goals we sought in the early to mid-1980s with expert systems. Because one of the aims of agents is to provide a continuity to the existing applications—as well as to revamp and renovate these applications—essentially we are interested in *morphing* expert systems into agents.

Morphing is a transformation ideally viewed online in real time, most often visualized by the user while it happens. However, the computation of morphing often requires hours of offline computing. Whether done in real time or offline, morphing is a metamorphosis from one *type*, or from one *state*, to another. In this chapter we look at morphing only as an example of:

- Transforming expert systems into agents

In Chap. 12 we will return to the notion of morphing and examine more closely the conceptual issues underpinning this process. In that case, we will be interested in:

- Morphing one agent into another agent

At least one of the ongoing projects on KQML has the objective of morphing expert systems into agents. In the background lies the fact that agents are geared to helping people use the technology. This has not been a top objective with expert systems, but the "help" principle should be more frequently observed as existing expert systems are morphed into agents.

Starting with the fundamentals, like many of the currently available expert systems, some agents use prescribed rules. Production-type expert systems do the same. The difference is that rule-based artifacts must now be adapted to changing circumstances that determine the agent's behavior.

Here is how Dr. Tibor Vamos, of the Hungarian Academy of Sciences, looks at the morphing of an expert system into an agent. If we consider a certain chunk of knowledge, the first problem is delimitation of the chunk. The crucial issue is how to delimit the necessary knowledge:

- From the viewpoint of the knowledge bank

▪ From the viewpoint of the agent's interest(s)—hence, indirectly, of the user's

An example from banking can help. Agents developed for savings banks would require that the knowledge about savings banks be separated from the general knowledge about commercial banks. How this should be done is a delicate design task because regulation and legislation vary over time.

Not only should the knowledge bank defining the mission of a savings bank be built most carefully but so should the specific functions within this mission. Rule selection can be quite different if the agent's master is:

▪ A senior bank executive

▪ A local bank manager

▪ An investment officer

▪ An important client

These are not issues that have preoccupied us that greatly with expert systems, but they have become very important with agents. Hence, from a system analysis and design perspective, they should constitute matters to be taken seriously in morphing.

There is as well a procedural aspect to be given due weight. As Dr. Vamos suggests, this has to do with *nonmonotonic* features of knowledge—and, by extension, of knowledge artifacts. No two agents have the same goals. Typically, agents have:

▪ Different interests

▪ Different knowledge

▪ Different backgrounds

Therefore, collisions of agent worlds will, quite likely, be unavoidable. This means that some features of nonmonotonic logic should be introduced combined with a support system able to detect a possible collision, define its characteristics, and provide alternatives in conflict resolution.

These ideas are also valid for the more general case. There are as well special considerations, for instance, related to different situation-dependent agent cooperation schemes that may not be possible to express clearly in a mathematical sense. When this happens, it makes conflict resolution that much more complex. This problem of conflict resolution among agents is indeed very important and will surely preoccupy system designers in the near future. Tibor Vamos has had the foresight to warn us, but luminaries in the agents' domain have failed to consider the conflict issue in their work.

Morphing expert systems into agents can be simpler when such interactions need not be considered. For instance, the artifact might be a rule-based agent that monitors electronic mail on his or her master's behalf, looking for key phrases to manage appointments. However, this too is a special case.

As we have already seen, KQML provides the facility necessary for the latter example. But rather than being simple straightforward orders, the filtering rules must be capable of learning how the agent's master refers to a given business opportunity or other event of interest to him or her. This is a major difference in mission between agents and expert systems.

An expert system may be written to mine databases for items the user considers important to him or her, according to some fixed criteria. Contrary to this relatively static solution, an agent will look up all or most of the databases attached to a given network to answer ad hoc queries by his or her master—which not only change over time but may also involve some uncertainty.

Functional Requirements to Be Supported by the Agent's Software: An Example with BargainFinder

Anderson Consulting has used KQML, Telescript, Java, and JavaScript to develop agents and demons. Most have been designed to do filtering, text extraction, testing, and backtesting. One of the better-known artifacts this company has made is *BargainFinder*, released in 1994.

Originally designed as an experimental project, BargainFinder looks around for bargains in connection to electronic commerce. Give the artifact the "go," and it will search online information regarding the best price of, say, a laser printer of certain characteristics the agent's master has defined.

BargainFinder typically takes less than a minute to come up with a number of references and prices relating to electronic commerce. Its activity resembles that of other agents that have been designed and implemented to search and recommend documents, products, or people to their master. In fact, BargainFinder seems to be so successful in performing its duties that some stores decided they don't want to see it around accessing their databases. But the majority of electronic commerce stores approached Anderson Consulting to get connected.

On the Web, BargainFinder is used between 800 and 2000 times per day. At Comdex Fall 1996, it was reported that some 90 percent of users have said they were really fond of a bargain the artifact brought to their attention, while 93 percent indicated they will use the agent again. Yet, BargainFinder is not as sophisticated as some expert systems have been. It works well for commodity products where price is the main reason for choosing a particular retail shop, but it encounters difficulties when more subjective criteria are used like after-sales service. If agents should be able to handle both qualitative and quantitative criteria, then BargainFinder is a marginal case. Marginal cases have led some people to think that agents are not necessarily knowledge artifacts (as we discussed in Chap. 1). But the majority of experts in the agents domain see them as artificial intelligence constructs. Hence the language we use must be able to handle subjective aspects of expertise. Lisp-based KQML can do that job.

Another intelligent artifact by Anderson Consulting is *LifestyleFinder.* It develops a profile of its master's interests and exploits a demographics database, coming up with focused answers. LifestyleFinder learns about the user's profile by asking questions:

- Which are your specific interests?
- What is the house you live in like?
- What vacations do you like to take?

These are typically multiple-answer questions that LifestyleFinder handles fairly well. Still another knowledge artifact is the *InfoFinder.* It browses information in databases and indicates relevance or irrelevance of various documents in regard to its master's interests, learning from the key sentences in the documents that it is looking up.

The *ContactFinder* is an agent with a different mission. It answers bulletin board questions. It also finds specialists for specific topics for research or for consultancy reasons. *ShopBot* is a knowledge-enriched artifact that contrasts to the way BargainFinder works. In its search, ShopBot employs:

- Pattern matching
- Inductive learning

ShopBot teaches itself how to shop in different online stores—but unlike a classical expert system, it does so interactively. As it receives information about the product its master is after, as well as about differ-ent variants existing for that product, ShopBot can be quite inquisitive, answering the prerequisites Dr. Edward A. Feigenbaum outlined for sophisticated software: to *investigate what* rather than simply following a *how-to* execution line.

The challenge of performing at high levels of competence is primari-ly a function of the program's knowledge of its task domain. Going beyond that level by learning requires a reasoning process.

For example, a current KQML—based project focuses on domain-spe-cific reasoning. Within the general software development landscape, domain-specific approaches are not yet generally appreciated because most of the classical computer scientists are uncomfortable with the specifics of domains. Yet, when software specialists distance themselves from domain-specific details, they take a leave from relevance to the real world. They also fail in their mission to design tools that allow users to express and capture domain-specific concepts and details.

Domain-specific software and the embedding of intelligence into the artifacts are integral parts of an evolutionary process that is irreversible. Expert systems developers know this because many of their artifacts in operation today are domain specific.

To a lesser extent, this is true of software like spreadsheets and word processors. Spreadsheets address an accounting-type computation. Word processing software targets text manipulation and document prepara-tion details.

The morphing of an expert system into an agent should preserve its domain specificity. But it should also add to its reasoning process an interactive and proactive behavior using the contribution of languages such as KQML.

Firefly, Marilyn, and Efficient Software Development[*]

Agents could effectively employ existing knowledge constructs in a process of *collaborative filtering*, with the agent working on the basis of what it has learned about its master. An example of collaborative filter-ing is *Firefly*, an artifact that recommends music and films. It asks each

---

[*]See also the discussion on software dependability in Chap. 10.

user to rate a number of artists. Then it compares those ratings with ratings other users made.

Working for a single user, the agent can build up a profile of its master's tastes. But the more references on preferences the agent has, the more accurate becomes its reasoning process—and therefore its output.

Firefly is a good example of an agent operating on the Web with the goal of making intelligent recommendations to its master. It does so by creating a three-dimensional case base, ordering its recommendations along an X, Y, Z frame of reference. The artifact carries user and organization identification codes protecting privacy in terms of informal consent and value exchange—or at least this is what its developers claim. In terms of privacy and security, this contribution goes beyond what direct mailers do by simply buying and selling information.

Other intelligent artifacts operating on the Web act as community builders. They search into catalogs and other databased information developing a targeting space. The goal is to enable their masters to leverage each other's knowledge on the Internet or the intranets.

There are, however, problems encountered with agents, just as there have been problems with expert systems. An example of failure to build an agent is *Marilyn*. Marilyn was developed by a Rupert Murdoch company to be a travel administration assistant. The artifact was supposed to know everything about the company's travel requirements and to take care of all its reservations.

Like many expert systems projects in the 1980s, this agent project was too ambitious, and though there have been lots of demonstrations of it, in the end the artifact did not work in a productive manner. Let's always keep in mind that such failures have also been experienced with all types of software—including many dumb programs written in Cobol or any other language. To be successful, knowledge artifacts must be focused on an objective and operate in a specific domain. They should not be written as "good for everything and for nothing"—like the policy followed with many Cobol programs.

Whether we use KQML or another language, it is wise to exercise prudence in the development of software. A good approach is the *fail-fast strategy:* If we are trying to build a complex artifact that has never been built before, it is prudent to focus on improving the learning curve, of ourselves and of the artifacts we are building, by starting with a small series of throw-away constructs through *rapid prototyping*.

Rapid prototyping helps to determine requirements, and it also gives feedback online, permitting the user to judge the suitability of the model. In this way, it provides the means to overcome poorly understood user requirements—which is a major problem in the development of applications software.

Typically, rapid prototyping includes the possibility of multiple iteration until the requirements phase stabilizes. The model that results can be exercised by its users to evaluate strengths and weaknesses of the programming product. This approach is most useful in detecting errors in the understanding of functional and structural requirements at an early stage of development. It provides an evolutionary process by means of online testing and/or incremental implementations—a process sometimes called *evolutionary prototyping*.

Evolutionary prototyping blends very well with artificial intelligence. One of the laudable contributions of knowledge engineering in software development tools and processes is the capability to have components inform other components about their own characteristics, functions, and properties.

Quite similarly, one of the lessons learned by companies with experience in rapid and efficient development of software is not to go for big modules—or big changes. It is wiser to move faster with smaller releases. Still another lesson is to be prepared for surprises, and not to panic.

Finally, in terms of software releases for electronic commerce, a good approach is what is now called *trialware*. Typically, trialware is downloaded on request but will work only for 30 days. A lasting copy is sent after payment—and payment will be made if the user organization (or individual consumer) is happy with what it is getting.

Agents for Browsing and Morphism: An Example from MIT

At MIT, a project being conducted under Dr. Henry Lieberman is building an agent that acts as a user's assistant in browsing the World Wide Web. In contrast to current Web tools that perform searches, the approach is to consider the search for information as a cooperative venture between the human user and the agent. Rather than searching a preindexed portion of the Web following keywords, Lieberman's agent, *Letizia*, infers interest implicitly from observing user actions. Then, it tries to stay just a few steps ahead of the user, dynamically searching its master's immediately accessible links.

The background notion of this project is that agent software can perform tasks automatically on behalf of a user. The agent can learn by observing its master's behavior, but there can also be cases where the user must instruct the agent more explicitly. *Instructability* is the high point of this project.

The user may present examples of behavior that the agent should follow and give advice as to how the examples should be interpreted. The agent gives feedback to the user so that the latter understands:

- What the agent knows
- What it is capable of doing

A sister project at MIT starts from the notion that current work in agent software relies mostly on domain-specific applications programmed from scratch or explicitly modified with an agent in mind. By extension it is possible to make a toolkit of protocols that permit an agent to communicate and control applications that have been constructed more conventionally.*

Within this frame of reference, KQML can be of help particularly if we account for the limitations of current browsing and searching tools as well as of database-mining expert systems:

- Agents should be designed for people, not for other programs.
- Agents must have consistent interfaces.

Morphing should see to it that the resulting agents embellish other computer programs, making them friendlier to people. Morphing should as well account for the fact that, because of a number of limitations, the currently available simple links cannot effectively serve an interactive environment, and most of the presently used approaches cannot be scaled.

As Part 2 will demonstrate, an upgrade to smarter communications protocols and database links is doable because agents are proactive. This is a basic reason that they can provide expert guidance to users who have to solve problems in and around a body of rules, regulations, procedures, or operating conditions that may be almost too complex to comprehend.

---

*See the section on morphing earlier in chapter.

Finance is a domain where interactive knowledge artifacts written in KQML can be of assistance. Speaking from experience in financial engineering, I would include in the implementation domains:

- Foreign exchange
- Equities and bonds
- All types of loans
- Derivative financial instruments
- Auditing and compliance
- Real-time risk management

In a way similar to the projects we discussed in connection to the ARPA/Rome Laboratory Planning Initiative, in finance, agents can be instrumental in planning, scheduling, and control operations, in logistics, and in database mining.

Other rewarding implementation examples in a networked environment should focus on the creation of intelligent agents to monitor and manage data streams by filtering, digesting, abstracting, and acting on behalf of a human master:

- Deriving knowledge from a large amount of information elements
- Distinguishing if data are scientific, financial, or legal
- Managing the data stream to present meaningful interactive reports

As explained in an earlier section, morphism essentially amounts to transforming rule-based expert systems into agents. An interactive interface to an expert system, for example, can greatly assist the end user—or even take the user's place. It can also give the agent access to the application's data and the user's behavior.

Fundamental to this morphism is a communications mechanism leading to a dynamic division of labor between the agent and the application software. Important contributions would tend to be situational, such as the agent's ability to comprehend *icons,* or generally, graphic design and visual examples.

A key feature of the morphism lies in combining representation and learning techniques from artificial intelligence with interactive graphical editors to generate programming-by-example solutions. From there, the next important step may be agents that inhabit computer-animated, three-dimensional worlds.

Finally, it is appropriate to add a brief reference to ARP's Palo Alto Collaborative Testbed (PACT), which has been designed as a testbed for cooperative research and knowledge sharing. Concurrent engineering research employs an informal, ad hoc approach to ontology, in which solutions are implicit, generated through a number of Email messages among agent developers:

- Knowledge sharing in PACT is done using encapsulated models and tool data

- Interface format PACT sees to it that agents communicate

The shared language is KQML. The interface is KIF. PACT uses both local agents as well as facilitators. These are responsible for providing interfaces, and a reliable layer of message passing. They route outgoing messages, translate incoming messages, initialize and monitor agent execution.

Communications occur between facilitators and between agents and facilitators, but not directly between agents. In PACT, consumer agents send requests to a matchmaker facilitator. Provider agents evaluate them by advertising capabilities to matchmakers. Consumer agents compare those capabilities to their needs. This project has shown that it is easier to have consumer agents express a need than to have agents summarize what they can offer.

Telescript and Agent Programming

As we have demonstrated, the morphism of expert systems into agents is part of the transformation taking place in networks. Whether conducted on a local area network (LAN), metropolitan area network (MAN), or wide area network (WAN), today's communications solutions are passive: They require the user to manually browse in search of items of interest. In contrast, a growing number of end users are seeking ways to turn passive networks into active ones.

One of the characteristics of *active networks* is that the tasks of searching, finding, and reporting are delegated to agents. Through morphing, manual browsing is replaced by automated services designed to seek and deliver items of relevance—and only those items—to the user.

Like KQML, *Telescript* by General Magic addresses this issue. It is an object-oriented, distributed programming language that helps to provide a software engine enabling the creation of active, distributed network applications. Four simple concepts characterize Telescript:

- Abstraction
- The concept of agents
- Places
- The Go command

Agents "go" to places where they interact with other agents to get work done on a user's behalf, by transporting themselves over the network. The software engine acts as a multitasking interpreter able to integrate onto an operating system. This is done through an interface: the Telescript API.

The careful reader will appreciate that whether we talk of Telescript, KQML, or other intelligent software platforms, the goal is to leverage the language in order to create active, personalized services. These enable users to better cope with their networking needs, which are steadily growing in volume and complexity.

Languages like KQML and Telescript simplify the creation of communications services by offering higher-level abstractions and built-in safety. In Telescript's case, abstraction, agents, places, and the Go command provide a simple but agile metaphor for distributed application development and usage.

Practically since day 1 of computing for commercial and industrial purposes, which started 44 years ago with Univac's installation at General Electric's Appliance Park, developers and users have spent less time handling the simple mechanics of programming than they have spent on hardware development. This has been just as valid about the underlying complexities in networking chores. By contrast, today the focus is on delivering value-added artifacts.

The value-added artifacts developed by Telescript are mobile agents. As with all object-oriented programming, the script consists of a collection of classes organized by subclassing into an ephemeral hierarchy:

- Telescript supports a form of multiple inheritance using the so-called mix-ins.
- Classes have features that are their externally observable attributes and operations.

Agent features may be public or private. Telescript's private features are visible in subclasses and also in the base class. Entire classes or features may be sealed so that they cannot be overridden.

Telescript does not permit incompatible signatures in subclasses. The language reference specifies a number of predefined classes that must be supported in every implementation by the engine (interpreter).

As with all object-oriented solutions, objects are instances of some class and inherit features from the top of the hierarchy. Agents and places are also objects, instances of various subclasses of *process*, the predefined abstract class. The object encapsulates its properties, which reference other objects.

Telescript's multitasking functionality is provided by process objects. Processes are multitasked preemptively, invoked by the engine, and scheduled according to priority. A process owns itself. But objects must be owned by one process. Those not owned are subject to garbage collection. A process can transfer ownership of an object to another process. This is doable *if* it owns that object and all others referenced by that object's properties.

The agent class is a subclass of process, which provides the sealed, private Go operation. Agents can request Go through a ticket argument that describes the *place* where the agent is trying to go. This can be done with varying levels of specificity *if* the Telescript engine can figure out where and how to route the agent, and *if* the trip is ultimately successful, *then* the agent becomes active, executing its next line of code, the destination.

In principle, the agent processes execute in the context of one or more enclosing place processes. Places usually provide a service API for agents to interact with and can be nested within other places. Every Telescript engine has a place. Typically, in processing an agent's Go, the destination engine requests that the entering operation give that destination the opportunity to deny occupancy. If no place satisfying the ticket will admit the agent, the trip fails.

Telescript Engines and Intelligent Networks

Consistent with the policy followed with KQML, it is not the objective of this chapter to cover Telescript in detail. Only the highlights follow, including processes, places, and *regions*—which help to define and delimit a Telescript engine. The Telescript region can consist of multiple engines with engine places running under the same authority. An agent may travel:

- Between places on a single engine
- On different engines in the same region
- To an engine in a different region

An agent will travel between engines *if* it has been serialized by the sending engine's encoder function. It must also be decoded by the destination engine.

This operational framework fits well within the Telescript network, which consists of interconnected engines. The language imposes no limit on particular network technologies that might be used. Main protocols are TCP/IP and UDP/PPP.

A Telescript engine provides platform-specific, code-enabling agent portability. Each process has a name, which is an instance of class Telename, and it features two OctetString-valued attributes:

- Its authority
- Its identity

A Telescript user is uniquely identified by an authority. Two processes have Telenames with the same authority if they are operating on behalf of the same user entity.

Telescript may intrinsically shield the programmer from hazards that would cause the engine to crash. Telescript engines do this through run-time-type checking with dynamic feature binding. For instance, the engine raises an exception if a program attempts to follow a null reference or accesses a feature that is unavailable or nonexistent.

The Telescript engine also features memory management, allocating storage when objects are created and performing garbage collection on unreferenced objects.

Telescript defines a number of built-in data structure classes as subclasses of the Collection class, using safe operations. Another feature is exception processing. Programs have the capability to catch exceptions, while uncaught exceptions usually result in process termination.

Telescript also offers a fine-grain access control over resource consumption and process interactions as well as public and private key authentication. These security characteristics are an increasingly important ingredient of network solutions.[*]

---

[*]See also Chap. 6.

As should be expected, because security is a major concern, the operator wants assurance that nothing unwanted will come by admitting an incoming agent. For control purposes:

■ The host wants to know who is responsible for the agent.

■ The agent would like to trust that the information it is carrying will not be disclosed arbitrarily.

This means that the platform must trust the agent and the agent must trust the platform—hence the need to provide security through a basic runtime safety mechanism, assuring safety and security at process, network, and systems levels. Conceptually, this is doable through appropriate software supports.

The Telescript engine may be considered part of a *trusted computing base* (TCB) providing a mechanism for controlled sharing as well as a reasonably safe process interaction. Security is enhanced through:

■ Protected references

■ Authentication for each process

References are protected by encapsulation of private properties and features, forming the basis for an object-oriented access control. There are also quotas and process privileges using permits, including control over creation of new processes and mediated protocols for meeting agents.

This contrasts to the way a typical C program operates. In any case, for any program, the developer must exercise extreme diligence to identify and control hazards like:

■ Referencing discarded objects

■ Accessing noninitialized pointers

■ Encountering pointer arithmetic errors

■ Copying in a string that is longer than the destination buffer

With mission-critical programs, these and similar hazards can have severe aftermaths. They also represent opportunities for system penetrators and other unauthorized users to abuse the system.

Local permits associated with places are another of Telescript's provisions for a restricted environment. The use of most security features, for instance, protecting against untrusted and potentially malicious agents or places, is discretionary.

In principle, agents can defend themselves, but they do not necessarily have to. To this end, good use can be made of permits of which there exist four kinds:

- Temporary, imposed on a block of code using the Telescript *Restrict* statement
- Native, assigned by the process creator
- Local, imposed by a place on an entering agent or on a process
- Regional, which apply within a particular engine or set of engines comprising a region

Temporary permits are useful for bounding the damage a suspect code might do. Native, local, and regional permits of a process are sealed public attributes. The same is true of the age and priority of a Telescript process.

In any particular situation an effective permit is computed by the engine, reflecting the logical intersection of all applicable permits. An effective permit value is true only if a given capability is true in all permits intersected. Only with a true permit value can an agent enter a place. The Telescript engine gives that place the opportunity to deny occupancy—an operation executed on a thread of control.

Other languages like KQML, Java, Safe-Tcl, and Oblique have similar but not necessarily compatible features. A common approach is to run an untrusted program in a restricted environment. A safe environment is said to be used, for example, by the Safe-Tcl interpreter. The latter partitions the runtime environment into different namespaces that vary from trusted to less trusted. We will talk more about security in networks in Chap. 6.

Agents in Networks, Mobile Computing, Security, Reliability, and Diagnostics

CHAPTER 5

Agents as Catalysts of Telecommunications Solutions

An increasingly more demanding marketplace, the accelerating pace of product development, and a growing business diversification see to it that financial and technical information has grown rapidly in volume. In a knowledge society, further progress is greatly dependent on the means whereby both *information* and *knowledge* are captured, transmitted, stored, retrieved, manipulated, and used. There is a continuous stream of information flows among business centers as well as between such centers and the client base. Intelligent networks have been instrumental in handling this data stream, but customer requirements are increasing.

Sophisticated networks have made it possible for industry to capture the unfolding new business opportunities. They have linked far away databases into one aggregate and helped in the exploration of new telecommunications frontiers.

If we wish to achieve better solutions and greater cost-effectiveness, the way to go is a more advanced organization of our resources. This means using new types of protocols, applying media solutions such as photonics, and involving artificial intelligence artifacts—all of which may maximize the advantages we obtain through networking. Based on my research in 1995 and 1996, Table 5-1 outlines the key components characteristicing of fifth-generation communications and computer systems, with agents at Number 1 position.

Some companies, including both user organizations and telecommunications providers, are building wandering agents capable of working across a geographically dispersed network. As we will see in this chapter, this can be of great assistance for:

- Effective telecommunications management
- The development of a sophisticated enterprise information system

Fifth-generation communications solutions come over and above the structure and facilities of the fourth generation, which have been characterized by peer-to-peer, any-to-any networks enriched with expert systems.

TABLE 5-1	**Agents**
Characteristics of Fifth-Generation Communications and Computer Systems	**Mobile computing**
	Personal communications
	Wired and wireless networks
	Gigastreams
	Asynchronous transfer mode
	Cellular telephony
	Multimedia
	Visual programming
	Network languages
	Virtual networks
	Seamless structural integration

Future networks will allow access to polyvalent systems and very large databases. They will not be bogged down by local bottlenecks and blocking. Autonomous learning agents will manage communications resources, and their services will be judged by how well they meet their objectives interactively while serving the network's users.

No longer will the end user learn from the interface; the interface will learn from the user. Soon, there will be many agents for telephony. AT&T, British Telecom, NTT, Deutsche Telecom, Bell Communications Research, MCI, and US West are among the carriers spearheading agent research. Many computers and communications manufacturers are also pursuing work in this domain.

Intelligent Networks and Their Agents in the Late 1990s

Shortly after the year 2000, the world's economy will be so networked and borderless that skilled, highly trained professionals from many nations will create a new international class. Some social scientists foresee a huge dilution of national power as economic and technological changes sweep goods and people across borders and telecommunications break long-distance barriers. The future's three most powerful scientific forces are:

- Communications technology
- Knowledge engineering
- Gene management

The prognosis is that, among themselves, they will change society's landscapes as we know it. Interactive telecommunications offers the possibility of uniting the worlds of work, leisure, and culture in ways no one has yet clearly envisioned.

Increasingly more sophisticated, knowledge-enriched network software will first target nodes and lines.* Then it will significantly surpass that achievement by bringing into being things that think featuring nearly natural intelligence, as we have seen in Chap. 1.

For its part, genetic mapping may allow us to preempt many diseases and dramatically manage population growth, fundamentally altering

---

*See also in Chap. 10 the discussion of Compass.

social trends. This will be reached in synergy between communications technology, knowledge engineering, and gene management.

- The able exploitation of the results obtained in scientific laboratories will largely rest on broadband, intelligence-enriched communications.
- Limited scope, parochial, nation-oriented networks are today's constraints and issues of meaningless discussions—not the next century's.

The complexity of required network solutions can be better appreciated if we keep in mind that half of all calls made by year 2000 are expected to originate from or terminate at a *mobile handset*. Such development will outstrip the computing and management resources of today's public networks—even if some carriers, like Nippon Telegraph and Telephone, employ about 20,000 software engineers to tend to:

- Routing
- Signaling
- Service problems

British Telecom suggests that at present it has 6000 exchanges that are being analyzed through the synergy of humans and expert systems. Ten to fifteen years down the line, this will look like the "old times," as network operators:

- Move from centralized to full distributed architectures
- Rely increasingly on agents—and generally intelligent network management systems

Intelligent software, therefore agents, could be configured to route calls quite reliably, convert protocols, assure secure communications, and better reliability. Telecommunications reliability will be increased by at least an order of magnitude through online diagnostics—which themselves will depend on agents.*

As we saw in Part 1, the notion of an agent has become quite popular. Announcements of products like the Apple Newton with its agent software, as well as General Magic's messaging agents, are evidence of significant interest in agent research and development. The critical issue in the emerging study of autonomous knowledge artifacts is assuring that their development is not oversold by the needs of marketing but is instead based on a results-oriented scientific approach.

---

*See also Chap. 8.

Quite independently to what has happened to General Magic as a company,[*] as we saw in Chap. 4, its Telescript is based on the notion of software agents prowling in search of service optimization and of conflict resolution. The vendor also bets on the fact that strict cryptographic safeguards should prevent mischief, but a secure system has yet to be thoroughly tested.[†]

Microsoft includes in its Internet offerings servicewide *find agents* that allow users to search for information on the World Wide Web. Netscape, too, incorporates intelligent agents to help users find data and automatically update files. Search agents are a good example of how communications, databases, and software resources merge.

There are as well metasearch artifacts, like the WebCompass agent, passing requests to other search tools, then processing the results. In this manner, knowledge engineering adds value to the more classical search engines. This works well in a modular manner:

- The first module is doing what a human user of the search tool would do: entering the search term(s) and actively searching the database resources.

- The second module downloads the documents returned by the search and analyzes these documents including natural language parsing.

For this purpose, the WebCompass agent employs a combination of statistical and heuristic methods to rank phrases in the document. It can also use conceptual clustering. After the agent has decided which documents are similar, it analyzes these similarities to produce a sentence describing that group of documents.

From that point on, this title acts as a hyperlink that can be used to navigate between related groups of documents. WebCompass combines facilities that include statistics, heuristics, text comprehension, and hypermedia—all supported through knowledge engineering.

CISCO's Pricing and Status Agents

In one way or another, practically all of the communications equipment companies as well as telcos work on agents. Some focus on agents as *per-*

---

[*]For a discussion on the reasons why General Magic skided, see H. Steinmann and D. N. Chorafas, *The New Wave in Information Technology*, Cassell, London, 1996.

[†]See Chap. 6 on security.

sonal communicators that let people send and receive e-mail and faxes by tapping on the screen of a handheld device. Others concentrate on programming languages for communications software that enable agents to zip along, retrieving information elements from distributed databases.

The field of intelligent software for telecommunications is so new and it is expanding so quickly that different companies have chosen different implementation domains. Some telecommunications equipment manufacturers and telephone companies bet their best brains and their money on agents employed to manage multimedia networks. Some telcos, like NTT, are working on a platform for intelligent, agent-based communications. Other carriers believe that agents can be used to move beyond the limitations of existing protocols and network hierarchies.

Among equipment suppliers, CISCO has developed electronic commerce agents with the goal of greater ease in doing business.* One of these agents is pricing CISCO products. Another provides greater efficiency in ordering and scheduling, end to end. This *status agent* helps the customer in knowing the status of his or her order in real time. Even if scheduling data change by the minute, the agent gives the client complete information on his or her order.

The fact that this intelligent artifact has been successful is documented by statistics: It is used 12,000 times per week, and its popularity is growing. A *pricing agent* helps buy currency, downloads prices on spreadsheets, and assists the customer in applying discounts to which he or she is entitled.

Another artifact, CISCO's *configuration agent,* works in a way similar to that of XCON, the seminal expert system developed in the early 1980s by Digital Equipment Corporation† to assist in systems configuration and to expedite and deliver to customers computers with much fewer errors than manual methods permitted.

The CISCO configuration agent helps not only the company's own personnel but also the customer in confirming the availability and suitability of the products he or she wants. It also assists the customer in communicating with CISCO by fax or e-mail. These commerce agents perform their duties end to end in a diligent manner.

---

*I chose CISCO's agents as the best example among those discussed at Comdex Fall 1996, regarding artifacts development by communications equipment vendors.

†See D. N. Chorafas *Expert Systems in Manufacturing,* Van Nostrand Reinhold, New York, 1992.

CISCO's principle is that, on the Web, a business-to-business connection helps in creating a virtual enterprise. The first major application has been in the publishing media, and it has had two versions:

- CISCO Connection Online
- CISCO Personnel Online

Both use *knowledge agents.* Through online publishing, CISCO has stopped the massive printing of documents on paper. Now customers can obtain what they need in information through the Web.

CISCO is also using agents to solve technical support problems. With assistance of intelligent software, the use of this facility is booming. At the end of 1996, the number of log-ins stood at 450,000 per month:

- Software upgrades are downloaded in 90 percent of all cases. The statistic is 60,000 per month.
- Electronic ordering reduces lead time by 3 days, and customers like it.

Telcos use agent technology in different ways. For instance, agents are employed for self-identification, a feature of signaling that tells the network that two callers are trying to establish communication. Other agents could be used to add a third party, by identifying the caller to a network control platform. Still others help in the switch in and out of the backplane that evolves as the infrastructure of the new International Standards Organization (ISO)—Open Systems Interconnection (OSI) architectural solution.

As we will see in the following sections, this work thoroughly restructures the OSI model developed by the ISO in the late 1970s. ISO/OSI has been *the* reference model in network architecture for nearly 20 years—but it has reached its limits.

Backplanes and Agents as Facilitators of a New Telecommunications Architecture

Agents are the facilitators of more efficient solutions, but they can also be the catalysts of a new communications architecture. Intelligent software can provide reliable network interface layers, routing messages on the basis of message contents and coordinating control activities. Such missions are projected based on the concept that during the next 5 years the moving gear behind the evolution of networks and their architectures will be:

1. The redefinition of mission-critical applications
2. New implementation environments propelled by mobile computing
3. The transition from legacy to luxury bandwidth
4. New network patterns promoted by interactive multimedia

Every one of these four fundamental reasons for change in telecommunications, and all of them in unison, will lead to a host of transition problems and associated technical challenges. One of the major difficulties in connection to current technology lies in the fact that enterprise network traffic will tend to a 50/50 split between data and voice.

Other challenges to the established order will be technicoeconomic in nature. Still others will center on novel issues presented by mobile computing, as we saw earlier in this chapter. Two of the most important developments projected by American telecommunications specialists, which will upset the current order, lie in the facts that:

- By 1998 or 1999, ATM costs will tend to be competitive to Ethernet.
- By 1999 or 2000 an ATM enterprise backbone, or *intranet,* with multicast will be available.

The *Internet* layer of the original TCP/IP protocol will be recast in terms of connectivity to the ATM enterprise backbone. By all evidence, network management based on the HyperText Transfer Protocol (HTTP) will be gaining rapid acceptance for applications that have been traditionally supported by other protocols.

Today, network hardware manufacturers find it much easier and less expensive to create HTML-based device management interfaces that plug right into a web browser by writing proprietary software. Not only with the expansion of the intranet market device configuration is moving to HTTP—but also tier-1 vendors use HTTP to extend network management capabilities.

HTTP-based network administration looks so attractive because of the implementation flexibility and the potential savings it offers. The overall concept can be assisted by creating Java applets to control the attached devices. Let's remember that Java was originally created to facilitate the development of embedded-system software. Hence, it has:

- A compact runtime approach

- A basic interpreter
- Library and thread support

Java applications are portable since the language specifies a machine-independent, intermediate byte-code that can be transferred between network nodes. Also, it is compiled on-demand by a local Java runtime environment. The problem is efficiency in execution, because downloaded applets need interpretation and the work of the interpreter can be a slow, time-consuming job.[*]

Whether or not applets are used, the more advanced architectural solutions profit from an increasing use of knowledge artifacts. Both mobile and wireless links are being supported in reference to the backbone and its tributary networks, as we will see later when we talk of mobile computing requirements.

Another very important concept that will characterize communications in the late 1990s and right after year 2000 is the feedforward and feedback *backplane*. The best way to explain the backplane concept and its functions is by reference to the International Standards Organization—Open System Interconnection (ISO/OSI) model.

Figure 5-1 refreshes the reader's memory on the ISO/OSI model and the functionality of its layers. The top layer is applications, which supports program tasks, user software, device ports, instruments, and so on. In short, it provides all services directly comprehensible to application programs. The other layers of ISO/OSI perform the following functions:

- The presentation layer transforms information elements to and from negotiated standard formats.
- The session layer synchronizes and manages data streams.
- The transport layer provides transparent, reliable data transfer from end node to end node.
- The network layer performs message routing for transfer between nonadjacent modes.
- The physical layer encodes and physically transfers messages between adjacent nodes.

As communications systems grow in size and complexity beyond the scope of their original design, the traditional architecture—its methods and software supports—is overwhelmed. Therefore, it becomes evident

---

[*]D. N. Chorafas, *Visual Programming Technology*, McGraw-Hill, New York, 1997.

Figure 5-1
A layered protocol architecture.

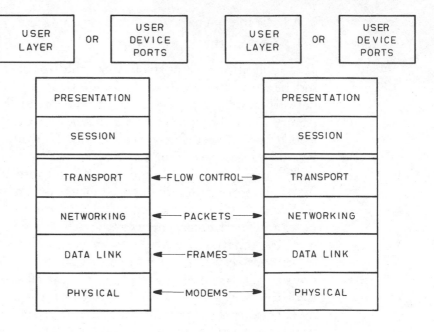

that quite significant improvements to the existing process are urgently needed.

During the last couple of years, work on new formal description techniques has progressed to the point that a communications architecture quite different than the one we knew is now feasible. The basic requirements for successfully developing an alternative to the old ISO/OSI are:

- Agents
- Backplanes

As seen in Fig. 5-2, the original ISO/OSI seven layers are divided into three better consolidated groups. These feature agent-supported *interface layers* between them. The backplane runs in parallel to this architectural structure of the old ISO/OSI. Notice that:

- Each communications mode is expected to have new protocols, which themselves will have embedded knowledge features—hence agents.
- In the left-most part of Fig. 5-2, a distinction is made under Resources and Applications between *wired* and *wireless* communications.

The new protocols in the making call for extensive development of tools and techniques to support formal communications methods through a shortened life cycle, with particular attention to online testing activities.

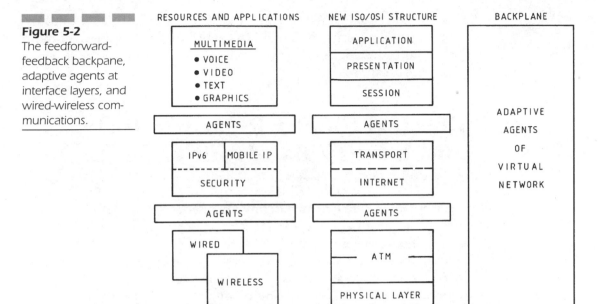

Figure 5-2
The feedforward-feedback backpane, adaptive agents at interface layers, and wired-wireless communications.

Some telecommunications researchers have begun to identify and propose solutions to these challenges, also suggesting the need for a test language standard.

Multimedia applications and the design of appropriate resources to meet requirements will attract the lion's share of attention at the level of the top three ISO/OSI layers. By all likelihood, the Internet Protocol, version 6 (IPv6), will dominate in the wired world, while a new mobile protocol will characterize communications in wireless systems. The two will work in unison interfaced through the backplane and agent layers:

- From local area and metropolitan area networking to the long haul, much more rigorous security algorithms will be necessary.
- With IPv6 these security mechanisms will focus at the transport and Internet protocol layer.

With *asynchronous transfer mode* (ATM), the bottom three levels of the ISO/OSI model will be collapsed into two—both in wireless and in wired communications. *Adaptive agents* will be the key connecting devices with particular attention paid to the complexity of interactions between subsystems.

The solutions to be applied in telecommunications will necessarily pay attention to the emergence of very high customer expectations for quality and reliability. As we will see in Chap. 7, this makes mandatory concurrent engineering practices and carries all the way into communications software engineering life cycles—where agents are destined to play a significant role.

Physical Clocks, Relative Clocks, and Luxury Bandwidths

The goal of the evolving architecture that this chapter has been describing is to support an organization-wide, user-at-a-terminal interactivity through a single *virtual network*. This must be seamless whether the user is mobile or operates in a confined space.

The model that seems to dominate views the computers and communications aggregate as the logical equivalent of a single, homogeneous structure which is highly distributed in a peer-to-peer manner. The virtual network is the Christmas tree on which hang:

- High-performance computers, workstations, appliances, special-purpose processors, multimedia database servers, and other functional units

- Important nodes as gateways to other networks that plug into the backplane and are integrated through an agent-supported, distributed operating system

From a user's viewpoint a single networked environment encompasses all available facilities. While admittedly we are a long way from reaching that goal, this is where the foremost telecommunications laboratories and top-of-the-line user organizations are headed.

Such an integrative approach becomes possible because two disciplines that originally developed as distinct and separate from one another are now merging. The one is *broadband communications facilities*; the other, practical developments in the artificial intelligence domain. Their coming together offers opportunities that change the way we communicate with our customers and our suppliers—in short, with our markets.

Not only new concepts but also new methodologies are evolving to confront the emerging environment. These new methodologies include knowledge engineering for up-front planning—as well as *simulation* for validation activities that go well beyond classical testing and verification.

Another requirement that is becoming felt is that in a user-centered design of the virtual network and its backbone, we must be able to identify dynamic customer-visible scenarios. This brings into perspective both of the following timing constraints:

- User specific
- End to end in the network

Therefore, specifications must include a growing range of features, and verification activities should be automated all the way to task execution, with an associated definition of sensitivity scenarios. Within such an environment:

- Network intelligence will be the franchise
- Customer information will be the product
- The combination of franchise and product will become the market opportunity

This market opportunity is global, and, in the late 1990s, as well as well into the twenty-first century, it will be propelled by agents. This is particularly true as manufacturing companies, merchandising firms, and financial institutions will increasingly pursue their customers and markets across geographic and political boundaries—using virtual networks.

The use of agent interface layers and backplanes will be particularly pronounced in the service industry, such as banking, while companies in other industrial sectors will use their networks and customer data to invade traditional financial markets. Let me add that none of the architectural concepts of today is well suited to face such requirements competently.

The new approach to network operating systems is to start from a dynamic specification of the user viewpoint of a system or service, considering particular scenarios from this point of view. Agents in the backplane must go beyond physical time to detect *relative concurrency* of communications events. This brings two clocks into the picture:

- The now classical *physical clock*
- A *relative clock* of communications concurrency

Both can be served through agents—and both must address global events. Physical time is important, but the communications system's distributed behavior should be based on relative time, allowing the derivation of ephemeral specifications that affect the allocation of network resources.

This scenario will effectively support a global events model based on a dynamic approximation to distributed physical clock time—which is

the sense of relative time to be implemented through agents in the backbone. Notice that this approach supplements the traditional concept of
physical time characterizing a communications system by means of relative clocks.

On virtual networks, the management of global events and of relative
clocks will require many backplane approaches supported by agents.
Another reason that network intelligence is a basic ingredient to enable
communications solutions for the late 1990s is a *luxury bandwidth* provided by:

- Fiber-optic networks
- Satellite radio pipelines

Both will be generating a profusion of new information services. They
will be the platforms upon which countless new products will be
designed, manufactured, and marketed—and will open a new era for
far-fledged applications.

As we will see in the following section, intelligent networking and
the implementation of photonics solutions and satellite transmission are
indivisible. The increasing use of photonics transmission systems in
public telephone networks brings forward the cleanest high-capacity carrier available, and its cost is dropping rapidly.

Luxury bandwidth becomes available by using light for digital information transmission. Fiber optics occupies less space while supplying
more channel capacity than conventional coaxial cables—but also poses
questions regarding real-time capacity management. Part of fiber's
appeal are the facts that:

- There are very high limits on the amount of traffic it can handle.
- It is immune to electrical interference.

It is as well quite clear that we have only scratched the surface of what
optical technology can do—and to do more, we need machine intelligence. Having automated their switching centers, enriching them with
expert systems for better performance, telcos run fiber cable to office
building, factories, and homes, delivering a wide array of new services.
These must be supported through agent technology at the lines and the
nodes.*

---

*See also in the next section the discussion on wireless communications.

Who Really Needs Network Intelligence?

Conceived in the mid-1980s by Bell Communications Research, the Intelligent Network (IN) experienced a difficult gestation. It also became subject to successive transformations in its definition of what IN *is* and *is not*. Only recently is the intelligent network really taking off through the use of knowledge robots. Like carriers everywhere, the U.S. regional Bell companies were becoming increasingly frustrated by the time, trouble, and expense of bringing new services on-stream. One of the salient problems has been the increasingly more sophisticated demands for telecommunications services posed by their customers. Another problem is the management of digital switches that form the core of most modern networks, as well as the development of new software releases.

Contrary to the old concept that new software releases must be installed on every switch in the network, a process that is costly, time-consuming, and prone to errors, in an IN, switching is separated from service features. The latter are provided via a different resource, known as a *feature node* or *service control point*.

In this manner, the ordinary switches function as they used to, passing calls that require additional processing via the common channel signaling system to the feature node.* With this solution, which becomes the new frame of reference, software for specific services can be developed by either equipment vendors, software houses, or network operators themselves. The establishment of separate feature nodes means that new services need not be installed in every switch, which greatly speeds up their networkwide delivery.

All problems, however, have not been solved with this approach. First, there has been difficulty in reaching agreement on standards. Second, it has become necessary to find a common platform on which both operating companies and equipment vendors can agree.

Because universal norms are not around the corner, major carriers have gone ahead with the delivery of key IN services, such as freephone and virtual private networking, using proprietary platforms. Another challenge regards the redefinition of what constitutes competition in telecommunications, and what this means to the bottom line.

---

*See also Chap. 8 about AT&T's time out.

Some carriers fear that a too-rapid development of an open network architecture would endanger their ability to reap revenues from new services. But practically all telcos agree that an intelligent network does not "just happen":

- It has to be designed through CAD and concurrent engineering.[*]
- It involves a collaborative effort between clients and vendors.
- Both nodes and links must be served through agents.

For profitability purposes, an intelligent network should show value differentiation and competitive edge. This means that design and implementation solutions must be experimented with in terms of structure, quality, capacity, and cost.

- The system must be served by means of schedulers, optimizers, and simulators.
- Online diagnostics and quality databases have to be exploited in real time through knowledge robots.

Simulation for experimentation on services and cost evaluation has become absolutely necessary, and the same is true of node and line intelligence supported through agents. Furthermore, as we will see in Chap. 8, there is a significant role for agents in network maintenance.

This answers the query posed by this section's title: The use of knowledge-enriched solutions is not just a better way of handling network problems; it is also a basic necessity. As distributed information processing and network technology become the fundamental building blocks of corporate information technology, the software that handles transmission and processing activities becomes increasingly complex.

These are background reasons that help explain the growing interest in the application of agents to networking. In my meeting in Tokyo with NTT, company executives underlined that the successful design of an intelligent network depends above all on:

- Sophisticated programming approaches
- An agile internode protocol
- The adoption of an overall software architecture

This is understandable since the functions needed by the carriers are largely performed by means of software. This statement is true from

---

[*]As discussed in Chap. 7.

intelligent CAD to the management of heterogeneous databases and the use of knowledge engineering—enriched diagnostics.

According to cognizant NTT executives, an intelligent network automates *fault administration* by detecting system or communication line faults and supporting recovery procedures. It also performs configuration management. An example of artificial intelligence implementation by NTT is the Knowledge Base Management System (KBMS—2). Its structure is shown in Fig. 5-3. Its applications include:

- Emergency fault handling for switching systems
- Fault diagnosis of crossbar switches
- The design of customized virtual private networks
- Computer-aided training of network operators
- Trouble analysis of computer software
- Sales support as well as after-sales service

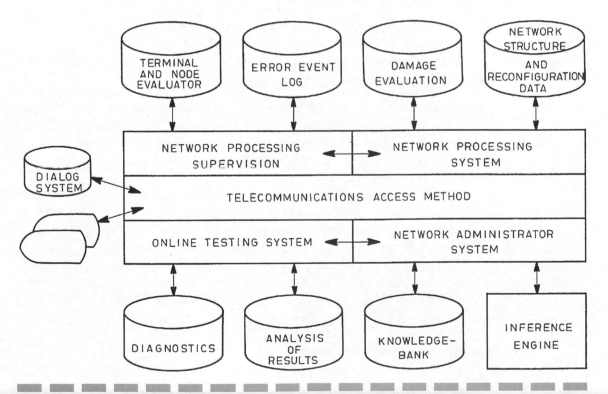

Figure 5-3 Methods, subsystems, and databases of an intelligent network.

These are among the research and implementation directions progressive telcos are taking. Agents are becoming integral part of network design, augmenting the capabilities offered by CAD and assisting in network planning, including topology, connectivity, and cost evaluation. They are also significantly contributing to the development of new income-producing network services.

Illocution and the Use of Agents for Mobile Computing Requirements

Mobile computing is characterized by a locality that migrates as users move. This contrasts to what we know about computing in a confined space.* Migration may alter the conditions of identifying the nearest gateway or server. Or the communication path can change in a way disproportionate to actual movement:

- A small movement by the user might result in a long path when crossing network administrative boundaries.

- Alternatively, an interactive communication may traverse many intermediaries, resulting in longer latency.

Agents must be prepared to follow on the aftermaths of these changes characterizing mobility in computing. Other agents should be tracking the risk of disconnection; the possible shrinkage in network capacity, because of fail-soft; changes in the bandwidth between the mobile unit and the gateway, and so on.

Similarly, in an operations sense agents must see to it that service connections are dynamically transferred and that load-balancing algorithms come into play. A good example is offered by the Personal Communications Network (PCN) and the requirements which it poses.

Personal communications will ultimately allow person-to-person calling independent of location, terminal used, means of transmission (wired or wireless), or other choices of technology. The market potential for personal communications services is expected to be huge, provided that low-cost tariffs are applied, but there are also a host of technical problems to be addressed.

---

*See also D. N. Chorafas, *High Performance Networks, Personal Communications and Mobile Computing*, Macmillan, London, 1997.

Current projections for the foreseeable future suggest that the maximum density for fixed-wireline telephones will not substantially exceed an average penetration of 50 percent of the population. In terms of wireline connection, this means approximately one connection per household, plus business use. By contrast, the penetration of wireless personal communications has the ultimate potential to reach nearly 80 percent of the population.

Wireless essentially means up to one connection per adult. A study done in 1994 by the European Union suggests that within the borders of the 12 nations composing the EU at that time, total user numbers could ultimately exceed 200 million. This should be compared to the then-total subscriber base for traditional fixed telephony of 153 million. In this, as in any other landscape:

- The prime mover will be the expansion of mobile communications into the personal communications market.
- The infrastructure will be not radio links but rather intelligent software artifacts.

Reaching out anywhere in the world where there is a market, American Telephone & Telegraph, Motorola, and IBM are each rolling out what they are calling *intelligent messaging systems*. These are projected to make practical, at any time and anywhere, communications provided by cellular phones, personal digital assistants (PDAs), and other technologies currently in the offing.

Intelligent messaging systems come to life because agents make feasible a dynamic development of mobile services based on software and terminal equipment. Sophisticated software helps to identify and route the message by the best method possible—whether over wires or airwaves, by digitized voice, fax, database to database, or other means.

Agents are also designed to send back confirmation that the message reached its destination. Another target is to use agents for passthrough among largely incompatible communications networks and heterogeneous computers—while making the system easy to use and its interfaces seamless.

Every vendor aims to offer in their network the services that will best attract public interest, and *illocution*—which means interactive messaging—is best supported by agents. Communications in a multiagent environment can be better understood by specifying the type of illocution that will reflect the contribution of artifacts. The term is borrowed from speech act theory, characterizing:

- An illocutionary force
- A messaging proposition

The illocutionary force distinguishes a command from a promise. The proposition describes the state of the world; that is, respectively, commanded or promised. By extension, the propositional part of a message specifies the state of the world to which the message applies.

Several applications rest on these concepts. AT&T's PersonaLink service is projected to browse electronic news automatically to find issues and documents of interest to the user. In this context, agents will be doing the legwork. They will be interactively responding to end-user requests, tying together incompatible systems, and dialing up services requesting information.

These intelligent artifacts will make the information superhighway work for the end user rather than force the user to learn about the mechanisms before using the system. Motorola has its own notion of a universal service. Called *Mobile Networks Integration* (MNI), it includes software and hardware to mesh various wireless networks, including cellular and paging, with corporate PC networks.

Motorola projects that its software would be installed in PDAs, portable computers, and cellular phones, as well as in the nodes that run phone networks and other communications systems. Code named In-Touch, IBM's service, which is still in the planning stage, is primarily aimed at the corporate market.

Sophisticated Software for Wired and Wireless Integration

During our meeting in London, Dr. Alan Rudge, the deputy managing director of British Telecom (BT), made reference to a research project by BT that he considers to be a brain teaser: a project undertaken to stimulate thinking both inside and outside the corporation. Its theme is the *Office-on-the-Arm*.

The Office-on-the-Arm can be considered today as the pinnacle of mobile computing. It is a miniaturization, and at the same time it is a concept promoting a dual aspect of systems integration, the way that it will probably be by the beginning of the twenty-first century: The project is a focused example on wired and wireless integration, as seen by

BT, and it involves the best in microprocessor power, memory chip density, and sophisticated software.

Even with few pioneering projects, there are two main areas where wired and wireless integration is vital in providing a networked service. One is fixed-mobile convergence; the other, common interfaces in a networked sense. Both are served through agents.

The customer and his or her call number are the two key elements in the fixed-mobile convergence. The way it has been practiced with telephony for over a hundred years, telephone numbering starts at the customer. In the opinion of leading telephone companies, this policy has to be preserved while both themselves and other network providers are looking for new services.

Another crucial technology problem is the common interfaces on a network. Telephone companies do not expect that total integration of wired and wireless communications will happen in the near future, but they are looking for solutions particularly in what has become known as the *radio tails* of the network—the last kilometer.

The radio tails are essentially the modern equivalent of copper wire and the local loop in the wired world. This last kilometer is highly regulated and has remained a practical monopoly, even in countries that pride themselves in having a deregulated telephone industry—like the United Kingdom and the United States. The limiting factor with radio tails is spectrum. Most competitors today fight for spectrum.

While questions relating to spectrum are in the process of being negotiated with the regulatory authorities who have been assigned this mission by the government, other challenges have to be faced by the telcos' own R&D laboratories. One of the most interesting is that of cost-effective approaches to wired-wireless gateways.

Figure 5-4 presents UCLA's WAMIS/NOS solution.[*] This research project addresses mobile computing, and most particularly the goal of making communications transparent to both the mobile user and his or her correspondent—regardless of whether the latter is fixed or mobile. Also, independently of:

■ Who initiates the communication

■ Where each party is currently located

As Joel Stark suggested during our January 1996 meeting at UCLA, there is a problem with protocol stacks to support mobility between networks.

---

[*]See also D. N. Chorafas, *High Performance Networks, Personal Communications and Mobile Computing*, Macmillan, London, 1997.

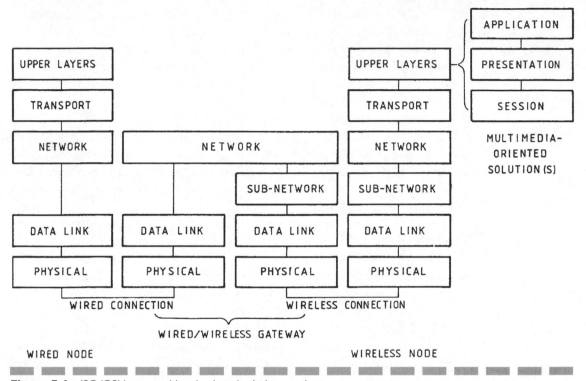

Figure 5-4   ISO/OSI layers, with wired and wireless nodes.

Nodes have to be reconfigured every time a user moves to a different network. This has to be done in a way that the open communications are not lost and services don't have to be restarted because of ongoing mobility.

The approach taken by UCLA's *nomadic router* in solving this problem is that of providing both *temporary* and *permanent* network and node numbers similar to that assured by Mobile IP. When done on the network level and not the link level, this helps to guarantee location independence. A nomadic router contains several agents. Some of these agents address device transparency; others, location independence.

Any new departure in communications technology evidently has prerequisites—for instance, doing away with current requirements that all link-level parameters that are device specific be manually configured.

To help in overcoming this constraint, the nomadic router provides device independence through intelligent artifacts. As experience is gained, the manual configuration is substituted by agents. Along this line of reasoning, in the years to come, applications will first describe their connection requirements. One agent can say: "The bandwidth requirements are *XXX* above minimum." Another agent may respond: "Required bandwidth not available."

Still another major challenge agents will have to face in connection with wireless is how to package the application's data stream so that it does not overburden the network. Novel paradigms have to be developed specifically designed for mobile computing, as contrasted to those already available for confined-space computing.

Knowledge artifacts and generally node intelligence will be crucial in connection with wired-wireless networks, as well as with pure wireless solutions, when it is necessary to deal with store and forward. An agent can advertise not only the current but also the expected level of changes using heuristics and database sunspots or blizzards.

Knowledge engineering solutions will be necessary in adapting for mobility whether the connection is intermittently wired or fully wireless and in providing a well-rounded communications environment that is reliable and consistent. A similar statement can be made regarding quality of service and its sustenance.

Agents on the Internet: From Error Control to Filtering

Dr. John von Neumann once suggested that errors and sources of errors do not need to be established specifically, in complete detail. They may be elaborated generically, that is, by some decisive traits which permit them to be identified, and then handled in an appropriate manner. In principle, a generic coverage may span an impressive territory, and this may be full of unforeseen and unsuspected details.

Prerequisite to a generic coverage is that we return to the fundamentals. The word *error* is one of those that has been used and misused in many cases, with different and often contradictory meanings. Basically, what we call "error" is not an extraneous and misdirecting accident but an important part of the process under consideration, on which we can capitalize.

The time series that we obtain from measurements are statistical in character, and their accuracy is that of a probability distribution. But there is as well the purpose for which statistics are taken, which helps define the accuracy we are after. This is what we would like an agent to do for us. Information providers on the Internet and other networks can nicely embed into their service(s) artifacts that:

- Present error detection capabilities at the source and/or the channel
- Perform goal-oriented evaluations since they know the purpose the data stream would serve

The errors' importance in modern engineering and finance is fully comparable to the other intended and normal critical factors characterizing a system in operation.* This is a basic concept of great service in information technology, with knowledge artifacts being the tools.

Much can be learned about how to develop and deploy such agents, from the way we estimate an order of magnitude. The "order of magnitude" accepts as normal a measurement error. For instance, we can estimate the number of books on a shelf at a glance, with some acceptable error. To count them precisely requires much greater time, which may not be justified by the goal we pursue.

This apparent contradiction between goals and means, or measurements and errors, makes it wise to look into the question of accuracy and precision a little more in detail. Accuracy is the overriding consideration: In all mathematical problems the answer is needed with rigor, with dependability. But this does not mean that it is also required with absolute precision.

In most problems of applied mathematics, including physics, the precision that is wanted is rather limited. With the exception of general accounting, which is regulated by law, the same statement applies in finance. The data of the problem are given only to limited precision anyway. What we need to establish is:

- The sensitivity of the result to changes in the data
- The limits of uncertainty of the result for known data

By and large, the precision of the input in physical problems, as well as in engineering, is often not known to better than 5 percent. Agents can be effectively developed to operate on that premise, and this is already happening in connection with agents on the Internet. If current projections materialize, every Internet user would have one or more personal *filtering agents* that would look after a whole range of operations. Filter-

---

*See D. N. Chorafas, *Statistical Processes and Reliability Engineering*, Van Nostrand, Princeton, N.J., 1960.

ing agents on the input stream will weed out unwanted information. The job of filtering agents in the output stream may be reporting by exception—for instance, the deviations.

Some agents will focus on accuracy and precision. Others will be constructed to sort through thousands of documents that come online daily or to mine databases, pinpointing issues of particular interest. The idea is to build *personalized agents* that:

- Assist their master in a multimedia environment
- Automate the transfer of information
- Make recommendations to their user—or users with similar interests

An example is *Webhound*, a World Wide Web document recommendation service developed at MIT's Media Laboratory. Through a sophisticated evaluation approach, Webhound automates the process of word-of-mouth recommendations for Web users. It does so by creating a personalized profile for each user based on significant features of documents on which the user provides opinions.

The artifact matches new users' profiles with profiles and recommendations from a universe of other users. The more document evaluation criteria each user gives Webhound, the higher the quality of subsequent personal recommendations is going to be. The agent relies on its users to submit opinions on new documents they discover while surfing the Web. This is significant inasmuch as the database of documents is rapidly expanding, being propelled by the user community.

Another agent on the World Wide Web is HOMR. Like Webhound it is based on automated collaborative filtering. Both make recommendations based on data about other users with similar tastes and interests. They:

- Compare user profiles
- Find out the user's nearest neighbors

As the user base for these services grows, the recommendations can become more refined. Agents smarter than Webhound and HOMR will be coming. We have already spoken in Chap. 1 about Things That Think, a project focusing on three research categories:

- Sensing technology
- Networking technology
- Knowledge engineering

It has as well been said that the goal is to make once-inanimate objects responsive to human needs and eventually emotions. Among the goals is the development of intelligent things able to sense the movements or feelings of their masters as well as to learn the users' habits. Filtering serves well in this context. A telecommunications applications environment other than the Internet that can be taken as a model of things to come is Project GreenSpace.

The Transition to a Telecommunications-Based Economy and Project GreenSpace

As the preceding eight sections help document, the transition to a telecommunications-based economy requires the establishment of a sophisticated infrastructure. This is characterized by interdependent basic investments in new technology, which is itself subject to rapid evolution and change.

One of the top two problems present in this transition is that new infrastructures have to be put in place worldwide. Local solutions are too limited because the revenues are a function of market acceptance, hence of usage. In turn, wider usage depends on suitable and attractive equipment, agile software, rewarding services, and imaginative applications.

- These will be developed only when the new infrastructures can reach a significant section of the user community worldwide or at least by major region.
- The markets for telecommunications products and services are mutually interlocking and characterized by the issue of critical mass and of sophistication.

One of the top problems present in this transition revolves exactly around the keyword *sophistication*—and the way it can be used to enlarge the market. In contrast with computing, telecommunications is of value to its users, and profitable to its suppliers, only when groups of people become established that are sufficiently large as well as able and willing to intercommunicate.

For this reason, building an international momentum and a concerted approach is of particular importance to all players: the providers and

Figure 5-5
A solution space for new telecommunications technologies.

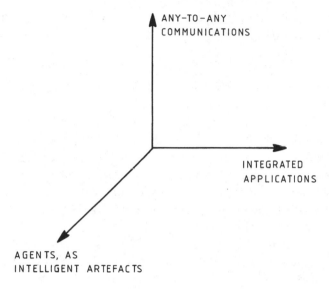

the users. The avoidance of fragmentation of markets not only across geographic but also across sector boundaries is critical to the overall economic justification of telecommunications investments. The solution space that is defined in Fig. 5-5 provides a frame of reference.

A growing number of experts think that one of the best domains for the new telecommunications technologies is the *global village*. The world as a *global village* is a relatively new concept underpinning the fact that a true global economy would depend on such key ingredients as:

- Business dynamism propelled by free markets
- Improved education, leading to further scientific and technological development
- A very imaginative implementation of information technology

This is the conclusion that was reached at the September 1993 Industry Summit jointly organized by MIT and Harvard University. The Industry Summit involved some 800 corporate, government, and academic leaders from 53 countries, as well as 100 workshops, interactive sessions, and plenary sessions.

The necessity of a global networking solution integrating science laboratories, businesses, and governments and their leaders was outlined by most of the 350 speakers, who placed emphasis on the need to create values in order to share values. Many speakers suggested that this should be done interactively through networks, without spending precious time in personal meetings.

A wide network-supported interactivity is what *Project GreenSpace* aims to achieve. The goal of this American-Japanese effort, which currently is in its fifth, and last, phase is the development of a telecommunications test bed for the global village.

On the American side, funding is provided by the National Science Foundation (NSF), Advanced Research Projects Agency (ARPA) of the Pentagon, NASA, and the National Oceanic and Atmospheric Administration (NOAA). Beyond these government agencies participate AT&T Network Systems, Bellcore, MCI, Sprint, US West, Evans and Sutherland, Silicon Graphics, Sun Microsystems, DEC, Intel, KSR, Ford Motor Company, and Boeing.

There are as well a number of universities taking part: University of Washington, MIT, North Carolina, Rutgers, Virginia, Illinois, and Central Florida. The University of Tokyo and Tokyo Metropolitan Institute of Technology participate on the Japanese side. Other Japanese participants are Toyota and Sharp.

Another objective of Project GreenSpace is to develop the concept of an international center for exploring the future of the information society. A basic aim is the development of sophisticated software able to get the network to act like a human manager. The network should appear transparent to the end users except in well-defined and expected instances. In these instances, agents would step in to aid each participant in performing his or her collaborative tasks.

Attention is paid to the fact that, in many cases, the network will need to automatically adapt itself to user requirements—for instance, in the case of latency, burstiness, dynamic range, frame rate, compression, and bandwidth—on demand. It will also need to adapt to shared memories, level of detail, robustness, topology, scalability, manageability, and protocols.

Protocols, Project GreenSpace suggests, need to be optimized for the types of transmission used for the long haul. Both new protocols and intelligent software are being born along, as solutions are implemented and stepwise refinements are made toward the realization of virtual-reality environments.

Still another aim of GreenSpace experiments is *haptic feedback*. Haptic feedback gives an impression of weight, momentum, and other forces and can be effective in producing a feeling of presence, satisfying interaction with objects in virtual space. The same is true of motion sensing, including:

- Procedural dynamics
- Parametric control

An example of *parametric control* is given by compound effectors. This control is realized by the mapping of many effects in a virtual space to a simple action on the part of the user—an action that can be assisted by agents within a telecommunications environment.

Finally, *procedural dynamics* relates to the fact that certain real-space simulations may need to have associated to them natural physical phenomena such as gravity. Others may need to exhibit different behaviors when collisions are detected. Such dynamics may be encoded into the objects populating a virtual-space environment within an expanding broadband communications network.

This solution will most likely underpin the new generation of *push software* coming out of Silicon Valley. Push artifacts are proactive and *event-driven*. As Harold Macmillan, the former British prime minister, formously observed when asked what determined success or failure in politics: "Events, dear boy, events."

CHAPTER 6

Using Agents to Increase the Security on the Internet and Other Public and Private Networks

If there is one thing that single-handedly can wreck a network, whether private or public, it is privacy and security—or, more precisely, the lack of it. This dictum is just as valid for the Internet as it is for any other network today, operating or being planned, though the present chapter focuses on the Internet as the better known among recent examples.

Today the Internet provides very little by way of support for secure communications. Even the stronger mechanisms said to be on their way do not seem to be failproof. It is, however, increasingly accepted that agents can play a key role in privacy and security. An agent designed to enhance privacy should be able to answer, among other issues, dynamic location queries, which requires:

- Knowing the location of all users on the network who may handle sensitive information
- Being able to protect messages as well as database contents against intrusion and misuse

An autonomous agent may protect privacy by denying some of the network users the ability to know another user's location or personal details. Other, mobile agents can operate in routing and logging telephone calls, logging meetings, or tailoring the content of electronic displays. There are two ways of looking at security:

- One is the rather practical approach, which means accepting that perfect security is impossible to obtain and appropriately adjusting the operating strategy.
- The other is the Ivory Tower approach, which involves searching for a world in which security is absolute—which is an illusion.

Security with online systems concerns the transaction itself, the transfer or transport of information (message or transaction), and the storage and retrieval in databases, as well as queries regarding transactions, balances, codes, or other database contents.

Because of this wide range of interests, security and privacy are important issues regarding the future of the Internet as well as of any other network. In principle, the digital world can be intrinsically more secure than the analog world, provided we develop the appropriate methodology and supporting software—but we have to work hard to keep the digital world secure.

One of the ironies of cyberspace is that, while it has been largely American developed, the U.S. government is one of the primary roadblocks to a good security solution. Current export laws—conceived to keep electronic privacy systems from falling into the hands of alien powers, terrorists, and drug dealers—preclude the global use of good digital security. Yet the people who pay for the aftermaths of poor security on the Internet and other networks are the legitimate users.

Facing the Expanding Nature of Security Risks

An increasing number of studies in the banking industry, as well as in more general themes concerning security and protection, draw attention to major corporate financial losses due to computer security risks. Of the 150 companies that responded to a Michigan State University survey, 148 reported suffering from computer crimes including the:

- Theft of credit card numbers
- Losses of trade secrets
- Software piracy
- Employees' snooping into confidential files

While Chap. 1 suggested, in connection to things that think, that there may be in the future intelligent credit cards which cannot be stolen because they recognize their owners, this *might* happen sometime in the future. It is not available in today's world.

A more disturbing finding in the aforementioned research has been a sharp rise in serious virus attacks. Code breaking seems to be another pastime. In many cases computer security is so low that hackers cost American business an estimated $3 billion per year. Rather than providing security, a number of generally available tools permit breaking into somebody else's system:

- Sophisticated scanners help in the theft of ID codes.
- Password files are meticulously collected over the years.
- Password guessers develop into code-breaking expert systems.
- Programs and keys are being bought from the hacker community.

Security threats are particularly disturbing because vital company resources are now held in databases, or they are being transmitted over the lines. In addition, the future of all first-world countries—their industries and their economies—will be determined by their ability to filter, store, retrieve, manage, and use the information that is created.

For this specific reason, Chap. 5 emphasized the use of agents for filtering purposes as well as for error detection, which can be extended to cover any deviation from what can be considered as correct practice. *If* we wish to enhance multimedia security, *then*, depending on the application, we must:

- Choose low-level protocols able to execute from/to verification, error checks, and other security routines.
- Implement high-level protocols, affecting encryption, executing conversion, and featuring file transfer characteristics.*
- Develop and use knowledge artifacts that learn to recognize their master, identifying friend or foe.

Clifford Stohl, one of the experts on network security, suggests that the Internet is not to be trusted: "The medium is being oversold, our expectations have become bloated, and there is damned little critical discussion of the implications of an online world."†

Other information scientists harbor exactly the opposite opinion, and, ironically, both lines of thought may be right, or both may be wrong. It all depends on the criteria being used. Thesis and antithesis characterize the current conflict between:

- The promises made by the people's network with an ideal free flow of information in cyberspace
- The harsh reality that corporations and government agencies must protect their computer systems and databases

This harsh reality is by no means limited to the Internet. Any other public network and any private network is open to about the same dangers. Internet comes more often under perspective because it has millions of users and it is *en vogue*—but private networks can be just as vulnerable to hackers and other intruders.

Not only computer criminals but also external hostile activities can prove to be major threats. For instance, if an alien power really wishes to damage America or Britain, it will hit its infrastructure, which is in very large measure controlled by computers from finance to transportation.

It is surprising that the IRA has not yet found that out, though the bomb which in early 1995 exploded in Canary Wharf was not far from such a target.‡ Modern terrorism can do more damage if it operates online through a network than with guns and bombs. This has not yet been a general realization, but it will not be long before it happens.

---

*See also the discussion in Chap. 7 on IPv6.

†Communications of the ACM, May 1995.

‡Later in this chapter, we will see how to protect a building's security through an example from the Lawrence Livermore Laboratory.

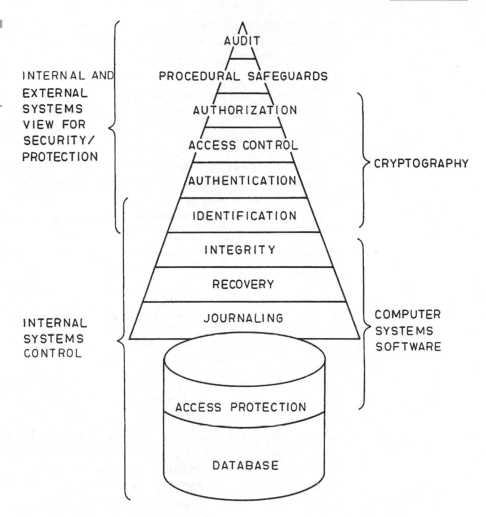

Figure 6-1
A layered approach to enhanced security, defined by a recent project.

Can we organize ourselves in a way that security is brought into perspective? The security pyramid in Fig. 6-1 comes out of a project that targeted a stratified approach with the aim to simplify the process of studying and implementing security measures, by attacking them level by level. Among the reasons for low-grade security were found to be:

■ The lack of precise goals as well as of a concept for security and protection

■ The absence of top management education on the need for security

■ The use of substandard security tools and the resistance by managers and other personnel in implementing what is available

Rather than giving to security its due weight, management often looks at security as demanding "too much work" and representing "unnecessary costs." Work, however, can be automated. Each one of the layers in Fig. 6-1 may be nicely served by agents.

Let me immediately add, however, that security with agents could be a double-edged sword. Remote agents may behave like viruses since they are small software programs executed on networked machines. The opposite is also true. Viruses could be disguised as remote agents that interact in unexpected ways with other people's computers.

Therefore, it is both important and urgent to define who is responsible *if* the remote computer has problems while it has *our* agent on it. Is it that our agent behaved wrongly, or was it triggered to do something that was not intended? Or, further still, was there a falsified environment that altered the security perspectives *our* agent was designed to address?

Careless Security Rules and False Claims

In a meeting in the Silicon Valley in January 1996, reference was made to a recent study in the United States which found that half of the surveyed high-technology firms and financial institutions were subject to computer fraud. Some even felt that it is better to keep this fact internal and not to announce it publicly—but practically all stated that they thought their security measures should theoretically have been adequate to prevent such happenings.

The person who made this reference underlined that to his judgment a good deal of the blame goes to the companies themselves and other organizations using networks. For instance, banks have the bad habit of handling messages of $100 and of $10 million by:

- The same process
- The same people
- The same procedures

There is no value differentiation. Neither is there a concept of risk in messaging. Yet every 24 hours in currency exchange alone, an estimated $1.4 trillion changes hands. On the average, that's about 20 percent of the gross national product of the United States.

Major security problems with financial aftermaths can also happen through accidental failures. Two years ago, subsequent to a computer failure, the Bank of New York discovered that they were $23 billion short in overnight funds, and they borrowed money from the Federal Reserve to save the day.* If the same sort of failure were to occur to the Federal Reserve system, which monitors 3 million financial transactions per day, then the black hole may be counted in trillions of dollars—and there would be no lender of last resort.

Therefore, both reliability and security must be addressed in a rigorous manner. To this end, in the mid-1980s the Swedish banks developed a well thought out vulnerability assessment method that is shown in Fig. 6-2. I bring it under perspective because it constitutes a good methodology.

This method keeps plans, results, documentation, and follow-up by computer. But its type of implementation is obsolete by today's standards because it was largely batch oriented. In other terms, the bullets in Fig. 6-2 are appropriate, though the support with which they are provided is not. This imbalance can be nicely corrected by:

- Developing one or more autonomous learning agents for each bullet as a node in a modern procedural network
- Writing personalized agents able to understand the security needs of their master, answering them in real time

This dual approach to software sophistication will boost vulnerability control and will help to put a tap on online crime. Let's, however, not forget that not everything will be a case of computer crime. Other issues need to be addressed.

An example is events such as endless mail-forwarding loops that are inherently unpredictable. These involve a number of unknowns, which can have disastrous consequences as there are no obvious solutions to remote software problems.

A different way of making this statement is that while agents can contribute a great deal to security, as we saw earlier, understanding how intelligent software may act is a prerequisite to grasping the challenges facing network managers. Agents might mutate technical problems. They may alter management issues that need to be addressed. Or they may increase the complexity of public network management, rather than simplify it.

---

*We talk more about this in Chap. 8.

Figure 6-2
Vulnerability assess-
ment method.

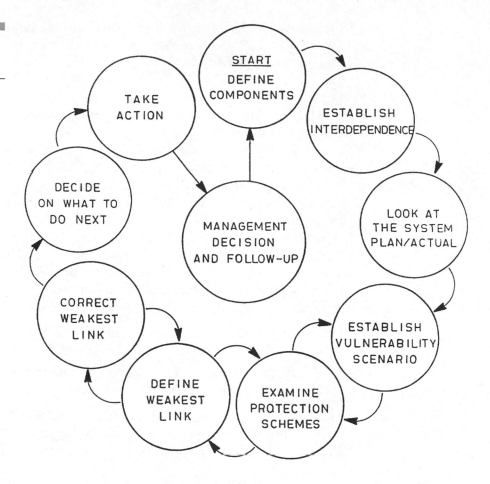

KEEP PLANS, RESULTS, DOCUMENTATION,
FOLLOW-UP BY COMPUTER

An increase in the complexity of network management is not necessarily a negative if the technical people responsible for operations understand what they are doing—which is not necessarily the case in general. Also, if top management has been careful in outlining the goals to be reached through security and protection, and in providing the knowhow and the means to do a clean job, security issues can be brought under control.

I choose to outline these issues in a generic sense because they are by their nature generic. Provided that the notions underpinning network security and the policies necessary to achieving it are well understood, we can proceed with practical examples. This is done in the following section taking the Internet as the frame of reference.

Examining Some of the Security Issues Connected to the Internet

To better understand the security issues connected to the Internet, it is appropriate to keep in mind that the people's network is not centrally managed, and it is open to use by anyone, including crooks, eavesdroppers, and impostors. While various information providers use technology to try to make it safe for business, security is not going to be the Internet's forte—at least not for the next several years.

New security holes are uncovered almost weekly, right after earlier ones are fixed, or at least recognized. "If consumers and merchants don't have a certain degree of confidence, [electronic commerce] is not going to work," says Carl F. Pascarella, chief executive officer and president of Visa USA, which has teamed with Microsoft to develop a scheme for safely processing credit card transactions on the Internet.*

In a similar frame of reference, Harris Computer Systems, a company that makes real-time software for NASA and Boeing, is offering *Cyber-Guard,* a program originally developed for the U.S. Navy. Comshare features *Detect and Alert* agents, which perform repetitive tasks and monitor targeted databases for significant changes. When a change is detected, an alert is flashed to the user and flagged on the user's monitor.

How safe can these artifacts be? In September 1995, Netscape Communications, one of the leaders in Internet software, saw the security locks on its Navigator Web browser program broken—for the second time in a year. The firewalls were torn down by a couple of graduate students; and a few weeks later, the same student pair said they had found a major security gap in software used at many Internet sites. A British team and a French graduate student cracked the crypto of Netscape Commerce Server independently of one another, on the same timetable. It took the French student 8 days using 120 workstations and two parallel supercomputers to search exhaustively for the key—about 64 MIPS-years of processing.† Other students, in their spare hours as hackers, identified a security flaw in the Netscape browsing software, resulting from a supposedly pseudorandom number generator whose use was too predictable.

---

*_Business Week,_ November 13, 1995.

†Communications of the ACM, vol. 39, no. 1, January 1996.

Many of the most recently uncovered Internet breaches open the way to what has become known as *bootstrap attacks.* Crooks can use the gap to intercept and alter copies of the Internet's publicly available software packages. *If* the software module's security routines were secretly broken, *then* programs that the corrupt package touched could be compromised, too.

Under current technology, agents can be of no particular service in this case. The risk is directly proportional to the race to create Internet software appliances—which is on at high speed. Virtually all leading consumer electronics companies are working on approaches to what is known as *Internet Lite*—inexpensive modules to bring the Net into the living room, which may become full of holes and viruses.

Among consumer electronics manufacturers, the emphasis is on gadgets: Philips, Thomson, Sega, and Sony are either retooling existing home machines or developing new ones that will bring WWW pages to the television screen. Their managers, however, don't really understand the risks involved with networks because they focus on entertainment products, forgetting that networked entertainment products are a different species than the one they knew. A security break that occurred in 1995 has been overlooked by many Internet users. Yet, this is the typical case of what is going to happen in a way with network appliances.

Not long ago, a bug made it possible to commandeer Web servers simply by sending a message that was too long for their input buffers. This same class of bug was responsible for the spread of the Internet worm that nearly shut down the Net in 1988—when a Cornell University graduate student, Robert Morris, Jr., and his self-reproducing viruses dramatically showed that it takes only one hacker to do lots of damage.

Such cases can repeat themselves at any moment, while other different incidents may arise. The fact that many security holes have not been sensed, have gone unused, for so long could mean that there are far fewer malicious hackers on the Internet than pessimists think, or, alternatively, that there are so many more opportunities for intruders.

The inexperience with the competent handling of security problems, as well as with what makes electronic commerce tick, shows through some of the pronouncements the chief executives of some companies make. Says Scott McNealy, chairman and CEO of Sun Microsystems: "My e-mail is far harder to get at than my hardcopy mail," which gets dropped off "in a tin box with no lock on it."

It may be that Sun Microsystems has the money and the sophisticated software to shield its Net computers from hackers. But the average Internet merchant will have to live with the nightmare that an intruder breaks in and steals thousands of credit card numbers or gives fake orders to ship, paid by unaccountable cybermoney.

Sometimes, time to market takes precedence over privacy and security considerations. In an apparent rush to launch its Navigator program into the booming Web market, Netscape's programmers did what the company admits was a sloppy job in coding security procedures. As we saw in earlier paragraphs in this section, the routine depended on random numbers to calculate encryption keys for each transaction. The way Navigator was programmed, these random numbers were relatively easy to predict, which made the resulting keys worthless.

Both security and the prevailing heterogeneity of protocols are fundamental obstacles in the way of electronic commerce. Companies active on the Net that aim to generate cyberbusiness have yet to agree on important protocols for sending payments over the network.

This might eventually be corrected through new and more potent protocols. In Chap. 7 we will talk of IPv6. But protocols alone will not do the job. Rigorous system solutions are necessary, and, to help in this direction, Fig. 6-3 presents a matrix that can be applied at the design stage to help sort out security and protection issues.

In conclusion, because security policies, methods, and protocols are so critical to the future of the Internet and to the digital economy in general, we have to be extra careful about the algorithms and heuristics we use, as well as about the methodology that we have chosen. The problem is that various players, including banks, computer vendors, software mak-

Figure 6-3
Building security in design stage.

	PREVENTION	REPRESSION
PHYSICAL	SECURITY RULES	INSPECTION
LOGICAL	SYSTEM STAGE INTEGRATION	ONLINE

ers, and major credit card companies, are all fighting for strategic position without a factual and documented basis on which scheme to back.

Security Software That Exists on the Internet

In my judgment, which like any other opinion can be wrong, what is available today in terms of security algorithms and associated software is one dimensional. We will speak more about this later on in this chapter, along with the Steinmann hypothesis. This does not necessarily mean that all current solutions are outright substandard. The problem is that they provide scant protection against sophisticated hackers. In Amsterdam, for instance, there is a Rent-a-Hacker market featuring hackers who have pretty good skills.

But there are some security mechanisms that are worth recording. One of the examples is a new approach to labeling Internet information developed by the MIT-based World Wide Web Consortium (W³C). This could help in sorting out the type of information going over the Net, using as its tool the Platform for Internet Content Selection (PICS). PICS works by labeling and grading, but it does not ban objectional fare. What it offers is a tool people can use to maintain privacy and to filter transmissions.

PICS itself is value-neutral, but it allows individuals and organizations to add descriptive or judgmental labels to any of the Internet's information offerings, including newsgroups and Web pages. In turn, this permits users to identify, and thus avoid, unwanted traffic—or shield children from offensive material.

The point can of course be made that though privacy and security are practically twins, a solution answering privacy's requirements does not necessarily solve all of security's problems—and vice versa. Even if over time PICS proves to be a valid answer for *privacy* reasons, it will not address the most basic security problems in the classical sense of the term.

A different approach, more tooled toward security, has been developed by VeriFone, a credit card authorization firm. VeriFone and its strategic partners—Microsoft, Oracle, and Netscape—collaborate on systems for merchants and financial institutions. But as has been already noted, such solutions are not foolproof.

VeriFone's device is small, like a network appliance. It is a keypad whose functionality on the Internet is embedded into a PC as virtual *point-of-sale* (POS) *software*, and a gateway aiming to provide a secure link. VeriFone will combine its partners' gateway software with its own payment system to link existing financial networks to the Internet. The importance that this development could possibly have in the near future comes from the fact that VeriFone is the largest supplier of credit card verification systems, using its Payment Transaction Application Layer (PTAL): PTAL is designed to be a bridge between existing payment networks, like conventional credit card swipes, and customers or merchants connected to the Internet. This method supports multiple payment options such as credit and debit cards, electronic cash, electronic checks, and micropayments.

VeriFone's approach consists of a software module on the consumer's personal computer and an interface to Web browser software from any vendor. On the merchant's server, the company accepts payments, communicating with the credit card firm's host computer for authorization, then proceeding with settlement. This is the classical example of one-dimensional solutions, which we will examine later in this chapter.

Other information providers on the Internet aim to offer some value differentiation. For instance, UUNet has installed Netscape Communications' Commerce server at its headquarters in Fairfax, Virginia. This application of the Commerce server:

- Generates and validates user identification codes
- Encrypts data for all users linked to hosted Web sites*

The strategy is to secure sensitive information sent across the Internet by using Netscape's Secure Session Layer. But UUNet also aims to protect electronic mail for business partners, as well as files stored on a server with Pretty Good Privacy encryption.

To promote this policy and gain market confidence, UUNet has set up a separate server to encrypt data before they are sent through the Web-hosting server. This solution also aims to avoid bottlenecks at the server. The fact, however, remains that, though superb for many applications, the Web is not yet suited for mission-critical chores such as order processing or accounting. This type of implementation will come on the intranet when more powerful encryption and digital signature tech-

---

*See also the section "Encryption and Cryptographic Keys on the Internet" at the end of this chapter.

niques will really permit users, both individuals and organizations, to secure their communications.

Higher levels of security will give momentum to Web authoring and management tools, as applications accessed over the Web become more interactive. The Internet Engineering Task Force's newest version of the remote-monitoring specification might help that process. One of the more actively contemplated solutions is the creation of a uniform security policy for browsers running Java applets. Browsers being considered for this task include Netscape's Navigator, Oracle's Power-Browser, Spyglass's Mosaic, Microsoft's Explorer, and some others.

The bottom line is that a uniform security policy enhanced by powerful tools makes sense because software, such as Java code, is downloaded and run over the Internet. Users want assurances that they are not downloading viruses or bugs onto their systems. Among the procedures presently being contemplated is the following: A Java applet would not be able to read or write to any *local* file. It would make network connections back only to the host from which the applet came.

This may sound good, but it leaves me unconvinced because the procedure may boomerang when the Java applet is supposed to make the connection only to its originating host. To provide for greater flexibility while security measures are being supported, developers should start to consider optional settings that would allow more leeway in handling Java applets as well as a number of other software subroutines.

Risk Control over Software Safety, Knowledge Artifacts, and Rigorous Procedures

There are many aspects to network vulnerability. Some of them have been examined earlier in this chapter, particularly in relation to security issues connected to the Internet. Others will be looked up later in the chapter. In between these two major groups of subjects comes an issue that is not too often discussed, yet it is a cornerstone to an effective and dependable implementation of computers and communications: No chain is more reliable than its weakest link—and the weakest link may be the safety of the software. Therefore, sophisticated software must be able to look after its own safety, security, and protection.

If no good answers are provided to software security within a fairly short, fast time frame, *then* in a fast-expanding network environment, software safety and integrity may become impossible to maintain. As a result, users will start closing their network borders because of the fear of an uncontrollable infrastructure and its aftermaths.

Reports of problems with Java's security come out of computer science labs. Problems on Web sites range from annoying to catastrophic—such as deleting crucial information from an end user's disk storage.* A growing number of researchers say that Java's defenses against *poison applets* are inadequate.

Some technology whizkids think that the theory behind Java is inherently risky; others believe the flaws are not in the theory but in the practice. "Java is not theoretically unsound," says Edward W. Felten of Princeton University. "But I think there is some reason for concern about whether one can build a system as big and complicated as Java without making mistakes that will compromise security. I personally run my browser with Java turned off most of the time."

Viruses are only one aspect of the problem. Software vulnerability has many facets connected both to applications and to systems programming. I see lack of dependability in terms of software safety as the Number 1 factor that will inhibit integration of private networks with a global Internet at least for the next 5 years.

Some efforts target this issue. As we saw in Chap. 4, Telescript is one of the languages that provide its own security rules. In the general case, for software safety, object-oriented languages use:

- Encapsulation
- Information hiding

Encapsulation helps in terms of engine protection through a perimeter drawn around objects. Access to an object's properties is through its public features, and these are supposed to enforce stringent protection strategies.

Operation wrappers can be effectively used for access checks around private features of a software module. Firewalls can be employed to identify the authorization of the requester. It is as well advisable to include identity-based access checks. Such checks may take different forms, but usually they will revolve around the current:

---

*David L. Wilson, *Experts Differ on Security Threat Posed by Java Computer Language*, The Chronicle of Higher Education, July 12, 1996.

- Owner
- Client
- Process
- Sponsor

Each one of these four pillars of a dependable mechanism should be secure. It is wise to employ *owner* references to any object. The owner is most often the current *process* supplying or manipulating the code being executed.

Contrary to this owner-process duality, the *sponsor* may be an unprotected reference to the process whose authority will get attached to the filials. In the realm of process creation it does make some difference who the current owner is—but much more important is the reference to the future user processes.

The *client* is the object whose code requested the current operation. A client's owner might in principle be another process with its own security and protection requirements, typically expressed in a list of:

- References to authorized object classes
- Authorized entities to implement an access policy

By and large, this type of solution places its bets regarding software safety, as well as database integrity, on the access method. While firewalls are one of the often talked about approaches available today for security and protection, based on my background with reliability engineering and risk management, I would like to see as well dynamic procedural solutions that classify software protection levels according to possible failures:

- *Catastrophic failure* means a severe problem affecting software safety and demanding immediate attention.

In such cases, normal business risk is high because services have been disrupted or are being disrupted. Hence the problem must be resolved immediately in a dependable manner.

- *Major failure* is one that demands immediate attention but is not catastrophic in terms of business risk.

Therefore, the software safety problem must be resolved within hours, before the current situation deteriorates.

- *Average failure* is one that leads to a problem whose impact is moderate.

For instance, internal accounting or customer services have not been immediately affected. The business risk is moderate but the problem must be resolved.

■ *Minor failure* describes a problem that has low to minimal impact.

In this case, the resolution might be deferred, to be addressed within a more general context. But even minor problems should not be lost from sight.

Catastrophic, major, average, and minor failures have associated *attribute features.* These may be passive or active. They may be dynamically called up by the process, be planted there for all cases, or come up by default.

Access control checks, as well as a finer grid of the definition of the four types of failure, should as well consider the possibility of *malicious* code. In Telescript's case, if the suspect call fails because of a permit violation, the engine raises a Permit Violated exception. This can be caught by the calling procedure.

If any of the native, local, or regional permits are violated, the system terminates the process with a Permit Exhausted command. There is as well a provision of what is known as *mix-in classes* associating security-relevant attributes with objects of those classes. In this case, the associated functionality is enforced by the engine.

Examples of this last reference include *Unmoved,* when an agent cannot take such an object along with it; *Uncopied,* when an attempt to make a copy of an object returns a reference but not a copy; *Copyrighted,* when copying is not properly authorized by a suitable Copyright Enforcer; and *Protected.* Once created, Protected objects cannot be modified.

There are, as well, restricted places like the *purgatory.* Agents entering the purgatory are given a quite restricted permit with sunset clauses and short timetables during which they may be operational. These features can prove quite useful in allowing agents access to underlying system resources, as well as in controlling the level of software safety we are after.

Planning the Security of Mission-Critical Communications Solutions

Not every risk connected to communications, computers, and software relates to the Internet. One of the better known security breaches is the

MCI calling-card incident in the 1992 to 1994 timeframe. Malicious software was installed on MCI switching equipment to record and steal about 100,000:

■ Calling-card numbers

■ Personal identification codes

These were sold to hackers throughout the United States and Europe. The sellers posted them on bulletin boards, and the result has been an estimated $50 million in unauthorized long-distance calls.

As this and similar experiences indicate, one of the major risks lies in the fact that the use of passwords to verify the identity of a person at a terminal is generically insecure on open networks. Packet sniffers operate interactively to record combinations of passwords and user names for later misuse.

Such pieces of intruder software have been implicated in dozens of major break-ins throughout America and Europe. Therefore, some experts suggest that an Internet or other network user should not be required to type in a password or reveal any personal characteristics that someone else could copy.* As an alternative, users could be asked to provide answers that depend on their knowledge of some secret item(s). This approach, however, is not only complex but also unstable and cumbersome, and hence, far from being foolproof.

One of the problems that makes secure solutions hard to implement is that people tend to see computer security issues as a technical problem. Therefore, they design firewalls and anomaly detection software. Anomalies are *outliers*, and, as shown in Fig. 6-4, they can be of two types:

■ Extreme events

■ Exceptional data

Firewalls provide some security that otherwise would not be available to users of systems connected to a network. However, even when things become safer, direct access to the corporate databases should be limited to machines with confirmed authorization.

A problem with firewalls is that of centralization and its delays. Forcing all communications to go through a single firewall point of entry assures that these communications have to pass through a stringently

---

*See also later in this chapter the section about tokens.

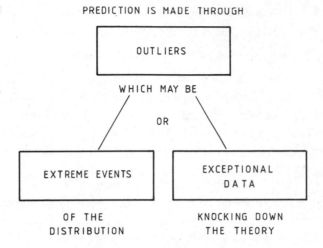

Figure 6-4
Events that do not conform to the prevailing theory are the motor of science.

and tightly managed system. This, however, creates bottlenecks, apart from the daunting task of managing firewalls.

As for exceptional data, agents can be written to detect extreme events and bring them to the attention of their master. This is doable, but technical solutions alone will not solve the problem. Technical solutions have to be backed by organizational approaches,* legal guarantees, and social solutions:

- Planning for security must be subjected to a rigorous methodology.
- Law enforcement must become sophisticated.
- Social values regarding appropriate computer usage should be promoted.

Ethical behavior is often difficult to achieve generically, particularly in a global setting, because different societies have different definitions of what is ethical and what is not. Answers are not straightforward. For instance, the ongoing debate on individual and workplace privacy highlights the lack of consensus with respect to ethics and privacy.

Legislatures and courts are being asked to resolve the ethical and legal questions raised by electronic surveillance, physical searches, and vulnerabilities plaguing e-mail, as well as to address privacy and security expectations regarding the use of the Internet. This job is becoming formidable because of:

---

*See also Chap. 10.

- The increasing number of computer users
- The growing diversity of applications
- The labyrinth of system interconnections.

Another impediment is the growing complexity of overall technological capabilities, which means a greater chance for privacy to be compromised. Together with ethical standards, organizational solutions can be instrumental in removing the risk of people doing things that they should not while still enjoying the feeling of freedom that the technology gives them.

In conclusion, planning for security is not easy, but it is doable within certain limits. For nearly 30 years, with online systems we have had a mechanism that needs updating to provide the necessary assurance. In its fundamentals, this mechanism has called for:

- *Logging* everything—messages, programs, and information elements—that is transiting through the system and/or reaching the database
- *Journaling* before and after images and the message itself as well as restart and recovery and control and auditing
- *Virtual keys*, which can be public, like DES of NBS (64 bits), or private, involving authentication and authorization

Practically every one of these three bullets can be served through agents because logging, journaling, and virtual keys are well-settled issues. The same is true of organizational solutions establishing the required levels of authorization: read only, read/write, add records, and delete. Any operation that we know how to do because of past experience is a good candidate for automation. But higher-level network security should be provided through imaginative innovation as documented in the following section.

Promoting Multidimensional Approaches to Security

The strength of logging, journaling, and using virtual keys, as well as the weaknesses of these methods, come from the same source: They are well known and settled. People and companies eager to protect themselves are using them, but hackers and other intruders know how to cope with them because they are too linear.

New approaches are therefore necessary in the security and protection front, and some projects are under way that aim to fulfill the objective of maintaining greater security in a communications and computing environment. Such efforts address:

- The security of the network operating system and its protocols
- The security awareness of system administrators
- The understanding of security by the system users

Standards organizations and industry associations, too, are trying to do something about security. For instance, The Open Group is developing a single-sign-on norm whereby users log on only once. This is also called *unitary* log-on. The current practice is to dedicate a password for each computer system that a user requires access to, but this results in too many passwords for individuals to remember. A single log-on, however, can be quite insecure in a systems sense.

In the background of different studies in the security domain lies the fact that security failures can have vastly different effects on a network than on stand-alone machines. This is true even if, from an analytical standpoint, they seem to be about the same.

There are two main issues pertaining to the security of operating systems: protection of information and protection of the functioning of the basic software itself. Experience reveals that not-so-secure operating systems usually violate principles like:

- Providing *complete mediation,* verifying that every access to every object is authorized
- Using software to implement *least privilege,* which would see to it that every process operates using the least set of privileges necessary to complete a job
- Featuring *least common mechanism,* by minimizing the amount of facilities common to more than one user

A few, more advanced security projects, however, suggest that while an analysis of strengths and weaknesses along these three bullets can be useful, the real solution to protection problems should be nonlinear. This contrasts with the fact that, by and large, security and protection have so far been examined as a linear process.

The way a linear process approaches security issues is shown at the top of Fig. 6-5. According to Dr. Henrich Steinmann, formerly executive vice president of the Union Bank of Switzerland, the security expert typically looks at his or her goal through a step-by-step procedure. This

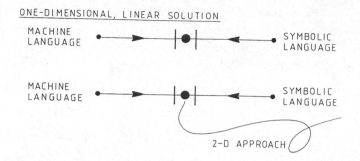

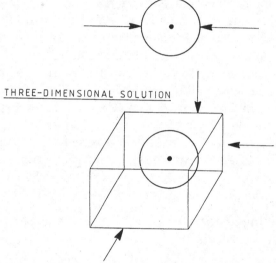

is a slow, costly, and painful process—particularly when the goal is to build a fairly complex security solution. This kind of limitation in the way we deal with our objectives is always present when we work through principally linear thinking. Therefore, from analysis and modeling to security and protection, we are increasingly interested in processes that are nonlinear.

As the second diagram in Fig. 6-5 shows, a person who employs a two-dimensional approach endows himself or herself with better tools because he or she has available an added degree of freedom. The goal of a firewall—but also of a hacker or other intruder—can be reached nonlinearly; and this is a better, more efficient method.

In terms of firewalls, a two-dimensional solution provides a more coherent security mechanism. In fact, a large number of current security flaws are a result of one-dimensional shortcomings, while other flaws are due to:

- Inflexibility of certain design features
- The improper shift of responsibility for security from system designers to end users

Dr. Heinrich Steinmann developed this concept in connection to security and protection, but it applies as well to other fields. The defenses built along a one-dimensional frame of reference, Steinmann says, may be superb. But an intruder who thinks in two dimensions will always reach his or her goal, passing through the nonguarded gate. This gate is visible to him or her, but it is transparent to those who have a one-track mind.

If the defenses are designed to withstand the security risks posed by 2D thinkers in the intruders' or hackers' community, then their attacks will lead nowhere—provided these firewalls are worth their salt. But an intruder who thinks in 3D will still be able to penetrate to the guarded treasure because 2D defenses are not planned to protect against the third dimension. This is shown in the last diagram of Fig. 6-5.

Notice that the level of one-dimensional and sometimes two-dimensional security measures often suggests that the system was not developed with a realistic notion of total security in mind. Yet, only total security concepts could guarantee some protection from vulnerabilities.

In other terms, without a coherent systemwide security mechanism, there is no systematic way to determine whether the aggregate is secure. Neither is there a systematic way to remove lack of security from it. Merely patching privacy holes as they are found cannot guarantee that other security flaws are not present, the fix of one flaw does not create several others, or the addition of a new feature does not introduce new security vulnerabilities.

In conclusion, 1D and even the more sophisticated 2D security solutions can be overtaken through the addition of a third dimension because 3D approaches practically add another degree of freedom.

Though the 2D solution is more flexible and better thought out than the 1D step-by-step security and protection methodology, eventually it builds its own boundaries that put limits on the evolution of security measures. A third dimension changes that, making it feasible to reach the goal much more directly. Agents can be quite instrumental in this type of 3D security environment.

Encryption and Cryptographic Keys on the Internet

Whether a private individual or a company, any user and every network needs to address risk types connected to security. Network operators and information providers should study the overall system requirements for authentication, as well as the chosen mechanisms and their embedding. Various approaches and some commercially available devices exist for:

- One-time passwords, including smart cards
- Randomized tokens
- Challenge-response schemes

For instance, handheld smart card devices can generate a token that can be recognized by a computer at an authentication site, the token having been derived from a cryptographic function. This might present better protection than the classical personal identification number (PIN).

Some devices generate a visually displayed token that can be entered as a one-time password, while others provide direct electronic input. These devices typically use one-key symmetric cryptographic algorithms such as the Digital Encryption Standard (DES) or two-key algorithms such as RSA, with public or private keys.

Other alternatives exist. The Signature Verification System (SVS) offered by one of the vendors is a signature capture and retrieval facility that enables storage of images for verification. It can be used by financial institutions for:

- Online verification of teller operations
- Back-office verification of incoming clearing instruments

Agents can be successfully used in conjunction with both operations, for instance, in regard to the process whereby multiple signatures are stored for an account or multiple messages are stored and displayed during verification.

While the sophistication of security keys and of other measures somehow increases their dependability, authentication must be easy for both authenticatee and authenticator. Here again the use of knowledge artifacts can make significant contributions.

The better solution is that the system should not depend on the secrecy of its cryptographic algorithms. The design of a token-generating device should make it very difficult for anyone to determine the internal parameters and nonpublic encryption keys. Agents have a role to play in this process.

Any solution providing authentication must be resistant to tampering. Every phase from design to implementation and maintenance should minimize the likelihood of accidental failures or the use of malicious code. Notice should also be taken of the fact that denials of service can result from tokens corrupted in transit. I can foresee agents able to do corruption identification.

Knowledge artifacts can play a significant role in connection to security and protection because the technical issues associated with this process have to do with codes, code breaking, and increasing complexity. To appreciate this reference, let's remember that each successive step in cryptography corresponds to a higher level in sophistication to be supported through software. Here is a brief history to keep in mind:

- In 1976, the mathematicians Whitfield Diffie and Martin Hellman developed the concept of public key cryptography.

- In 1985, David Chaum, a computer scientist, proposed PKC, a technique for anonymous transactions that enhanced public key cryptography.

- In the 1990s scientists at Sun Microsystems suggested an Internet standard called the Simple Key Management Process (SKIP), which automates the exchange of keys and allows the keys to be changed rapidly during a transaction.

- Also in the 1990s, Philip Zimmermann developed smart security software known as Phil's Pretty Good Privacy (PGP), which was banned from use abroad by the U.S. federal government.

However, on January 11, 1996, encryption on the Internet got a boost when a U.S. federal prosecutor dropped the 3-year investigation into whether the Internet distribution of the computer encryption program violated U.S. laws about exporting munitions.* This means nobody will be prosecuted for posting Phil's Pretty Good Privacy.

"I'm just really pleased the sword of Damocles is not over me anymore, and I wonder why it took so long," said Philip Zimmermann, explaining that his software turns computer messages into a jumble of

---

*Because the PGP code seems to be unbreakable, it has been legally classified as "munitions," making its export without a license a felony. It's amazing what bureaucrats can imagine—but the court knocked down that rule.

numbers and letters unreadable to anyone except the intended recipient. Zimmermann also developed PGP Phone, a software program that turns a computer equipped with a microphone into a rather secure voice telephone.

Agents Watching after Security in Buildings

So far we have treated issues connected to logical security—DES, SVS, PKC, SKIP, and PGP, for example. But it would also be wise to take a look at ways and means of assuring trusted security systems in buildings. This is a never-ending subject because it evolves as technology leaps forward. Therefore, I will limit myself to two references:

1. Today, some of the more sophisticated solutions grant access to a building by analyzing a person's fingertip, voice, or retina (biometric identification).

These solutions tend to use knowledge engineering artifacts. A good example of the use of expert systems to advantage in security assessment is provided by the Lawrence Livermore National Laboratory (LLNL). At LLNL, artificial intelligence constructs monitor systems and events such as:

- Security alarms
- Equipment alarms
- A variety of sensors
- Radio communications

Rather than building complex artifacts, LLNL chose to write a family of simpler models, each oriented to the control of a single event. The following is an example:

If   \<a relevant event A has occurred>

and \<Event A is a member of a class of events that imply an intruder>

and \<An intruder class incident is in progress in the same area>

Then   \<Associate event A with the incident; create task to reassess priority of incident>

While agents cannot make unsecure systems secure, they can help to maximize the effects of security measures by ensuring that the security mechanism that is in place is properly utilized and that system weaknesses are compensated for as much as possible.

2. Tomorrow, robot guards may sniff a visitor's body odor, using a superkeen nose like the one invented by two scientists from Tufts University.

David Walt, chairman of the Chemistry Department, and John S. Kauer, a professor of neuroscience, have patented a system that combines fiber-optic sensors and neural network software to identify various smells.

This approach has an array of fiber sensors that detect different chemicals. By analyzing the combined reaction of a bundle of 10 sensors, the neural network could identify up to a million compounds. The researchers also suggest that artificial sniffers might as well detect oil leaks or diagnose diseases based on metabolic changes in a patient's breath or sweat.

While these solutions are not for tomorrow, they do point toward a trend to use increasingly sophisticated technology. There is no doubt that knowledge artifacts have a key role to play both in logical and in physical security. The doubt is if companies have the needed culture to exploit to their profit the potential of high technology.

CHAPTER 7

Using Agents in Concurrent Software-Hardware Network Design

Software-hardware codesign refers to the concurrent, integrated study, evaluation, and specification of communications and computers systems. Conceptually, such an approach is not new. What has changed is the complexity that it involves because of the increased diversity of applications employing embedded software solutions.

Among the reasons propelling the need for concurrent software-hardware design are advances in key enabling technologies that need formal methods for their handling. Such methods are neither solely hardware nor strictly software oriented. Other reasons are:

- The amount of customization today necessary for many state-of-the-art implementations
- The growing requirement to decrease the cost of designing and testing new systems
- The nature of applications raising issues like time to live (TTL) connected to hops between nodes, as well as address limitations regarding end systems.*

Software-hardware codesign has become important with modern high-performance networks because it supports the dynamic generation of changes in the style and environment of the tasks in which our tools are used. It also supports consideration of the effect of new developments in utilizing computers, communications, and software—as we will see later in this chapter when we talk of tariffs.

Deregulation has allowed new entrants into the market. These companies, however, must be able to compete against established monopolies that have enough political clout to make life very difficult for their rivals. It is not enough to argue that new entrants can offer a service more cheaply than the monopolies; it must be also established that greater efficiency will sustain that advantage in the longer run, and as local, long-distance and international carriers are linking up together to form global networks, software-hardware codesign becomes a "must."

The work we are doing in cooperative software-hardware development environments is that of linking, via a network, distributed software production bases with end-user nodes. As the network expands, it necessarily involves a wide range of constituent technologies, including:

- Giagastream communications
- Real-time decision systems
- Multimedia applications
- Distributed deductive databases

The development and implementation of sophisticated applications already span a broad area and embrace issues related not just to technical issues but to ergonomics and social psychology. Advanced research

---

*See "Internet Protocol, Version 6, and Network Flexibility" later in this chapter.

on networks involves both optimal communications methods and styles of work. Both can be enhanced and made more cost-effective through the use of agents.

The Role of Agents in Concurrent Modeling Procedures

Every one of the applications examples that we have seen in Chaps. 5 and 6, as well as a wide range of other implementation cases, can be significantly improved through the use of agents. For example, Securum, a Swedish financial company, uses agents in choosing lists of repairs for its real estate holdings. Knowledge artifacts are also:

■ Developing the specs of the intervention

■ Evaluating the cost of labor and materials

■ Establishing intervention timetables*

Assisted through agents, modeling procedures are elaborated, and the adopted solution can even propose a budget. Once a project has started, agents follow the progress of the construction or maintenance work, evaluating the planned versus the actual project.

While this example comes from financial projects connected to real estate, once the procedure is established, it can be nicely applied to networks. In its realm of operations, Securum uses agents to control actual versus budgeted expenditures. In a way similar to the one we saw in Chap. 6, knowledge artifacts are bringing their master's attention to:

■ Exceptions

■ Salient problems

This permits management to concentrate on crucial issues and therefore to take timely action. Rather than spreading the available resources thin over a wide range of activities, some of which may be well under control, the chosen solution concentrates on salient factors and exceptions.

The same principles can apply to software-hardware codesign, and in general to cooperative work. Continuing increases in the complexity of networked environments and the constant effort to gain early market advantage are driving designers to computer simulation of systems and processes.

---

*See also in Chap. 10 the example of Compass, of GTE.

Engineers and executives at Ford's five design centers around the globe talk to each other daily and exchange designs across the Atlantic through video conferences and computer nets. Although many cars will be global—particularly midrange models—details of styling and specification must still be tailored to regional markets. Once this new operation is in full swing, Ford expects to save as much as $3 billion a year.

The Internet is another good example of concurrent engineering applications not only because it provides the communications facility but also because its supports are being globally tested—even if the provided Internet infrastructures are local. Other reasons that software-hardware codesign of Internet services is important are that:

- Multimedia implementations pose quite diverse requirements in terms of channel capacity.
- The time distribution of network load and its peak(s) fluctuate during the 24 hours of the day.

Developed by the National Center for Supercomputing Applications (NCSA) on the basis of file transfer statistics by volume, Fig. 7-1 shows the very significant difference that exists among audio, video, text, and image channel capacities.

Statistics on past activity help us inasmuch as they provide a basis to forecast future events. The simulation of complex systems and their key

Figure 7-1
World Wide Web statistics by volume during a 24-hour period.

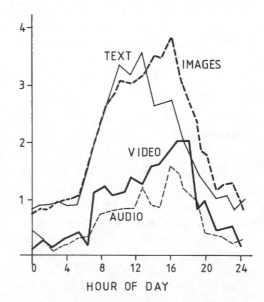

components permits designers to unify the software and hardware domains by using an integrative model. It also makes it possible to explore software-hardware tradeoffs. Assisted by simulation, codesign helps the engineer to:

- Perform system decomposition
- Proceed with software-hardware partitioning
- Evaluate performance characteristics and functions

Agents can be instrumental in this function by bringing to their master's attention outliers, discrepancies, and incompatibilities. An early awareness of their existence supports design continuity and makes it feasible to maintain consistency between the software and hardware descriptions. As design refinement proceeds, software-hardware tradeoffs can be explored at various stages. This leads to more efficient implementations, as well as to improvements in reliability and cost-effectiveness.

Agent-supported interactive solutions are a timely innovation for current design practices. Codesign does away with old concepts that rest on the separation of hardware and software paths early in the design cycle. Traditionally, these design paths have remained independent, having had very little interaction until system integration. By then, it was too late to identify incompatibilities and correct failures.

Many network design failures have been due to the fact that systems engineers often specify hardware without fully appreciating the computational requirements of the software. Also, they do not track necessary changes to software functionality due to:

- Decisions made during the hardware design phase
- Changes in usage requirements, like the multimedia example shown in Fig. 7-1

The result of such widespread practices is defective software-hardware interfaces as well as suboptimal coordination in technology investments. When the software and hardware are finally combined, system integration problems invariably call for modifications of software and/or hardware leading to:

- Significant cost increases
- Schedule overruns
- Performance losses

In conclusion, simulation, prototyping, and improved design automation tools allow complex systems to be studied fairly quickly. This is very important as the decision to allocate functionality to hardware or software is not straightforward. We must consider all options, and we can benefit from knowledge artifacts that operate online to serve their masters in allocation and in optimization.

Why Agents Can Assist in an Integrative Approach to Common Tasks

Simulation models both performance and functional attributes of the software-hardware system at an early development stage. As explained in the preceding section, agents can help in identifying discrepancies and also in providing the bill of materials and cost estimates of the system-to-be.

Based on a current project, Fig. 7-2 presents a block diagram of the component parts entering into an integrative approach to network design. An agent tracks logical issues involving design aims and objectives. Another agent audits gateways; still another interfaces. The latter come into the job stream after the project has passed the logical design

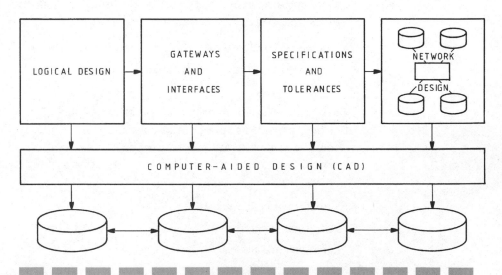

Figure 7-2   Taking an interactive approach to common tasks.

audit—but they may also return the project to the previous stage pinpointing issues that need review.

More sophisticated are the agents that do the final auditing of specifications and tolerances. One of the knowledge artifacts currently projected will use the help of a simulator of the production process to precheck possible failures in quality after manufacturing. In another project of a similar dimension, the agent addresses value analysis premises; still another assists in automatic documentation and its updating.

Five years ago, in a network project assisted by agents, engineering plans were developed in concurrent fashion. Intelligent artifacts effectively tested whether the grand design had been observed by the different engineering teams that worked in three different companies. Expert systems:

- Did value analysis in regard to the choices made of components, as well as of labor content and its costs
- Examined if parts that are reusable had been employed or if new specifications were developed without a real need
- Searched for possible discrepancies in the specs between the different design teams, as well as for synergy between mechanical, electrical, and electronic plans

Today, if I were to redo this project, I would not use static expert systems but dynamic agents. There are major benefits to be gained from online interactivity, and the experience that has been accumulated since then clearly points to the wisdom of real-time software-hardware codesign.

One of the better examples of the need for agents in concurrent, collaborative work is the development and use of models for environmental studies. These typically require input from different professions and subsequent evaluation by a number of specialists with different backgrounds.

Sorting out the large number of factors in climate prediction has always been a complex problem. The more so if special effects have to be accounted for such as the impact of deforestation in the Amazon on a given regional climate or the effect of a warmer atmosphere on the melting of the earth's ice caps.

A number of different professional fields can contribute expertise to this problem. To address the issue of climatic changes and their possible aftermaths, MIT scientists use recently developed simulators that describe the physical processes over land and in the atmosphere. The model is run under a number of hypotheses, to simulate the climate that is being observed and its associated conditions. Then, the researchers change certain parameters such as those describing reflection of solar radiation and surface roughness.

One module of this model projects the resulting changes in terms of climate. Another module helps to investigate how rain is intercepted by the canopy, that is, the leafy treetops. In the Amazon, around 10 percent of the annual 2 meters of rainfall strikes the canopy and evaporates without ever reaching the ground. Both modules make use of knowledge artifacts.

Another experimentally supported research area, which falls under the same reference of codesign and parallelization, is that of developing a description of spatial variability of soil moisture and how it relates to topography. Here again, different professional disciplines must contribute to establish the complex relations of hydrologic processes over large areas. Soil moisture depends on the climatology of the region and is very much a function of rainfall. There are, however, indications that the interaction works both ways: Soil moisture in turn influences the amount of rainfall.

One of the problems presented with such interdisciplinary approaches to modeling is that of synonyms and homonyms. Practically every project team and every research laboratory uses its own terminology. This poses difficult problems in document handling, which can be assisted through the use of agents as suggested by the block diagram in Fig. 7-3, which is based on a Japanese study.

Object View Agent Links (OVAL) is an MIT project that also tackles intricate issues associated with document handling. It can link a variety of tasks by providing seamless connection, and it makes feasible different views when looking at information elements. Originally designed to be a general platform for cooperative work, OVAL can be customized by its users, and it operates with semistructured and unstructured information.

The OVAL project involves 14 agents that move messages into and out of folders, for various kinds of premises. To create an agent, users fill in the fields:

- The folder to which the agent applies
- One or more triggering conditions
- A set of rules they wish to implement

When the agent is triggered, it will apply the rules to the objects in the

Figure 7-3
A sophisticated system for document handling developed in Japan.

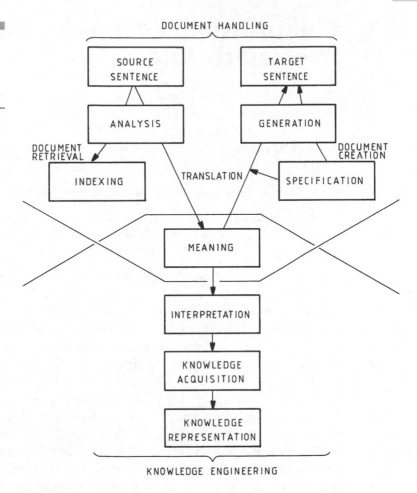

Apply To folder. Rules are created with a straightforward sequence of menu picks and forms. Rules also move conversations with premises from the user into folders. Some of the agents employ all-objects-of-a-type folders. These are maintained by the system so that it always contains all objects of a specified type.

Through this and similar agent-supported approaches, diverse teams of people in different companies and/or countries can routinely work together in real time, concurrently rather than sequentially. Knowledge engineering—enriched systems as well as networked sensing devices can effectively interconnect different laboratories among themselves and link them directly to the production line and from there to the marketing and sales effort.

Compression, Filtering, and Bandwidth Allocation

Like all highly interactive real-time applications, concurrent engineering is a bandwidth-intensive task. Solutions are therefore necessary to save channel capacity. While technology expands bandwidth, it also provides the means, through *compression* and *perceptual coding,* for making some of the bandwidth requirements more manageable.

- Compression encodes digital bit streams in a way that can be effectively decoded on the receiving end.
- Perceptual coding is a lossy compression technique that removes features from an image or sound stream.

Perceptual coding works on the premise that what is removed would not be easily noticed by the user. We can send images, animations, sound, and text streams across to each participant at the start of a session, using commands to cause them to be played locally. For greater effectiveness, these commands can be knowledge enriched again highlighting the use of agents. From start-up to termination, the cross section of the bandwidth on the network changes with each phase of a session and with the command system we are using. Since bandwidth is not unlimited, it is wise to apply data compression technology for delivery of digital information, whether purely audio or multimedia.

The principle of data compression is simple: To deliver an image over a network quickly, the communication channel must either be sufficiently large or the information should be tightly packed. All solutions adhere to this principle, but some do so better than others.

In 1995, researchers at MIT developed data compression software that could have a significant impact on the race to provide high-quality image and video data over ordinary telephone lines. In Internet applications, for example, this approach could allow cybershoppers to:

- Download multiple catalog images in a fraction of a second
- Click on the page that captures their eye
- Zoom and pan around the image in a seamless manner, to further examine product features

Other applications include computer graphics, databasing, archiving, digital television, teleconferencing, and telemedicine. The software is based on *wavelet theory* and differs from today's standard compression algorithms known as *Joint Photographic Expert Group* (JPEG) for still images and *Motion Picture Expert Group* (MPEG) for video.[*]

The problem is that neither MPEG nor JPEG is capable of achieving high enough compression ratios without loss of quality. At the same time, they represent a heavy drain on processing power, and therefore current delivery of images and video over the Internet has not been that practical.

In terms of the ability to pack large amounts of data into tiny volumes, without overcharging a computer's processing unit, wavelets are a significant improvement over the Fourier transform—based JPEG and MPEG. They can do a better job at capturing key features in an image without losing sight of the intricate details that are present. By breaking down an image into smaller blocks for more efficient processing and preserving image quality, wavelets make it possible to develop a technology allowing the manipulation of finite-length data.

Another technique of service to concurrent engineering and other real-time jobs is *filtering.* Numerous applications in science and technology require the use of filters to selectively pass, accept, or reject various components of an incoming signal. But filters invariably suffer from one problem connected to the passband they feature—its center frequency and width.

The center frequency and width of the filter's passband are difficult to control precisely. This is especially true in the case of filters that are intended to be very selective. The challenge is practically synonymous with filters having extremely narrow passbands. Agents could help with problems that are associated to filtering.

Massaged data streams affect the network bandwidth requirements by reducing the capacity requirements of each process running on the network. Based on current studies and projections, Fig. 7-4 shows a likely distribution of network capacity roughly split 2 to 1 between production and management. The best way to look at these figures is in a just-note-the-difference manner:

- Real-time video tends to take the lion's share: about 45 percent of available capacity.

- Two other production processes, real-time audio and burst data, account for roughly 10 percent of capacity each.

- Control data describing participants' behavior consumes some 20 percent, and another 15 percent will go for network overhead.

---

[*]D. N. Chorafas, *Visual Programming Technology*, McGraw-Hill, New York, 1997.

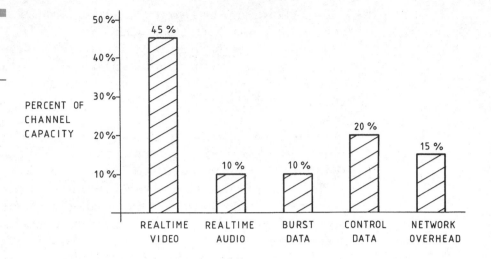

Figure 7-4
Expected channel
capacity allocation
with megastreams.

Under the term *real-time video* come different features, from real-time simulation and virtual reality to high-definition television. Hence, it can be split into finer-grain components that have in common live images of high digital resolution.

Real-time video requires a megastream of 2 Mbps or more. By contrast, audio, including stereo, can be supported on 64-Kbps lines with signals that are better than voice quality. Future applications will also call for a distinction between:

- *Sustained* digital streams with continuous transfers for extended times, often for the duration of the session

- *Short-burst* transfers of large amounts of data, mainly at the beginning of a session

What this means is that we have to rethink classical perspectives on communications. The frame has changed because both the infrastructure and the implementation requirements are evolving. We cannot manually control the design process—we need knowledge artifacts to help us.

Sensory information data streams, for instance, will be of sustained type and may come from tactile input or similar processes. Sustained digital streams will also originate from instrumentation. The source of interactive data may be not only computers but also position orientation, gestures, and so on.

Each one of these implementation references has its own characteristic bandwidth requirements that will evolve in accordance with projections for the coming state of the communications art. In the runtime phase of a session, the bandwidth traffic will be predominantly continuous media information such as video and audio streams and control data describing the participants' behavior.

As this discussion demonstrates, we can categorize digital streams carried on the physical links, switches, routers, and up to the network interfaces. In terms of software-hardware, any quantitative evaluation must account for a constant network overhead due to packet header and other routing information tacked on by the various network protocols.

The Need for Multiprotocol Software to Be Used in Networks

Those of us who used networks in the mid-1960s learned to work with the start-stop line discipline. Not only is this protocol still active, but it also constitutes the large majority of applications because it is simple and very inexpensive—but it cannot handle sophisticated implementations or high-bandwidth requirements.

The choice of appropriate protocols is one of the best examples that can be found in engineering to justify the need for software-hardware codesign. As the two-dimensional map in Fig. 7-5 demonstrates, no single protocol can ever match the huge range in response-time requirements and in transmission speed:

■ Legacy applications with channel capacity that goes up to the 64 Kbps ISDN require and use a number of protocols from start-stop and bisynchronous (BSC) to X.25.

■ A number of line disciplines characterize the range between 64 Kbps and 74 Mbps—a difference of three orders of magnitude in transmission speed.

■ Still other, much more efficient protocols have to be provided for 3-digit megastreams and for gigastreams—some of them still waiting to be invented.

There are reasons other than channel capacity for the proliferation of protocols—for instance, mobile and wireless communications[*] and secu-

---

[*]See also Chap. 5.

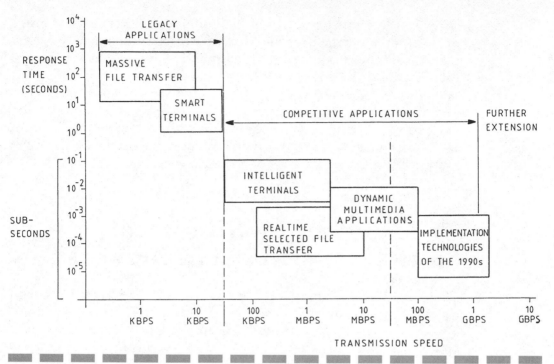

Figure 7-5   Legacy and competitive applications with their acceptable response-time levels and data transmission requirements.

rity—which we discussed in Chap. 6. We will return to security issues when we talk of Internet's IPv6 later in this chapter.

Basic principles in protocol design are *functionality* and *dependability.* The currently emerging multiprotocol software for base stations will allow wireless networks to handle growing traffic from any type of mobile phone. It will also permit service providers to:

- Avoid supplier lock-in
- Maximize use of existing infrastructure

Agents can contribute to ongoing improvements in digital signal processors, enabling a single base station to handle multiple protocols for fixed and mobile applications. Such development could have as big an impact on wireless communications as client-server architectures had on computing.

The dual effect of agents and multiprotocol structures is compounded by the fact that wireless has moved from what used to be broadcast radio to a mobile computing business. Relying on silicon chip—based digital signal processors (DSPs), the new technology turns the base station into a facility that handles all the modulation requirements for an incoming radio signal. Then, it converts this signal bit stream for effective transmission across the network.

Knowledge-enriched software has still another role to play. While the advent of multiprotocol solutions should be welcome, reasonable approaches cannot ignore the most important issue in local loop competition: the right to interconnect at a fair and reasonable price.* Besides this, legal frameworks are, by the force of things, a necessary complement to new technical solutions.

Given the reasons that have just been outlined, network access and interconnection is a key goal of current negotiations on basic telecommunications services within the World Trade Organization. It is also an issue of increasing concern to standards institutes, which have to work not only with conflicting technical requirements but also with pressures by vendors.

Still another good reason for developing network intelligence served by autonomous interactive artifacts is that users want greater simplicity, higher capacity, lower cost, better performance, and increased interoperability out of their networks—all at the same time. Choosing a standard and getting the vendors to observe it would clearly be the preferable strategy, provided that:

- There are *real* standards.
- The user organizations have the muscle to make the vendors follow them.

Even then, getting to one protocol, or just a few, requires a blend of technical knowhow and the ability to build consensus. Everyone favors standards as long as the "standards" selected are those that they happen to be using already or that serve the products in an advanced phase of development. Experimentation on multiprotocol software is so crucial because more and more network managers have to make these difficult choices. Some of these practitioners see encapsulation and gateways as means to make unwanted protocols transparent.

Encapsulation† uses the carrier protocol to transparently transmit other protocols (payload protocols) across the backbone. It permits users

---

*See also the discussion in the section "Agents, Competitive Access Providers, and the International Telecommunications Market" later in this chapter.

†The concept of encapsulation is discussed from a data viewpoint in Chap. 10.

to keep the backbone network simple, ideally running (perhaps) only a single protocol, such as TCP/IP or the newer Internet Protocol, version 6 (IPv6).

In its way, encapsulation improves a network's performance since it is often easier to tune a single routing protocol as well as to control congestion. The problem with encapsulation is the increased overhead that comes with extra protocol headers. Straight encapsulation requires that all of the overhead packets, such as acknowledgments, are encapsulated and carried across the network. This happens all too frequently since each transmission through the network creates similar overhead packets in their carrier protocol.

There are also some other problems such as the extra node hops that are introduced. The message is sent from its source to the encapsulator and to the nearest backbone router, then across the network to the target backbone router, to the deencapsulator, and on to destination.

Another problem with today's encapsulation approaches is that most are proprietary and require that both ends of the connection be managed by software from the same vendor. Therefore, a somewhat better strategy for reducing backbone protocols is to actually translate from one protocol to a standard backbone protocol using gateways.

At the bottom line, however, there are really no ideal solutions in protocol translation and interpretation. This explains why many user organizations have a strong desire to begin eliminating legacy protocols, also to decommission unsupportable older network solutions. Decommissioning is another challenge that, to be effectively done, requires software-hardware codesign and the use of agents.

Internet Protocol, Version 6, and Network Flexibility

The Internet so far has no rival in its role of the precursor of the global information superhighway. Politically and socially, the basis of its popularity is that it mushroomed as a people's network. Technically, its power rests on a suite of more than 100 TCP/IP protocols, based on two core line disciplines: Transmission Control Protocol (TCP) and Internet Protocol (IP). TCP manages the data flow, and IP gets the packets from sender to receiver.

For the last few years, the Internet has practically doubled in size every year, a growth rate that is unprecedented. Planning for the future, designers are currently working on the next generation of Internet protocols known as IP, version 6 (IPv6),[*] which is projected to run well on:

- Wireless and other low-bandwidth networks
- High-performance networks, such as asynchronous transfer mode (ATM)[†]

IPv6 is able to handle multimedia and, as we will see in the section that follows, it also enhances security, though to what extent has yet to be tested. Many communications specialists now look at IP, version 6, as the next-generation IP. It includes an array of improvements over IP. One of them is addressing.

For instance, in December 1994, in the course of an Internet seminar in Beijing, the Chinese stated that they would eventually like to have 1 billion addresses at their disposal.[‡] In other countries, too, every computer user would eventually like to be connected to the Internet—and in a few years there would be several billion devices requiring an addressing technique that is adequate and dependable.

Reference was made in the introduction to time to live (TTL). The IP contains an element TTL implemented as an 8-bit header field in every IP packet. The sender of an IP packet sets it to an initial value, typically around 30. This denominates the number of hops or forwarding routers the packet is allowed to pass.

TTL is an identifier between source and destination. In its original conception, this mechanism was implemented to prevent looping packets from crashing routers or saturating whole links in networks. But its usage has been extended.

Typically, under normal conditions, each router decrements an IP packet's TTL value by 1 while forwarding—therefore keeping a count. It may, however, even decrease the TTL value by more than 1 per hop. This will depend on the time the packet was queued in the router. A value of 1 is subtracted from the TTL value for every second the packet gets delayed in the router.

But such approach is no more dependable as there are too many variables affecting transmission time. To cope with network growth, a new mechanism has been created to inform the sending end system about

---

[*]Which came to life as "IPNG," for "IP New Generation."

[†]See also D. N. Chorafas, *Protocols, Servers and Projects for Multimedia Realtime Systems,* Macmillan, London, 1997.

[‡]*IEEE Spectrum,* September 1995.

packet loss on the way to the receiver. If a control packet indicates that the TTL value reached zero before the IP packet arrived at the intended node, the router may increase the TTL value for packet retransmission. Some communications experts look at this procedure as patching over the original design. Patches can become messy, and the best way to handle them is through agents.

A knowledge-enriched approach improves upon the original IP design by providing a dynamic adaption to the actual load and topology of the Internet. It can also assist in a faster accumulation of experience through quality databases.*

Quality databases mined through agents can be of help because in many systems the option of adaptive TTL we just described has never been implemented. Instead, a fixed value of around 30 is used. But as the Internet approaches the limit of 30 routers between end systems, a number of problems rise on the horizon.

Not only will new addressing protocols and time-to-live considerations be necessary but also much better techniques for address management. Agents can assist in making solutions quite flexible because the steady introduction of new classes of devices changes rather quickly the perspective of what needs to be done.

There is still another major problem beyond the fact that TTL is limited in the number of hops and the current IP runs out of address space: The original version of the Internet Protocol takes more time than expected because of ATM implementation:

- *As is,* the IP does not capitalize on ATM services. This has to be done through special software.

- Also, security was not initially addressed in the IP. But it has been subsequently embedded into version 6.

The question then is *when* will the Internet go to the IPv6? And when it does, what will be the costs and the advantages of converting to the new discipline? Pros say that the IPv6 presents at least three major benefits in connection to the points made in the preceding paragraphs:

- It finds addresses in a network more quickly than the current IP.

- It integrates well with the asynchronous transfer mode.

- It is quite efficient for multimedia transmission.

---

*See Chap. 8 and Chap. 10.

One of its functions is enabling time-sensitive data to find paths through the network even if some areas may be congested. A digital stream is broken up into a narrow channel for low-definition video, and a wide channel for higher definition. Should no congestion take place in the network, then all channels are passed. If congestion occurs, some channels are dropped gradually. In this fail-soft way, priority video gets through the network, even if it may be of poorer resolution.

The adoption of the IPv6, after it becomes operational, is expected to come relatively fast. Some companies like Sun, Hewlett-Packard, and DEC, as well as router vendors, are working on it with beta releases. By 1999, it is expected that when a user buys an operating system it will include the IPv6.

Not surprisingly, given the Internet's modularity, many vendors expect to start the implementation of version 6 at the consumer end. Then, as applications and services come on-stream and user demand picks up, vendors will probably deploy multicast routing capabilities inside the Internet.

With this development projected to happen from the bottom up, the change in networking concepts will be at least as great as that due to the telephone. This, of course, is just a projection because both technology and the market's whims change so fast that it is difficult to predict how well all that comes about and what will be the actual results. We just have to live through the experience.

The IPv6 and Enhanced Security on the Internet and the Intranets

The most striking thing about the Internet architecture and its implementation is its *simplicity.* This makes its growth easier and also leads to *flexibility.* Users did not need to change anything in the Internet in 1993 when the Web was deployed. It was implemented by simply changing some piece of software in the attached devices.

The flexibility of the Internet is further demonstrated by the fact that it is practically unnecessary to change something significant on the Internet to run voice or video. This latter statement, however, is conditional: When users run voice over the Internet, they often hit congestion somewhere due to a combination of bandwidth shortage and inadequate traffic control.

Video-on-demand, on which so many telcos are currently working, may be based on the Internet but not necessarily on the old IP. Either there is at present, or there will be, an IP address on every visual device in the office and in the home. This will be able to handle a multimedia transport protocol. But, by all likelihood, it will not be one of the line disciplines we presently use.

Forward-thinking communications experts believe that not only the line discipline will change but also our culture in the way we use the network. A great boost in this cultural change will be the use of agents. Practically everything that was said in the first three paragraphs of this section is open to the employment of knowledge artifacts.

A similar statement can be made about mobile computing. To be served in an able manner wireless communications will require their own specialized protocol(s) and custom-designed agents. Both wired and wireless communications will require high security. This, too, will be served well through agents as we saw in Chap. 6. Figure 7-6 brings, once more, this concept into perspective.

Given that security is a major concern of a growing number of Internet users, a critical question is: "Does IPv6 bolster security?" And if yes, "Why?" and "How?" The fact that there are no uniform security protocols and policies—or even agreements on standards—is indeed a big issue.

The answer to the questions asked in the preceding paragraph comes by means of a critical aspect of IPv6, which requires that its implementation must support a consistent policy on privacy and authentication. But, as we saw in Chap. 6 in connection with security algorithms, the problem is that export regulations tend to restrict the more advanced encryption techniques.

Because "this" or "that" type of restrictions are not expected to be lifted soon, IPv6 designers have modularized the design so that certain components can be deleted without upsetting the protocol. Interestingly though, a vendor cannot claim its product conforms to the IPv6 without the full security mechanism being implemented on it.

Still the IPv6 does not address database security. What it does is authenticate and maintain privacy of packets that flow between machines. This helps in handling security threats existing in the current Internet, like:

- Source address spoofing
- Source-related routing attacks
- Password sniffing or tampering
- Connection hijacking

Figure 7-6
Both wired and wireless IP will need to serve multimedia and to benefit from high security.

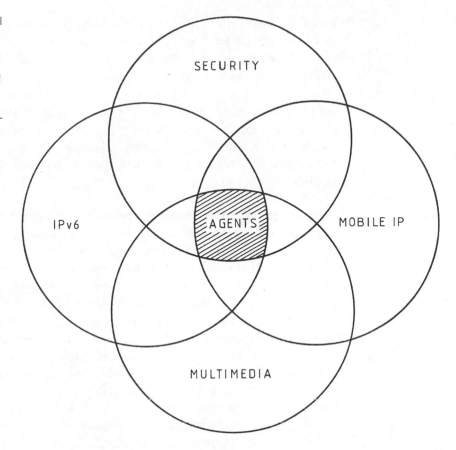

But it falls short of covering all security aspects. The concept of the IPv6 approach is to generate a packet, keep it safe, sign it for authenticity and only then send it through the network. This way it does not matter how many routers it goes through, as it cannot get exposed until it gets to the target computer.

Let me add that a good security mechanism must, as well, include the denial-of-service policies that the Internet has started to experience—as some users pound other users' machines with messages and prevent them from doing their primary work. For many applications, particularly those that are mission critical, security is both:

- A process
- A product

Trusted systems solutions on a network will eventually require certification authorities, which are presently not in place. Actually they may never be there, given the Internet's fully distributed structure and the fact that nobody has control over it.

Good organizational solutions can make the difference. One of the approaches toward somewhat greater security is that taken by Sun Microsystems, which provides a virtual private network. The user encrypts data on one end, and then he or she does not mind how it goes on the other end. Because the encryptor is on the network, not the desktop, it doesn't require applications to change. On the other hand, when the encryption is on the network, it is easier for hackers and intruders to tamper with it.

Besides this, there is always the possibility that after an Internet message gets to the target machine and becomes plain text again, it can be tampered with. Hence, at the application level the user needs to protect the information at his or her disposal.

No matter how we look at the security problem, there is no denial that the end user should play a leading role in assuring the security of his or her programs, data, messages, and transactions. This is no job to be done manually. Hence, the use of agents is to be valued—and it will remain so with or without the IPv6.

One of the characteristics of a good network security solution is that it should not be vendor specific. The IPv6 promises to provide that vendor independence. But above all, valid security approaches require the cooperation of people. There are many things people can do wrong, thereby defeating the technical security mechanisms.

The vendor-independence requirement, expressed in the last paragraph, is part of the new trend. As they emerge, new protocols will probably reflect a platform-free design concept. This contrasts to current practices. Today, for instance, television is transmitted in a way very dependent on how the TV set works:

■ The signal is completely related and bound to the manner in which a specific piece of equipment receives it.

There is a lot of inflexibility in the current transmission because it is wired to transmission devices and receivers conceived long ago and characterized by inflexibility:

■ But a digital solution breaks that linkage between transmission method and presentation, while agents increase the degrees of freedom.

Researchers say that when they started to work with video over the Internet, they discovered that there was a lot of flexibility. They could change the frame rate, the pixels, or the compression ratio. This is important because today several projects look into an Internet TV channel, some focusing on knowledge artifacts able to capitalize on the bandwidth advantage.

Agents, Competitive Access Providers, and the International Telecommunications Market

There are many ways of capitalizing on the broadband channel, and these are best studied through concurrent software—based engineering—both before and after the grand design of the network is done. Current practices vary. Some happen to be application specific; others are end user oriented; still others are focusing on the market edge that competitive access providers can gain.

There are today in the United States some 50 or so phone companies known as *competitive access providers* (CAPs). About half the states allow this sort of competition, and the CAPs have been steadily building state-of-the-art phone networks. The financial cost is significant. Huge capital expenditures and heavy borrowing have kept all of the major publicly traded CAPs in the red. But some are beginning to show quarterly improvements in cash flow, which solidifies their market presence.

To survive in a competition with the giants, CAPs must assure that the pricing of their products is very dynamic not only because that's how the market behaves but also because its inherent complexity leads to complex tariff structures, as we will see with Mercury's One2One. That's where *autonomous learning agents* have a major role to play.

There is plenty of purpose in optimization, and knowledge artifacts fit well the CAPs' strategy. By using high tech, they can keep tariffs low, and an alternative phone company could become a *carrier's carrier*—selling local service on a wholesale basis to long-distance companies or other users:

■ Wholesale or volume discounting, already the norm in the United States, could spread worldwide.

■ Discounts of 80 percent on the nominal retail tariff could start becoming commonplace.

■ A massive surplus of capacity could drive down prices further and further.

Both vendors and users capitalize on knowledge artifacts. Agents have been developed that search on behalf of the user for the best tariff deal, the cheapest bandwidth, and the lowest phone company charges. As electronic spot markets similar to those for other commodities develop, agents go to these markets:

- Each hour of the day
- Each day of the week

Agents experiment on tariffs within the intended environment of usage. Then, they report to their master on the lowest costs and best functionality they can get. This way, knowledge artifacts bring a new way of looking at telecommunications functions and the optimization of their costs.

This will profoundly affect network design in the years to come. User organizations able to develop and deploy competitive access agents can capitalize on the profound changes now under way in telecommunications. In the longer run, the different telco monopolies and their governments will find it impossible to protect their physical frontiers from the invasion of cost-effective competitors:

- Cheap long-distance telephone service is the new market.
- The tool is *callback,* which allows major phone users to save big money.

User organizations save money through foreign, often American, dial-tone services that permit callbacks to make intercontinental calls. AT&T, MCI, Sprint, and different independents provide this service, which some countries, particularly in Asia, have outlawed—in a last-ditch effort to erect barriers. Agents can help the telcos on the defensive but also the end users who optimize their costs. Rather than depending on silly barriers, the telcos can mine their databases and take marketing action. User organizations can effectively employ knowledge artifacts to unbundle tariff structures and experiment on cost swapping within *their* operations environment.*

With the excess capacity in international telecommunications, U.S. telephony companies have been moving to undercut existing phone rates. While China, South Korea, and Thailand made callback illegal, many other countries instituted restrictions on advertising in an effort

---

*For a practical example of how this is done, see also D. N. Chorafas and H. Steinmann, *Intelligent Networks: Telecommunications Solutions for the 1990s,* CRC Press, Boca Raton, Fla., 1990.

to keep the low tariffs from being known. Yet:

- Low-cost services are vital to all industries for their survival when they get free from the suffocating hand of government protection.
- Callback services are a sharp reminder of the need for industries to become more cost-effective or perish.

Agents able to capitalize on competitive opportunities are an integral part of the technology that has begun to obviate the need for costly cable laying to serve remote areas. They can integrate in their search cellular technology and the forthcoming introduction (within the next 3 years) of satellite phone systems. The developments will sharply increase the need for knowledge artifacts.

Britain provides a good example of where this could lead in the medium term. The Mercury subsidiary of Cable and Wireless (C&W), which was licensed in 1984 as the country's second national carrier, found it hard to compete against the entrenched might of British Telecom. BT responded by:

- Cutting its own tariffs
- Creating barriers regarding the terms on which it interconnected with Mercury's calls

As a result, C&W made a successful diversification into mobile telephony, where it can benefit from a wider spread of technologies. This is done through its Mercury One2One subsidiary,* owned jointly with US West, whose services were launched in September 1993.

An interesting case study is One2One's past policy with its off-peak local, free-of-charge calls. While its existing customers still benefit from no-cost-attached, the company has abolished free evening calls for new customers. Local weekend calls, however, will be free of all tariffs. In effect, One2One now features three tariff levels: Gold, Silver, and Bronze:

- The Bronze tariff addresses low users.
- The Silver tariff is for high users.
- The Gold tariff includes national options and international calls.

As diversified tariff schemes of this kind multiply, and as its networks become fully global, there will be plenty of scope for agents in evaluat-

---

*At the moment, One2One covers Greater London, the West Midlands, the South Coast, and northwest England, but it plans to cover 90 percent of the U.K. population by the end of 1997.

ing competitive access providers and their costs. In fact, providers will increasingly become a diversified lot including resellers of simpler bandwidth, suppliers of end-to-end circuits, and operators of international gateways handling traffic from different carriers. There is plenty of room for knowledge artifacts and agile software-hardware solutions for profits.

CHAPTER 8

Agents in Network Reliability, Diagnostics, and Maintenance

The goal of a network is to provide the appropriate *infrastructure* for an increasingly intense communications environment. The network must be able to act as an *integrator* of attached resources* whether these are homogeneous or heterogeneous, making them available to the user community in a seamless and cost-effective manner. As private and public networks are interconnected into larger systems, we are increasingly facing situations calling for the effective integration of networks. The aim is that of developing *one logical network* able to service any and all multimedia communications requirements.

---

*See also the necessary architectural characteristics in Chap. 13.

Rigorous network design and *reliability* standards must guarantee the full availability of attached facilities. The protocols must be efficient, providing a distributed platform for current and new services. This must be done in such a way that the network provides to its users a strategic advantage.

Within the context discussed in the preceding paragraphs, first and foremost the use of agents aims to sharpen the network's cutting edge. Knowledge artifacts serve well the objective of using high technology to improve upon the management of computers and communications resources:

- Planning, implementing, and controlling network reliability
- Monitoring communications events taking place in real time
- Endowing the network control center with artifacts that assure quality of service

One way to look at a network in terms of planning and control reasons is as a structure of successive management layers like that shown in Fig. 8-1. Autonomous, learning agents will be most helpful at each layer and for each supported function also throughout the implementation topology and its local characteristics.

To steadily improve upon network reliability, tier 1 companies spend between 10 and 20 percent of the cost of the network on its management, including quality control, online diagnostics, and monitoring through knowledge artifacts. For leading firms, this strong commitment to the dependability of the network is based on studies that have been instrumental in determining that:

- When high technology is used, the company's competitiveness is improved while communications costs are swamped.
- If communications capacity were lost for a few hours, the experience would be financially painful.

The use of agents in network management allows companies to keep the adopted solution flexible and responsive to business requests. This increases the market appeal of the company's business and permits optimization of applications, making them more cost-effective.

As we will see later in this chapter, enriched by knowledge engineering, network control services have the overall objective of guaranteeing uninterrupted communications between end users. These may be *humans*, whether authors or device operators; *processes*, therefore programs; or *processors* and *storage media*, from network nodes to attached computers and communicating databases.

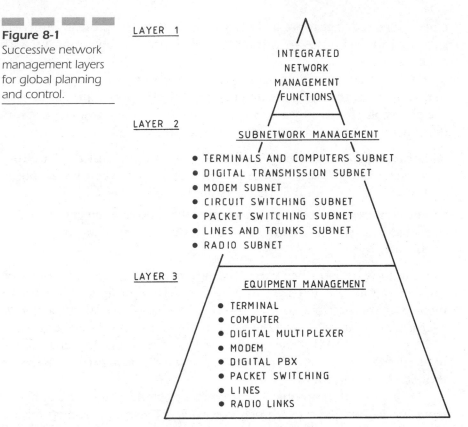

Figure 8-1
Successive network management layers for global planning and control.

The Gain from Using Learning Agents in Network Operations
==

The introduction to this chapter placed emphasis on reliability. As we will see, reliability is not an ability but a probability of nonfailure. Dr. John von Neumann speculated that one could design machines that, under suitable conditions, would repair themselves. But at his time, more than 50 years ago, a practical discussion was rendered difficult because the technology was not that far advanced to make this hypothesis possible.

According to the von Neumann hypothesis, human-made systems are operating with much more unstable materials than nature does: "A metal may seem to be more stable than a tissue, but if a tissue is injured, it has a tendency to restore itself, while our industrial materials do not have this tendency, or have it to a considerably lesser degree." But then von Neumann added: "I don't think, however, that any question of principle is involved at this point. This reflects merely the present, imperfect state of our technology—a state that will presumably improve with time."*

A notable advantage of agents in connection to rigorous network management is that they are independent of emotional questions or of the attention that at any particular moment is being paid to network dependability by people supposed to look after it:

■ The Number 1 problem with manual diagnostics is that their accuracy varies with the skills of the person exercising the control action, as well as with the mood of that person.

■ The Number 2 problem is that manual diagnostics, even activities supported by offline computers, cost too much money. They are not cost-effective.

Some 10 years ago when expert systems constituted the first practical implementation of artificial intelligence, AT&T designed and implemented at the network control center of Dallas—Fort Worth a knowledge artifact that supported the work of experienced network engineers. It did its job so well that the number of graduate engineers per shift was reduced from 7 to 1; an 85 percent reduction in personnel costs, which showed at the bottom line.

The use of autonomous, learning agents could improve upon that score, but it won't be a free lunch. Network managers are sometimes led to the erroneous notion that vendors are creating integrated network management systems that will do the whole job for them. Those who think so will be disappointed. What network managers really need is a global view that focuses on an integrated network management perspective. Figure 8-2 presents an example which emphasizes that operations and maintenance are only two of the key functions.

The use of agents able to learn from the day-to-day work they do is important because network management should be a preoccupation of a communications project: end to end and in life-cycle terms. Responsibilities start at the planning phase. Using von Neumann's reference as background, the principle is that support systems must ultimately repair themselves.

Agents can be written to bring this principle to life. One of the first tasks is to establish service-level agreements with the users, such as busi-

*F. Brody and T. Vamos (eds.), *The Neumann Compendium*, World Scientific, Singapore, 1995.

Figure 8-2
Integrated network management: necessary to support the whole life cycle of networked services.

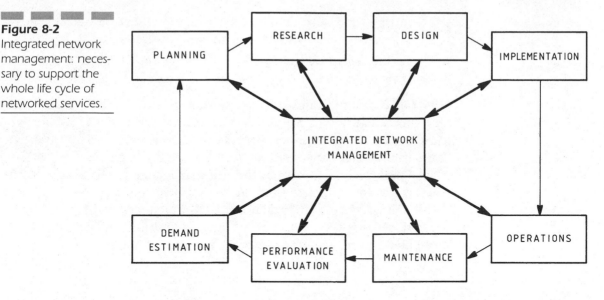

ness units and line manages. Topics covered in such agreements might include capacity, cost, reliability, response time, and other targets of specific business application.

Agents can interface among people and functions entering such agreement(s), as knowledge artifacts are instrumental in providing support for integrative functions, to be served by different network components in a coherent and efficient way. Part of the mission should always be to realize real cost savings through greater automation and fewer staff members.

Such artifacts cannot be bought off the shelf, at least not at the current state of the art. No single vendor, even the best at managing his or her own devices or software, can do the whole job for the user organization. The task is too complex, and vendors simply do not have competence in every area. Success in network management always depends on the particulars of the user environment.

Within a given environment, a concept such as network availability involves standards that each user organization defines in its own way, even if there is agreement that they generally fall into functional network management domains such as configuration, channel capacity, performance, reliability, security, and accountability:

■ Monitoring through agents the development in service demand, as suggested in Fig. 8-2, enables developers to anticipate and plan.

■ Measuring the volume and quality of network services makes it possible to verify the bills and hold people responsible.

■ Evaluating the service rendered by hardware and software components, by individual users, enables cost allocation to be corrected.

Classical communications software cannot do this job. All of the necessary functionality will never be available in software packages, nor will it ever be completely calibrated to standards. However, it is no less true that reliability standards are not the same for all companies.

Like performance measurement and management, reliability is a proprietary network characteristic. The way in which a user organization is able to manage its resources determines, to a large extent, its profits from network investments. That's how the contribution of learning agents should be seen versus the cost incurred in their development.

Network Reliability Standards

Reliability, as stated in the preceding section, is not an ability. It is the probability that under established operational conditions and for a specified period of time, a system, subsystem, or component will operate without failure. This definition is very important with all human-made systems and most particularly with mission-critical applications.*

From the rigorous studies that were done in the 1950s in the United States by Dr. Werner von Braun, Dr. Robert Lusser, and Dr. Erich Pieruchka on the reliability of guided missiles, there are today available mathematical tools which provide the basis for rigorous solutions in regard to network reliability. Mission-critical systems must be assigned requirements in terms of catastrophic failure probabilities through a process that involves:

■ Statistics on component and subsystem mortality, hence failure rates

■ Risk assessment for a given environment and application requirement

■ The allocation of a reliability factor—for instance, a failure rate of less than 1 per year

---

*See D. N. Chorafas, *Statistical Processes and Reliability Engineering*, Van Nostrand, Princeton, N.J., 1960.

Theoretically, failure rates can be checked by testing the product. Practically, tests for high-end reliability are at the boundary of what can be assured by means of laboratory-based evaluations. There is no alternative to online follow-up and analysis—a job agents can do very well:

- Collecting real-time statistics
- Mining quality databases
- Analyzing and testing
- Reporting their findings in real time

Networks are dynamic entities that must operate 24 hours a day, 7 days a week. Their configurations, their software-hardware components, and their traffic have an impact on reliability—and therefore they should be taken into account from the design level throughout the entire life cycle.

- Contrary to traditional techniques for dimensioning that assume stable traffic statistics, it is wise to collect and exploit dynamic information.
- Traffic models must be used to make feasible predictions on the expansion of network resources and the competitive evaluation of service-specific features.

Agents can have a dual role: as collectors of dynamic network statistics and as examiners of the content of the quality database kept by the network control center. Knowledge artifacts should be specialized by major area of responsibility. Figure 8-3 shows a solutions which I adapted in

Figure 8-3
All functions of a network should be supported through expert systems and agents.

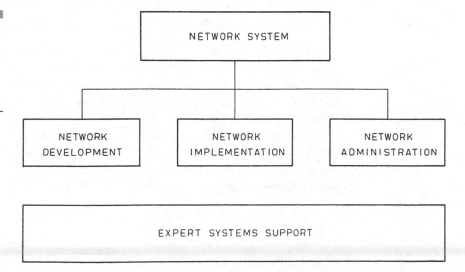

the late 1980s in the design of a financial network. At that time we were using static expert systems rather than dynamic agents.

Studies must be undertaken on the impact of multiple service provision such as traffic supervision, flow control, overload handling, rerouting, and fault management. Also studies should be made on the impact of ad hoc service creation like characterization of user traffic, user-network signaling under overload and congestion, and the like. Very important is an analysis of the impact of multimedia operations, and the study of changes to the media stream, used during the interactive presentation of information.

Both the security and the reliability mechanisms must be examined for their impact on traffic flows, replication strategies, modular structure of the system, failure-mode analysis, and fault detection and recovery. These are demanding tasks and they require knowledge artifacts to be sustained.

The relationship with quality of service and associated modeling should definitely be taken into account. In this domain, as in so many others, knowledge engineering can make a significant contribution— further documenting the wisdom of using intelligent agents.

But knowledge artifacts are not written in the abstract. It is therefore a legitimate question to ask what kind of reliability standards user organizations establish for their networks. There is no universal answer to this query, though leading companies tend to adopt the following benchmarks:

- 99.9 percent availability for digital circuits
- 99 percent availability for analog circuits
- 90 days or more mean time between failures (MTBF)
- 2 hours or less mean time to repair (MTTR)—hence restore—service

For any practical purpose, fault-tolerant hardware does not exist—in spite of vendor claims. Neither is software answering to that call. The catchword *fault-tolerant* is deviating attention from the real issue because the most crucial problem is a complex one, that is, *hardware and software reliability.**

In calculating the mean time between failures and mean time to repair of our network and its attached devices and systems, we must be conscious of the fact that low reliability can be a real killer. A target reliability for mission-critical systems is now set at:

- *1 FIT,* which stands for 1 failure in 10^9 hours

---

*See also D. N. Chorafas, *Handbook of Data Communications and Computer Networks,* 3d ed., McGraw-Hill/Tab Books, New York, 1991.

This metric is particularly crucial with massively parallel computers and large networks, where 10^6 processors would imply 1 to 10 failures per day. This is not seen as unreasonable if we have the technology to really manage it. Systems solutions, however, need:

- *Checkpoint computations,* which are not commonly implemented by network programmers
- *Agents and expert systems* for diagnostics, including the ability to quarantine faulty components

For reliability purposes, knowledge-enriched software must be developed and implemented to handle the growing challenges. Programming products for sophisticated system management must map faulty processors out of the address space and dynamically execute *reassignments.*

It is unwise to program links directly because we don't know if the wires are there—and, in case they are, for how long they will stay. Links may be virtual. In other terms, to manage our network in an able manner, we should be keen to change our past practices:

- We should employ knowledge artifacts to help us do a neat job.
- We must be able to virtually program the network.
- We should use reliability management procedures for dynamic component mapping.

Designing for reliability should follow a strategy of extreme simplicity with low component count redundancy. To do so, we need *algorithmic efficiency* to handle mission-critical communications components as well as to affect the necessary tradeoffs.

Such goals not only require a very careful network design, online registration, operational statistics, and experimentation but also sophisticated knowledge-enriched tools for *reliability analysis.* Understanding the causes helps to reduce the chances that the same types of reliability problems will recur repeatedly in the future. Both the agents and *we* must learn how to learn.

Facing the Risks That Exist with Human-Made Systems

With complex radio-and-fiber-optics networks, mobile communications, and personal digital assistants, risk assessment could demonstrate almost any type of conclusion, depending on the *assumptions* we make and the *frame of reference* we are using. Results obtained through risk assessment may also be employed for devious purposes, with parameters or interpretations influenced by company politics.

Quite often, an a priori assessment of risks and failure causes can be undone by carefully examining the audit trail. *Retrospective* studies should therefore aim at correcting risk evaluations that have been hindered by uncertainty. In the 1991 Middle East war, for instance, the Patriot missile was touted as highly successful, but in subsequent analyses, the estimates of its effectiveness were seriously downgraded, from about 95 percent to 13 percent. The reason given for such low performance was that the system had been designed to work under "much less stringent" conditions.

Like most business and industrial communications systems, those designed and implemented for the military have not been originally projected for real-time operations. They were not conceived for sustained deference in situations requiring a real-time response. As new requirements emerged, the *software* was rewritten for the mission, but the *hardware* was not changed.

As an example of what this means in practical terms, the clock drift over a 100-hour period resulted in a tracking error of 678 meters and was blamed for the Patriot missing the Scud missiles it was supposed to kill.

Nevertheless, while failures always can and do happen, there are significant potential benefits from using advanced software—such as agents—and a sound system infrastructure. Still, we have to keep in mind that the extent to which such effort can provide results tends to vary from one case to another, often dramatically. Much depends on how long-term considerations have been factored into realistic analyses of:

- Costs
- Benefits
- Risks

Reliability and security in connection to real-time performance requirements must be thoroughly anticipated to be effectively analyzed in regard to the behavior of a complex system. As I will never tire repeating, reliability must be built in during the design phase, with clearly defined requirements for:

- Day-to-day maintainability

- Longer-term availability
- Component reusability

This means that for all factors on which failure risks may depend, we have to consider a priori the possible range of variation that would result during adversity in operations. Short of this, deficiencies are very difficult to overcome a posteriori, and therefore they will subsequently come back to haunt us.

The subjects of which we are talking are not new. What is new is the realization that while many designers do their best, big systems cannot be effectively approached through largely manual solutions or even by means of classical CAD:

- Knowledge artifacts that work interactively are necessary to guide the designer's hand.
- Assisting in every step of the design process, agents must mine databases and report on performance tests.

An equally important issue concerns the attention that should be paid to the choice of components and their eventual replacement. Figure 8-4 presents statistics from IBM's banking terminal 3600 and its successor 4700. Notice the difference in number of failures over 30 months after each terminal's market introduction.

Figure 8-4
Strategy in system design: failures at least as low as those replaced.

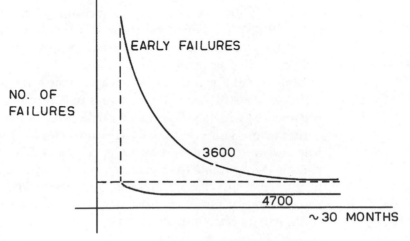

In all the work that we do in connection to network reliability, we have to keep in mind that there are still enormous gaps between theory and practice. Much of this is due to intrinsic limitations of technology and of the people who use it. An added factor is the complexity of solutions we are after.

- Big systems are not small systems that grew over time.
- Communications networks are big systems whose specific requirements are in a constant state of change.*

There are many examples of computers and software being improperly matched to one another and to a particular situation. Serious failures have involved an unwillingness to believe a diagnosis indicating anomalous events, as well as annoyance with critiques on performance and pitfalls in designing a system to meet critical needs.

Experience shows that even the most carefully projected network may have serious flaws or include component parts that are being misused. Therefore, agents can provide able assistance in technical auditing. Classical testing and formal verification can have deficiencies, such as the:

- Intrinsic incompleteness of on-time testing
- Difficulties of carrying out a thorough verification

At the same time, given well-defined and reasonable reliability requirements, talented and diligent people with adequate financial and physical resources can build networks that satisfy stringent requirements most of the time—over relatively short timeframes.

It is good to remember that, as technology rapidly evolves, even the best reliability solutions tend to be relatively short range. In the longer run, fully guaranteed behavior is not possible to achieve—and this is independent of whether or not we use people in the operational loop. Reliability could be improved with agents' mining quality databases.

People are still needed, albeit in small numbers, because there are inherent risks in relying on software systems operating under critical requirements. This is especially true in complex cases controlling real-time environments. But unreliability is also a fact with human components. It is impossible to foresee all potential disasters, and it is often the unforeseen events that are the most destructive. These tend to bring up a combination of circumstances involving both people and computers, working in a noncoordinated fashion.

---

*See also the section on AT&T's time out later in this chapter.

Hence, while we must anticipate the occurrences of catastrophes in using computer systems in critical applications, we must also be flexible with our solutions. What many communications experts fail to appreciate is that agents can be a great help in assuring the needed flexibility.

The drawback with high-tech solutions is that many communications and data processing professionals are very slow in adopting new concepts and practices. This is true even if prototyping and knowledge artifacts present very interesting possibilities that could lead to results that are realistic. Cultural change too often proves to be the bottleneck.

Software Reliability in Telecommunications: AT&T's 9-Hour Time Out

Mid-December 1989, AT&T installed new software in 114 switching systems of the Number 4ESS class. The goal was to reduce the overhead required in signaling between switches. But then a workhorse 4ESS switch in lower Manhattan malfunctioned and sent out trouble messages to others across the country.

At the root of this failure was a particular *improvement* which, design-wise, made sense. After successful recovery from a failure, a switch was supposed to signal to other switches an implicit recognition of having resumed traffic. But there was a latent flaw in the recovery-recognition message from the previously affected switch to the other switches in the neighborhood. The avalanche came in a month's time when, on January 15, 1990, one of the switches experienced abnormal behavior. It signaled that it could not accept further traffic, recovered, and then resumed sending traffic. A second switch accepted the message from the first switch and attempted to reset itself.

Quite unexpectedly, this well-intended software improvement ended in a nightmare in AT&T's long-distance network. With this, every network operator and every telecom was reminded of just how fragile a software-based communications system can be. Traffic on the network slowed to a crawl as malfunctioning code turned a routine procedure into a long disruption. As public networks grow in complexity, they also become more vulnerable. Software problems are almost inevitable and they can happen on every network at any time.

The crash of AT&T's long-distance network has been all the more of an eye-opener because of the exceptional standards of quality the company has set for itself—which are, by and large, observed.

At first, it was not clear if it was a computer virus, a hacker, sabotage, or just overburdened exchanges that caused such widespread blockage on the network. Then, the fault was diagnosed as a software bug in the common channel signaling Number 7 systems that form the backbone of digital telephone networks.

AT&T put up a remarkable effort in responding to the time out. But what took place is a dramatic example of how the national economy, as well as the world economy, depends on the efficient operation of telecommunications.

Network breakdowns are obviously not unique. The same can happen with computer systems. As we saw in Chap. 5, in 1986 the Bank of New York suffered a major failure in its computers and could not deliver securities for 28 hours. This obliged it:

- To borrow $20 billion from the Federal Reserve for 1 day at the cost of $50 million
- To face an estimated aftermath of $0.05 per share in earnings in the fourth quarter of 1986

Ironically, the software bug that brought AT&T's network to a crawl was put into service as part of the company's efforts to improve its performance. The improvements that, as we saw in the beginning of this section, started in mid-December 1989, were intended to shorten the time of network reconfiguration to the level of 1 or 2 seconds.

The default procedure that is followed in such cases with telephone systems is routine: The switch taking itself out of service signals to another switch to stop sending in traffic. This procedure, however, backfired because of the software defect. A cascade of events took place when the second switch shut itself down, and it signaled a third switch, which notified another switch and then shut itself down, and so on.

In the short span of 20 minutes, all 114 of the 4ESS switches on the AT&T network were jammed. Monitoring the signaling networks provided evidence that the Signaling System 6 (SS6) network was operating normally. This led the control center to conclude the problem was with the Signaling System 7 (SS7).

Agents can make a significant contribution in early diagnosis. Indeed, in AT&T's case, this early diagnosis saw to it that in spite of the SS7 time out, the company's network was able to complete about 50 percent of attempted calls. Old technology can still render a good service, at least as a backup. The lesson to be learned is that no network is foolproof, and

TABLE 8-1

Milestones in the AT&T Experience from Failure to Recovery

1. *Monday, January 15, 1990, 2:25 p.m.*
   Switch trouble noted at AT&T Network Operations Center, Bedminster, New Jersey.

2. *2:45 p.m.*
   Network blockage spreads. Bell Laboratories called in. Some processes put on manual control.

3. *4:30 p.m.*
   Problem pinpointed to SS7 network. Network traffic sent to SS6 trunks.

4. *7:00 p.m.*
   Bell Laboratories prepares a set of software overwrites.

5. *10:00 p.m.*
   Software overwrites sent and uploaded online to switches nationwide.

6. *Wednesday noon, January 17, 1990*
   The AT&T network is again functioning normally.

no solution can give 100 percent guarantees. But there can be a well-organized effort to overcome the accident when it happens.

Table 8-1 shows the milestones from failure to recovery in connection to this example. As we saw in the preceding section, like all human-made systems, networks do not operate at 100 percent reliability. Network administrators must always be on alert.

Prior to the AT&T time out, there was the worm that brought down almost the entire Internet in the United States. Both these cases, and many others, suggest the need for technical and legal safeguards, as well as the necessity to carefully study third-party liability for damages. This is another reason why the use of agents as database miners comes into the spotlight.

There is need not only to determine the legal and contractual relationship between network operators and users but also to exploit the letter of the law and the contractual clauses when an accident happens. Tier 1 companies have been successfully using agents on matters of compliance for some time.

Applying Lessons Learned from the Time Out to Other Communications Systems

In the early days of telephony, connections were made by operators who plugged wires into switchboards. Since the time of the Strowger switch, this process has been automated, but the automation process came in stages. Here is a reminder of the most important milestones:

- In 1891, the first automatic—but electromechanical—dial system was patented by a Kansas City undertaker, Almon B. Strowger.

- Also electromechanical but an improved version was the Step-by-Step switching system, first installed in smaller cities by Western Electric in 1921.

- The Number 1 Crossbar was introduced in 1938, but it did not become popular as new technology in switching centers until after World War II.

- This was followed by Crossbars Number 3, Number 4, Number 4A, Number 4A/ETS, Number 5, and then by Crossbar Tandem.

- Software control first came in May 1965 when Number 1 ESS was first put into service by AT&T.*

- Number 1 ESS was followed by Number 2, Number 2B, and Number 3—but the real explosion in software switching came after the 1968 Carterphone Decision by the Federal Communications Commission (FCC).

By lowering the monopolistic walls in telephony, at least in the United States, the Carterphone Decision unleashed a Golden Horde of software products, bringing computers and software in a big way into the network—from regional switching centers and city centers to private branch exchanges (PBXs).

That's the history. Now let's look at the mechanics. The tones that telephones produce as callers dial numbers activate a series of computers at telephone switching facilities. They can as well activate agents leading them to:

- Search databases
- Select specific routes
- Avoid congested trunk lines
- Make other fairly complex decisions

Knowledge engineering is important because this can happen for millions of calls at a time. The most complex software ever written in the world is *switching software*. Classical programming would not do the needed job. We have to use the most advanced software concepts.

---

*Bell Telephone Laboratories, *Engineering and Operations in the Bell System*, Western Electric, Indianapolis, Ind., 1977.

But all machines and all software modules can fail. The irony of what happened with the AT&T 9-hour blackout is that the first switch recovered quickly and sent out a burst of backlogged calls. That was a valid design decision, but the burst overwhelmed the second switch, which needlessly shut itself down because of a bug in its program.

If agents had been used in this connection, diagnosis and recovery might have come faster. With manual searching and testing, it was nearly midnight before engineers stamped out the bug by sending overriding software to the switches. It took some time to diagnose the cause of the failure, which is a prerequisite to correcting it, and the failure had a snowball effect: The same problem that hit the first switch propagated iteratively to all other switches.

The bug problem manifested itself in subsequent simulations whenever a second message arrived within too short a period of time, estimated to be of about 4 seconds. The problem was finally analyzed and eliminated by reducing the messaging load of the network, after the 9-hour, nationwide blockade.

Autonomous learning agents might have been instrumental in sorting out this problem as the bug that caused all the trouble was nothing special. It arrived in software that was loaded into the company's long-distance switches, and it was embedded in the kind of upgrade that AT&T makes often.

As if to document that testing is no cure for everything, this bug had eluded three layers of testing, lying dormant for over a month until a confluence of conditions brought it to life. A minor programming change triggered a catastrophe.

Industry experts say the potential for such cascading damage is inherent in the network features of Common Channel Signaling System Number 7, a high-speed message system that identifies a path for a call by *asking* switches whether they are free to handle it. This approach was selected because it slashes the time needed to set up a call, and it also makes possible services such as automatic credit card verification.

Reportedly, the cause of AT&T's long-distance service shutdown was traced to a C language program that contained a *break* statement within an *if* clause nested within a *switch* clause. The intervening *if* clause was in violation of expected programming practice, but the origin does not need to be ascribed to the programmer. It might as well lie with the computer or the compiler.*

---

*Communications of the ACM, vol. 33, no. 7, July 1990.

TABLE 8-2

Accidents per Million Departures Involving Loss of Aircraft (Excluding Military Incidents or Sabotage)

McDonnell Douglas DC-10	2.52
Airbus A320 and A321	1.73
McDonnell Douglas DC-9	1.21
Boeing 747-400	1.19
Boeing 737-100/200	1.15
Lockheed L1011	0.91
Boeing 737-300/400/500	0.62
McDonnell Douglas MD-80	0.51

This type of software failure can happen with any human-made system, aircraft being another example. All kinds of aircraft are today software controlled, and they have a very different track record in terms of accidents. Accidents per million departures for different aircraft types are shown in Table 8-2.[*]

The statistics in Table 8-2 are not telling about only mechanical failures. They are compound, involving as well software bugs and human error. Originally it had been said that the cause for the crash of the Birgen Air 757[†] was most likely instrument failure. But then it was found out that human error played the major part.

According to the black box, which was finally recovered, the plane did not climb fast enough while the instruments showed it did. Air turbulence on top of the wings saw to it that the plane nose-dived. The pilot probably panicked or was not trained enough to attempt an eleventh-hour rescue. Knowledge artifacts do not panic, and agent technology might be of service in eleventh-hour cases.

Fault Tolerance and the Cost of Network Failures to the Users

In computers, communications, and software, the concept of fault tolerance is a vital process. It emerged in the late 1960s as an attempt to produce reliable enough solutions in connection to weapons systems. At the

---

[*]Newsweek, September 11, 1995.

[†]The Turkish airline that took off from the Dominican Republic with German tourists aboard.

time, the need was for designs that would keep systems going even after a fault occurred. The system needed to behave:

- In a fail-soft manner
- With minimum degradation of service
- Without corruption or loss of data

The first commercially available fault-tolerant option was the Tandem Nonstop System released in 1976. When working correctly, each attached processor would send a regular message down the bus identifying its uptime status.

With message exchange, it was the job of the operating system to detect whether a module had become inoperative by the absence of such message(s). But this solution is not easily portable to all computer aggregates because of differences that exist in architectures. Multiprocessor systems can be either:

- Loosely coupled
- Tightly coupled

Both can be served by agents but of different types. A *loosely coupled* fault-tolerant aggregate consists of a minimum of two semi-independent processors interconnected by a dual high-speed bus. Each processor runs its own operating system and has its own memory and input/output controllers.

In a loosely coupled system, each processor shares multiported peripheral controllers with at least one other processor as in the Tandem Nonstop architecture. By contrast, with *tightly coupled* architectures there is the risk that a failure would propagate, closing down the whole system.

Telephony is, by its nature, a tightly coupled architecture. Generally, in computer systems of this type no pairing or load balancing is required between individual processors. Each processor can access the entire database without involving other processors. But there is a difference between hardware and software supports. In a hardware sense, any similar unit backs up a failed device. But in terms of software, all similar units have the same programming modules—though different types of systems might back up one another.

This, as we saw earlier, happened with the backup of the SS7 by the older and less sophisticated SS6. A significant improvement can, however, be made through the introduction and use of autonomous agents as testers, able to learn by experience, as shown schematically in Fig. 8-5.

Along this frame of reference, agents have been successfully developed

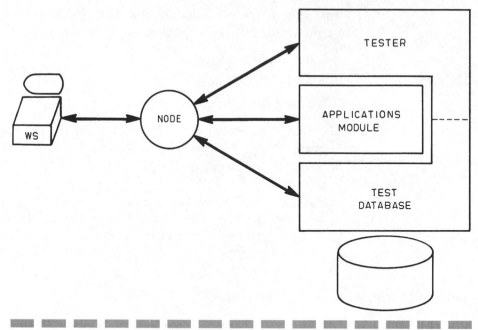

Figure 8-5   A tester program is not enough. There should also be a test database.

and used by Network General Corp. for network analysis reasons. They help in solving performance problems characterized by a great deal of network-connected information and plenty of choices in terms of a possible course of action.

One of the agents discussed at Comdex Fall 1996 is a protocol analyzer running on workstations (WSs). In terms of networked applications, its domain of competence is typically the client-server type. The client may be:

■ A Web browser address

■ A remote file server

■ Another device

A different network agent deals with problems associated to network switches. In fact, a whole family of agents has been designed to use service databases and monitor traffic and to follow up on network performance and automatically adjust to thresholds.

Network General has developed a *network object model* that understands interconnection of all objects connected to the network. It provides a correlation of alarms across multiple items, and it also understands how system performance relates to network features and status information.

In this and similar applications, in the background of a knowledge-enriched implementation, lies the fact that today's large client-server networks, and the processes running on them, create a complex performance analysis problem:

■ Information overload sees to it that we need a multitier analysis, through intelligent agents able to correlate this data.

■ Interactive knowledge engineering artifacts have a vital role to play both in middleware and at the clients and servers.

In Network General's implementation, middleware downloads to agents when performance degradation is noticed. The agents gather information on system processes, perform end-to-end, response-time measurements, and actively implement performance-tuning modifications. Agents may also modify priorities of system processes in a proactive way. They know how to affect the operation of the database server or Web server.

Middleware agents may modify parameters in the routers and switches. They do so by understanding how the system performs and which traffic factors relate to network efficiency. They are as well able to modify *priorities* in the system in order to assume that first-priority functions get through ahead of others.

Agents in Electronic Commerce and in Daily Business

Because of the competitive advantages they offer to their users, agents are increasingly employed in electronic commerce. Typically, they are able to move from one node to another, bringing with them encapsulated data and rules that allow them to negotiate on behalf of their owner issues connected to electronic transactions.

It is generally expected that before the year 2000, which essentially means within the next 3 years, agent technology will pervade information technology. By doing so, knowledge artifacts will change desktop working practices and, with them, many of the support services in the office and at home:

- Agents will arrange meetings, keep calendars, and manage time schedules.

- Agents will explore databases and libraries, retrieving the information their master wants from online sources.

- Agents will also constantly carry out repetitive tasks, enriching them with intelligence.

Agent technology will alter the way in which today we conceive workflow applications, and it will provide flexible, easily updated process automation. As we saw in the preceding section, in the example with Network General, agents will be instrumental in telecommunications, helping to develop enhanced services on the Internet, the intranets, and the extranets.

Precisely for these reasons companies such as AT&T, US Sprint, and British Telecommunications have begun to bring on-stream key products based on knowledge artifacts and associated technology. US Sprint, for example, has designed *Clearline*, a wide area network supervision application. Clearline uses an intelligent agent to:

- Correlate alarms

- Detect the origins of failures in communications

In the preceding section, we examined the services provided by AT&T agents in connection with fault detection capabilities (see also Fig. 8-5). The agent in each attached workstation or other processor—and in the network's nodes—checks for all types of errors or malfunctioning and takes appropriate action if a fault is discovered.

This kind of proactive action significantly improves system integrity—that is, the degree to which it tolerates faults which, when processed by normal software on the network, will produce failures. Agents can help in:

- Online detection and diagnosis

- Fault tolerance through the isolation of errors, hence confinement

- The prevention of further damage

- Recovery by restoring a stable, consistent system state

Such solutions evidently cost money, but failures are even more costly. A record 148 million phone calls had been attempted during AT&T's 9-hour outage. This was 3 million more than the previous record during the San Francisco earthquake of October 1989. Confused and frustrated callers tried repeatedly to get through. When the dust settled, it turned out that AT&T had gotten off easy.

Owing to the observance of Martin Luther King Day, many offices were closed, and business calling was light. While all publicly switched, long-distance traffic—including toll-free 800 lines—was affected by the time out, dedicated private lines were not. This left important government and some business communications intact.

Certain companies fared worse than others. The 800 service of American Express was badly snarled, leading the company to consider spreading its business among several carriers. Similarly, MasterCard's point-of-sale authorizations were severely hampered, affecting merchants seeking approval for credit card purchases.

All of the $30 billion communications systems of du Pont were affected, and when the company lost access to its phones, data transmissions between its R&D operations and its Cray supercomputer were lost. Days later, MIS and telecom staff at the Wilmington, Delaware, du Pont headquarters were still assessing the impact. At the same time, Marriott hotels were getting only 10 percent of their usual volume, though the company uses MCI for 800 calls. And Arizona Telemarketing, which places 4000 to 9000 calls a day, sent its 40 employees home.

There have evidently been marketing aftermaths. Although outright customer defections were few, both Sprint and MCI reported a surge of inquiries regarding their services, and MCI noted a substantial increase in calls over its network in the 48 hours following the debacle.

However, all told, AT&T got a good grade in handling the whole issue, both from a public relations and from an engineering viewpoint. Could all that snarl happen again? The answer is *yes!* No carrier and no users are immune from a repeat of the 9 hours of chaos that gripped America's long-distance network. The shocking aspect of the outage, and the reason for believing it might not be the last, is how routinely it began—and how far-reaching were the consequences.

Improving Software Functionality through Knowledge Engineering

Major snarls like AT&T's 9-hour outage don't happen every day. However, the experience of leading telephone companies, during the last 10 years, demonstrates that day-to-day network troubleshooting, diagnostics, and maintenance are all textbook cases for the advantages presented by knowledge engineering.

Twenty-four-hour availability definitely calls for the automation of diagnostic reasoning and the use of expertise embedded in agents. Such applications capitalize on the fact that most network equipment emits a stream of status information through a secondary channel, which typically ends in a printed report.

Hence, diagnostics information is available in a standardized, consistent format—even if on an awkward medieval medium. But the existence of the printer port makes expert system interfaces easier to build, while at the same time an integrated agent application can actually intervene:

■ Switching traffic to fallback lines

■ Bringing backup equipment into operation

There is enough experience that has been built up over the years in telecommunications, through expert systems, to talk in a factual and documented manner about what can be achieved with agents. An example is *Compass* by General Telephone and Electronics (GTE).* It performs analysis of diagnostic messages of telephone switching. The knowledge artifact:

■ Examines maintenance logs from central offices

■ Suggests appropriate maintenance action

Compass is operational in many GTE telephone operating companies, providing guaranteed diagnostics and maintainability of existing switches. Its knowledge bank has captured expertise from the best telephone engineers employed by the firm—and the expert system industrialized this expertise.

Another GTE knowledge artifact is *Prophet.* This is an acronym for *Proactive Rehabilitation of Output Plant using Heuristic Expert Techniques.* Prophet is a troubleshooter for telephone lines and terminals, and its contribution is to:

■ Assist in trouble analysis

■ Help control center staff in identification of local loop problems

■ Interface to GTE operating systems for preventive maintenance

Another expert system, known as *Proactive Management for Customer Access Facilities,* identifies bad sections of cable that may need repair or

---

*In Chap. 10, we will use Compass as a case study on how to build up an expert system—and by extension an agent.

replacement. As these examples help document, telephone companies are eager to bring high technology to the local loop level.

Until recently, the main impact of technological change has been on long-distance calls. Now, however, a significant amount of interest is being focused on the classical local loop. This connection links the end user to the nearest exchange and is usually made with a twisted pair of copper wires, a technology unchanged for almost 120 years. Improvements are urgently needed because:

- Local distribution accounts for roughly 80 percent of a network's costs.
- Current estimates indicate that it costs around $1200 to $2000 to connect a new customer with copper wire.

Such investments are still made even if less expensive and more flexible alternatives have become available. For instance, a less costly way is to run telephone services over the same system as cable television.

Also, breakthroughs in laser design achieved in the late 1980s make it possible to send analog television pictures along optical fibers. Furthermore, optical fiber solutions make sense because both telephone and cable systems have increasingly acquired optical-fiber backbones.

The other alternative is the use of wireless transmission.* Wireless has great flexibility and fairly low cost, allowing the development of networks competing directly with fixed wires. It is estimated that if local telecos were to rebuild virtual local loops with radio, the cost will be about $800 per subscriber.

But whether we talk of twisted pair, coaxial cable, optical fibers, or wireless, knowledge artifacts are necessary to beef up the quality of service. Network operators should be satisfied with nothing less than the best—and agents can make a significant contribution to quality, as we will see in the following section when we talk of network control center functions.

The Challenging Task of a Real-Time Network Control Center

Problems connected to network control centers (NCC) interest telephone companies, network operators, information providers, and user organiza-

---

*See also D. N. Chorafas, *High Performance Networks, Personal Communications and Mobile Computing*, Macmillan, London, 1997.

tions. Satellite operators and wireless communications solutions at large are also impacted.

To the user organization, a network control center provides a wealth of functions, which can be appreciated within the context of day-to-day network operations. Many organizations give to the NCC not only control but also planning functions that require provision of:

- Statistical and historical information on the management of a network's configuration
- Resource utilization references, including bottlenecks and uptime and error rates
- Other performance data on network devices, including switches and communications lines

The pillars on which NCC duties rest are shown in Fig. 8-6. These involve networkwide supervisory activities executed through testing lines, switches, modems, data terminating equipment (DTE), software, and information elements. An NCC should support journaling and security,

Figure 8-6
A network control center (NCC) rests on three pillars.

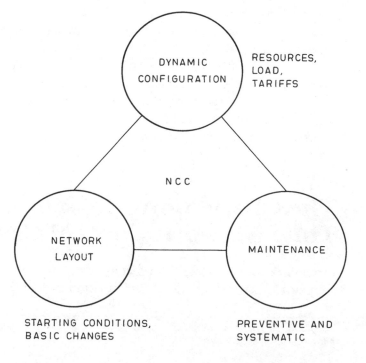

as well as quality control of databases. This is best done with knowledge artifacts able to make:

- Playbacks
- Real-time analyses

The network control center should provide for fail-soft action, which is tantamount to assuring data for dimensioning studies, and also for restart and recovery. Autonomous learning agents can contribute to every one of these functions, most particularly to:

- *Supervisory activities:* Downloading, loopback, and fault detection
- *Quality history:* Analysis, experimentation, and suggested corrective action
- *Projections of possible failures:* Identification, provision of bypass, and parallel synchronization

Other functions in which agents can be of assistance are the assurance of a consistent image of network operations, personalized to the end user; the online evaluation of reliability, availability, and uptime of the network and its components; and security and protection issues, of which we have spoken in Chap. 5.

The operating facilities to be followed up by agents will generally focus on constant monitoring of network resource status, gathering of information on the operating conditions of different devices and lines, and securing the efficient operation of all attached devices and software modules. The maintenance requirements will include:

- Continuous logging of facts and figures
- Loopbacks and other tests done to locate any errors being encountered
- Intelligence-enriched trouble and fault diagnostics
- Preventive maintenance for greater network reliability

Most of these activities are known from the more classical network operations, but complex wired-wireless setups, as well as wireless systems, require still more sophisticated approaches. Because overall network reliability of a radio-and-fiber-optics structure becomes enormously critical, the use of artificial intelligence can be instrumental in assuring a higher network reliability. Therefore, it comes as no surprise that tier 1 corporations are:

- Building agents for error analysis and error prediction, and error control
- Using simulators for terminal emulation, line and node management, and intelligent database access

Knowledge engineering artifacts are used to provide friendly interfaces, support advanced graphics, and assist in overall automation of operations. They also contribute to network testing procedures—both of total structure and of selected parts of the communications system.

"There used to be a case when the network was very simple," stated a senior telecommunications executive during our meeting. "It was just dumb terminals. But now we must care for intelligent machines, provide sophisticated services, develop and employ powerful software. It's a different ballgame."

Though NCC solutions vary from one company to another, some of the more advanced organizations have adopted a sophisticated network management structure. Their strategy is device independent and vendor independent, aimed to provide integrated management functions through:

- Control databases
- Knowledge artifacts
- Intelligent interfaces

As we have seen through a number of references, this supports handling of network diagnostics and maintenance in a multivendor environment. However, not all companies follow this approach—and those who don't have the higher costs and a larger number of troubles.

Old school friends are too much attached to their preferred vendor to capitalize on the opportunities offered by agents and by an open architecture. Blinded by the vendor, they are awfully unaware of what technology now offers in terms of network reliability and of the major cost benefits they can gain through an open vendor policy—as well as through the analytical approaches technology makes possible.

PART 3

Applying Agent Technology in Business

CHAPTER 9

Boelter's Agents

In his keynote lecture to Comdex Fall 1996, Bill Gates mentioned *agents* as one of the main issues that will characterize the coming years in the industrial and business use of computers. For instance, in connection to Office 97, Microsoft has embedded Outlook—an agent acting as a personal information manager with e-mail, calendaring, and group scheduling. In this as in practically all other present-day applications, agents perform as the end user's assistants. They also increasingly become animated characters. In Microsoft's case, there is a choice of nine agents, including Einstein and a perky paper clip that offers tips.

Bill Gates thinks that in the coming years computers could understand how their masters work and learn from them in an implicit fashion. Workstation software would adapt to individual users' needs and requirements, learning automatically from the way people actually interact with their computers.

Such adaptation can nicely be based on the user's profile, as well as on other criteria relating to the workplace—whether local or remote. Just as important is the development of self-healing hardware and software features. If there is a problem with a machine, it should be intelligent enough to automatically identify a failing part or retrieve a software upgrade across the network by acting as an autonomous engine.

Efforts toward machine intelligence are laudable, and time will tell if the projected breakthroughs become real. The probability that this happens is proportional not just to the mathematics we built into our artifacts but as well to the background of their developers in the humanities, and to the developers' ability to embed into their constructs much more than mechanics.

This sounds as a strange, if not provocative, statement. But even more awkward is the resistance to accepting the role the humanities can play in the evolution of technology. "The philosophical bent in Part 3 would be more accepted by a European audience than in the USA," I was advised. "[It] may not be accepted by the American techno-business [public]."

To say that I will be sad if this rejection of the humanities indeed proves to be the case is to state the obvious. But beyond that, my writing about the need to bring philosophy, and more generally the humanities, into technology is not exactly my own finding. I learned it in 1953 as a graduate student at UCLA from my professor L. M. K. Boelter, who was the dean of the Department of Engineering.

Dr. Boelter often lamented that students came to engineering without a background in humanities because he saw that this is a handicap in their study of technology. Rigorous learning of engineering as a discipline needs to be broad based, polyvalent, and crossdisciplinary.

We must be paying attention not only to the nuts and bolts of engineering design but also to philosophy and history—including the history of science. This is one of the most valuable lessons I have ever learned, and it is a professional responsibility to transmit and explain Boelter's dictum.

The Source of Creativity: Not Agents, but Ourselves

"One is somehow impoverished by looking up the answer, or asking somebody to find it for him," L. M. K. Boelter taught his students, "because as we should appreciate for every person personal accomplishment is found in creativity. There is both pleasure and pride that accompanies creative tasks."

Boelter's dictum is valid with all scientific problems, not just computers, and with many managerial problems as well. The difficulty in following this advice is primarily conceptual: Except in rare cases we have not been taught and have not been trained to be truly creative. Instead, disincentives are put to creativity. Those who challenge the "obvious" are often taken as heretics.

One of the examples the old master of UCLA's Department of Engineering would take to show the pleasure of creativity, and the results, was how our society has developed scientific laws and how vulnerable these may be to new findings. Even minute new evidence, let alone evidence that is factual and documented, can knock out widely accepted scientific law and postulates. This is the bridge which links science to philosophy, as we will see in the following section.

Dr. Boelter took as an example the laws of thermodynamics. The first law, thermodynamics, also known as the "conservation of energy," states that energy can be neither created nor destroyed. The first was conceived in the 1840s by Hermann von Helmholtz. In a way, it is the easiest of the three to understand, and it held its own over time.

The second law of thermodynamics governs the direction of the flow of heat. It holds that during every transformation of energy, a certain amount is dissipated. Therefore, it is unavailable for doing work. The third law of thermodynamics is the science of heat. It essentially dictates that no object can reach the state of absolute zero. As we will see, this is the weaker law of the three.

The second law was originally formulated in 1850 by Rudolf J. Clausius, and it stood on its own as a separate thermodynamic principle. But it also evolved over time. In 1872, Ludwig Boltzmann identified atomic disorder as an essential thermodynamic quantity and restated the second law of thermodynamics in its current form:

In any physical system, disorder increases naturally, and work is always required to reserve this trend.

Boltzmann's major contribution, which has a direct relevance to the development and use of agents, was in showing how disorder, as expressed on the atomic level, relates to heat flow. The basis for this discrepancy is to be found in the *statistical nature of order:*

■ In any system, whether in physics or in a business organization, because of a great number of possible configurations, disorder is more probable than order.

■ The odds against molecular order in gases, liquids, and solids—or in products, markets, and organizational units—are so high that over time increased disorder is virtually certain.

Anyone who thinks he or she has circumvented either of these two laws of thermodynamics, Boelter taught his students, would be considered frivolous unless he or she provides solid proof. But then Boelter took exception to the third law of thermodynamics, which is not as well understood as the other two.

The third law was formulated in 1906, by Walther Nernst. For this, Nernst won the 1920 Nobel Prize in chemistry. Prior to formulating his law,* Nernst had to reach an understanding of absolute zero. The hypothesis he formulated is that:

Absolute zero (first discussed by the physicist Guillaume Amontons in 1699) signifies the absence of disorder.

But it does not necessarily require an absence of motion—which somehow seems to contradict the first hypothesis.

According to this understanding, which in essence is a tentative statement, the approach toward absolute zero is one of perfect order. In this path, each successive step is more difficult in its execution than the preceding one. Embedded in this approach is the concept that the described relationship is no accidental property; it is an attribute of all matter.

Or is it not so? As an answer, take notice of the concept which, in 1953, I learned from Llewelyn Boelter: Any hypothesis is based on suppositions that may or may not be true. Therefore, in connection to the third law, he added the statement that physics may have other secrets which we have not yet discovered—though we might be in the process of doing so.

---

*Which software developers often fail to do regarding the constructs that they build.

Dr. Niels Bohr phrased the same concept a little differently: "The opposite of a correct statement is a false statement. But the opposite of a profound truth may well be another profound truth," and the two profound truths might contradict one another.

Both Bohr and Boelter were right. In 1953 the dean of UCLA's Department of Engineering had no inkling of what would be the result of an experiment at another American university 44 years down the line. His reasons for challenging the "obvious" were of a philosophical nature.

If an experiment on absolute zero currently conducted at the University of Florida meets with success, *then* the third law of thermodynamics could be relegated to the graveyard of scientific history, like so many other laws.

"Divide and Solve": A Good Example of Cultural Change

As we have seen in the introduction to this chapter, Boelter's dictum has been that when current technology reaches a limit set by physical laws and when it breaks out of established design principles, there is no point in trying to bulldoze our way through it. The best strategy on how to proceed is to:

Circumvent the old structures by appreciating their limitations, and starting afresh along a different path, using the past to prognosticate the future.

This is what we should do with agents, and more generally with software. We should be smart enough to recognize that for the last 15 years we have been at the limits of what classical programming approaches can provide. If we don't learn from our past mistakes, we will be condemned to repeat them.

The use of agents in business and industry should not be seen as just a new departure but also as an opportunity to change our conceptual frame of reference. If we fail to do so, agents also will fail, and their impact will be lost in the dust of history.

Few people really appreciate the effects of cultural change on their profession, all the way to their everyday life. Yet, without cultural change, the tools we use become gimmicks that have no roots, and therefore they are short-lived.

To preempt the query of the reader who might ask: "What has this to do with *agents?*" the answer is that cultural change and the success of agents highly correlate. Are we looking at knowledge artifacts as a way for fast bucks or as a deeper cultural evolution with lasting effects on software technology?

Another valuable lesson L. M. K. Boelter taught his students back in the 1950s was the technique of dividing difficult problems into small, manageable ones. He repeatedly stated that this concept of "divide and solve" applies to many cases besides those amenable to numerical computation. I suggest that the reader follow this advice:

- The interactive intelligent artifacts that we use today are *Boelter's agents* because most of them abide by the "small-and-manageable" rule.
- "Divide and solve" is not just a good strategy for building complex software but as well a valid approach to most engineering and business problems.
- Small, flexible agents can be built in hours or days. Large monolithic Cobol programs take years to build, and often what they provide is substandard.

When we build huge software constructs by the book, we deny to ourselves the pleasure of creativity—and we rob the users of the programming product they need and its competitive advantages. Those developers of agents who emulate in their work bad practices established over the years with Cobol are preparing themselves for a great deception.

We gain a great competitive advantage by analyzing the lessons taught by the history of science. James Clerk Maxwell (1831—1879) once remarked: "It is when we take some interest in the great discoverers and their lives that [science] becomes endurable—and only when we begin to trace the development of ideas that it becomes fascinating."

One of the most fascinating stories I have heard on how the minds of great scientists works is Fermi's *piano tuners*. This is also one of the best examples of how to approach an order-of-magnitude solution in connection to a problem with many unknowns. In his teaching, Dr. Enrico Fermi asked his students: "How many piano tuners are there in Chicago?" Part and parcel of this question are:

- The improbability that anyone knows the answer
- The number of unknowns that it involves

This type of problem has no standard solution, and that's exactly the point Fermi wanted to bring into perspective. But it is possible to make assumptions leading to an approximate answer:

- *If* Chicago's population is 5 million, an average family consists of 4 people, and one-tenth of all families own pianos,
- *Then* there will be 125,000 pianos in the city, as an order of magnitude.

If every piano is tuned once every 5 years, 25,000 pianos must be tuned each year. If a tuner can service 4 pianos a day, 250 days a year, this will make a total of 1000 tunings a year. Therefore, there must be about 25 piano tuners in Chicago. This answer is not exact. The number of piano tuners could be as low as 15 or as high as 40. But as an order of magnitude, it is the right answer.

The metaphor of Fermi's piano tuners and Boelter's "divide-and-solve" strategy have much in common. Both show that even if at the outset the answer to a complex problem with many variables is unknown. There are ways to reach the problem's solution. We can proceed on the basis of different hypotheses. We then arrive at estimates that fall within an acceptable range. This is one of the secrets in building intelligent artifacts.

- *If* our hypotheses are nearly correct.
- *Then* calculation errors tend to cancel out one another.

As a whole, it is improbable that all of our errors will be overestimates or underestimates. The order of magnitude is the best strategy with difficult problems. This concept is part of the philosophy of science.

Deviations from the correct assumptions will tend to compensate for one another. Therefore, the final result will converge toward an order of magnitude that stands a good chance to be right. Think of Fermi's process when you contemplate a software system's design.

Those people who question the relevance of this chapter in a book on agents should take notice of Boelter's dictum, Fermi's approach, and Maxwell's thoughts. I heard a critique by a person who saw an early draft of this text that he "did not find between the pages the procedure needed to build an agent."

- Yet, the necessary procedure for building agents is not only between the pages but as well between the lines.
- Eighty percent of the solution of *any* problem is conceptual. The nuts and bolts make up the other 20 percent.

If we miss the conceptual part because we are in a hurry, because "it has not been invented here," because of disregard for fundamental issues of grand design, or for any other reason, then what we produce will be wanting. Sooner or later this will be found out. Abraham Lincoln once said: "You can cheat all of the people some of the time, or some of the people all of the time. But you cannot cheat all of the people all of the time." Agent developers should understand and appreciate Lincoln's dictum.

The Importance of Logos in Mathematics and Science

My advice is that philosophy and the humanities have a great deal to do with technology at large, and most specifically with agents. As explained earlier in this chapter, not only new tools but also a different culture are necessary to break the current software bottleneck.

This different culture is well reflected in the work of L. M. K. Boelter. A couple of people who read an early draft of this text have asked me how is it possible that in 1953 Dr. Boelter thought of agents? So to speak, at that time simple business-type computer applications did not even exist. The answer to this query rests on two pillars:

1. The late dean of the UCLA Department of Engineering always thought of *metaconcepts* in science, and the No. 1 quality of his teaching was his ability to give *perspective*.

2. In 1953, the new field of scientific investigation in business was *operations research* (OR), and Dr. Boelter was fascinated by OR.

Prior to writing this chapter, I consulted my notes from the UCLA years. With some surprise, I found out that a good deal of what Boelter said about the need for humanities and for philosophy to enrich the analytical spirit that should characterize operations research studies, fits hand-in-glove with agents. The fact that Boelter's thoughts on OR apply to agents, shows foresight and insight—as does all work characterizing a great scholar.

There is no better all-American example to substantiate Boelter's thinking that *philosophy and science are twins* than Benjamin Franklin. He is known as one of the founding fathers because he helped to write both the Declaration of Independence and the Constitution. But Benjamin Franklin also was:

■ A *scientist* whose experiments with electricity are known worldwide

- An *inventor* of the Franklin stove and the bifocals among other things
- A *philosopher* who founded the American Philosophical Society*

In his quest for a humanities background in technology, Dr. Boelter was very fond of ancient Greek philosophers. He was fascinated by their way of blending philosophical concepts with science. This, he used to say, helps to circumvent the argument that somehow surfaced earlier on in the twentieth century and still can be heard from time to time, that philosophy and metaphysics are not really rigorous scientists' stuff.

Mathematics, and especially geometry, was for Plato the example of pure reasoning. Mathematics provided an idealized, abstract, immutable way of looking at concepts and problems—detached from human affairs and close to absolute truth. To Plato's mind, mathematics was the perfect intellectual training for philosophers. No wonder than that the students of Plato's academy acquired a solid mathematical education. Among them was Aristotle, whose thinking dominated the physical sciences for nearly 2000 years.

This, however, was one viewpoint. In ancient Greece the opposite concept was taught by Isocrates, the orator, a man with great influence on historians, writers, and politicians. At the center of Isocrates's philosophy stood *logos*, the word:† Language has brought us together, founded cities, made laws, and invented arts. Language is what made us human.

The irony of this logos versus mathematics controversy is that while Plato insisted on the study of mathematics, from Aristotle's time until Sir Isaac Newton (1647—1727) and Gottfried Wilhelm Leibniz (1646—1716), physics was largely a narrative. Logos was at the kernel, at least in its beginning.

Logos has also been at the core of simulation and computation—from antiquity to our time. Archimedes discovered the law of the lever when he found that a balance beam is in equilibrium when the ratio of the weights is equal to the inverse ratio of the length of the lever arms. Like any other equation, this one expresses the likeness between two seemingly unrelated quantities: distance and weight. In this, as in so many other scenarios, until the law was phrased, the underlying likeness was hidden.

---

*The Autobiography of Benjamin Franklin, Wordsworth American Classic, Hertfordshire, U.K., 1996.

†Remember what Dr. Bohr said about a profound truth (p. 231). See also the section on Autonomy's agents later in this chapter.

In a similar manner, through his penetrating ability to perceive hidden relationships, understand their meaning, and therefore establish laws, James Clerk Maxwell noticed that the four known equations of electricity and magnetism nearly form a striking pattern. When he worked on the systems of signs and rules (which we call "mathematics") for the electric and magnetic fields, he got back almost the same equations he had started with:

- The algorithms Maxwell used showed him a hidden relation: The oscillating electric field gives rise to an oscillating magnetic field.

- This also works the other way around, which led Maxwell to realize that reciprocity could produce a state in which oscillating magnetic and electric fields could mutually sustain one another.

As in Archimedes's case, this conceptual discovery led Maxwell to two important applications of his theory. The prediction of the existence of *radio waves* and the explanation of the nature of *light*. Both are powerful theories of classical physics—and while both have been the subject of significant further evolution after Maxwell, at the beginning there was logos.

In the twentieth century, Albert Einstein developed his theory of gravity in a similar manner. He postulated his equations on the basis that they were simple and consistent. Experimental proof for the theory of relativity was almost entirely lacking in 1915. Only a tiny anomaly in the orbit of Mercury—one small piece of evidence—served as documentation for Einstein's bold vision.

- Ten years later, Dr. Werner Heisenberg depended on experimental evidence to validate Einstein's theory.

- What convinced him he was on the right path was the coherence of the master's approach.

Once again, some readers might ask what all this has to do with agents, and the answer is, a great deal. The examples I have just provided document Boelter's opinion that the humanities and the use of narratives (scenarios) are indivisible parts of science. They also follow Maxwell's dictum about the interest we should take in the lives of great discoverers.

As intelligent artifacts, agents should have a humanities background in their database, or at least a thesaurus accessible to them. They should not only learn from their masters and their peers but also from the lessons of history. We will never be able to program into an agent all that it needs to know. The major contribution of schools and colleges is to teach *how to learn*. And this should be also embedded into the intelligent artifacts we are building.

Software Research, Dependability, and Contrarian Thinking

Two research contracts from the U.S. Department of the Navy have been awarded to Software Productivity Solutions (SPS). Both are studies on leading-edge R&D. One of the contracts, "Tempus, A Realtime Measurement Project," aims to predict the performance of a real-time system early in its development. The other, "Rapid Application Prototyping and Development," applies a model-based architecture to support rapid prototyping.

Both real-time measurement and software prototyping address the needs of reducing development costs while improving system quality. From development to testing, and real-time usage, we can make profitable use of artifacts able to judge the dependability of other chunks of software. In this connection, agents can play a key role.

The technological part of the software dependability challenge is an old problem that goes back a long time. Its origins lie in fault tolerance. Like reliability, dependability of an artifact depends on the absence of significantly weak links. However, software systems today are riddled with weak links, even if they are supposed to be dependable programs. Apart from embedded bugs that escape testing, there are misuses that exceed the coverage of fault tolerance.

Procedural weaknesses can completely undermine the intended robustness of software. In terms of usage, the human part of the equation is always perplexing because anticipating all possible human behavior is very difficult.

The sort of problems that come up in basic software and in applications software do not necessarily mean that the human component is inherently unreliable. What this reference means is that the whole system of software development and usage leaves much to be wanted because it is not engineered for human use. For instance, the C++ draft standard:

- Is more than 700 pages
- Is revised three times a year

Nobody can keep track of these changes in a dependable manner. But failing to do so means off-standard behavior during C++ program development, testing, and operations. This decreases the dependability of the human component, without being specifically the fault of "this" or "that" computer user.

Therefore, with software, as with every other human-made system, one of the important challenges facing us is to be able to develop dependable aggregates out of less dependable components. This is especially critical when the solutions we provide have to rely on the behavior of people—hence on unknown factors.

Properly designed, focused agents can make a significant contribution to software dependability. They can improve results all the way from formal testing to analytical techniques used in runtime. They can also inform on the behavior of a malfunctioning component and derive future expected behavior as a function of current results.

Implemented through agents, this approach is most critical to the effort of detecting vulnerabilities that cannot otherwise be localized. As software increases in complexity, it is becoming impossible to analyze its dependability without structural and functional analysis done at runtime—which the agents should perform.

In connection to software dependability, agents can provide input not only for analytical studies but also for contrarian thinking. What was said earlier about the importance of logos and of scenarios can come to life through an ingenious procedure and the right input. The strategy does not need to be different from that followed by Bill Clinton in preparing for the debate with Bob Dole.

The president's sparring partner was former Senate majority leader George Mitchell. After the simulated debate with Mitchell, Clinton told reporters, "He beat me like a drum." It was later reported that in the mock debate Bill Clinton was unable to stay cool. He became frustrated and testy. This simulation, however, was instrumental in winning the real debate with his Republican opponent.

George Mitchell had clobbered Clinton in the mock debate in exactly the same way software developers and testers should clobber their artifacts. In the role of Dole, Mitchell bored in on Clinton's greatest vulnerability. "The issue of trust," Mitchell began. "Where are the files? Will he pardon his friends and associates? How can one trust the president and his record?"

A similar principle exists in the testing of software dependability. Agents can be used to advantage to provide real-time diagnostics and other online support. These agents will be that much more focused on the job which they will be required to do if their designer has a tough challenger who:

- Criticizes all functional and structural aspects of the artifact
- Through an open debate, of which should exist a record, shreds the agent's specs to pieces—both before it is built and right after

British Petroleum had developed a different method, also based on logos, in an effort to significantly improve knowledge acquisition for expert systems. It tape-recorded a session involving an old hand in oil exploration, who taught a couple of young engineers the secrets and the rules of the profession.

This was done subject by subject and step by step in an interactive manner, with the young engineers asking questions when a rule was not explained in a comprehensible manner. *Boelter's agents* can greatly benefit from this approach. They would do even better when their developer is challenged by a colleague regarding the validity of the hypotheses and of the rules.

Database Mining and Knowledge Discovery in a Data Warehouse

Database mining is a term that has been often used in Parts 1 and 2. It is also a popular concept in connection to inference, information harvesting, the finding of useful patterns in databases, knowledge extraction, information discovery, and the newer term: *data archeology*.

The best definition of *database mining* I have found, albeit one that is folklore, is "torturing the data in computer storage until it confesses." The torture is done through algorithms of all sorts—more often through heuristics. The process can be nicely executed online through agents, provided that they are following basic principles characterizing scientific research.

This approach parallels of concept of Sir Francis Bacon (1561—1626) who defined the aim of science as "putting nature to the question." Database mining does precisely the same in connection to all information elements which we can access and we suspect have some relevance to the subject of our study:

- Raw data rarely prove to be of direct benefit to the user.
- The value of an episodic memory rests on our ability to extract infor-

mation in a way that helps us understand the phenomena affecting the data source.

This has been classically done through personal experience, when the experimenter or the analyst became intimately familiar with the data and with what has been governing the data source. Traditionally, the process has been largely manual, with analysts acting as database-mining engines.*

But manual processes can no longer cope with the mountains of data generated by modern industrial and financial systems. Mathematical statistics is at the heart of the inference through validation of hypotheses, exploratory data analysis, and pattern recognition—which are part of database mining.

There is another reason for using agents in data mining. As image databases become popular and the complexity of queries increases, conventional approaches no longer deliver. In conventional databases, the software can look for exact matches only of specific keywords. It does not support:

- Query by image
- Query by multiple content

By contrast, advanced software solutions use knowledge engineering techniques that observe, for instance, the relationship between words. The more sophisticated agents know enough about English syntax to expand their search and find complex matches. More recently, some researchers prefer to use the term *knowledge discovery in databases* (KDD), by which they refer to the overall process of unearthing useful knowledge from data.

A number of KDD specialists say that their approach is broader than database mining because it includes data selection, data preparation, data cleaning, and data quality procedures. It also involves the incorporation of the appropriate prior knowledge and interpretation of the results of mining to assure that useful knowledge is derived from the data.

Other KDD proponents add that there is a growing need for *knowledge and data discovery management systems* (KDDMSs) as second-generation database-mining solutions. They want KDDMS support to manage KDD applications, just as a DBMS helps to manage business applications.

Still others prefer to talk about *online analytical processing* (OLAP) as an

---

*See also in Chap. 12, some practical examples on database mining.

architectural extension of the data warehouse that has been equipped with data-mining features. Not everyone agrees with these differences and their definition. Some people think that it is not sensible to differentiate between:

- Data mining in a data warehouse
- An OLAP process containing customized data

But at the same time there seems to be a developing consensus that agents are an indispensable part of the armory necessary for operating at a higher level of sophistication than the one supported by a data warehouse.

To my mind, the argument about the name of the procedure, rather than its contents and fine mechanics, is like the trees that hide the forest. KDD, KDDMS, and OLAP tend to draw attention away from the fact that today there is a significant trend toward databases that contain not just numeric data but also large quantities of multimedia information of a nonstandard data type. This includes:

- Nonnumeric, nontextual information elements
- Graphical data and animation

Often, the time series or database content is a nonstationary, temporal, spatial mixture of numeric textual and graphical information elements, as well as voice and other digital streams. Such plurality of substance makes more complex the algorithm searches. The model we use may overfit the data, resulting in poor performance, or it may simply not answer the requirements posed by massive data sets, intraday time series, and high dimensionality.

Both accumulated volumes and fast data streams must be accounted for in connection to every competitive data management system. Not only do we have terabyte databases with millions of records and large numbers of attributes and variables but also we must be able to handle subsecond data feeds, and do so ad hoc in real time.

Taken together, these references create combinatorially explosive search spaces, as well as an increase in the chances that classical data-mining algorithms will result in patterns that are not generally valid—hence, the need to use agents for testing, apply approximation methods, and introduce dimensionality reduction techniques. The incorporation of prior knowledge and intelligent artifacts can be of significant assistance in sophisticated database mining.

Agents for Screening, Publishing, and Reporting

The massive data sets with which we increasingly have to cope have induced an increasing interest in using a sample to predict properties. The basic assumption behind this approach is that the sample is representative of the population in terms of content and probability distribution.

■ With all processes of prediction, our primary interest is in accuracy rather than in precision.

■ Often, prediction methods assume some regularities in the probability distribution and accept constraints typically supplied by human experts.

Elements of this approach were supported by Autonomy, a company that presented agents as programming products at Comdex Fall 1996. Its artifacts are self-learning along the path described in the preceding sections. The user can also teach them about how he or she likes them to behave in the future, to better serve the requirements of his or her job.

One of Autonomy's agents specializes in content screening and publishing. It accepts user questions (not just keywords), and after mining the database, it suggests items relevant to the query—also creating hyperlinks in function of the user's expressed interests. This agent:

■ Works on the Internet

■ Reads the contents of each Web page

■ Understands the context in which words are used, in the sense discussed earlier in the chapter

A key contribution is user profiling. The agent employs its master's profile of interests to monitor, evaluate, and retrieve information on the Internet, as well as to build a dynamic database. One application, assisted through this facility, helps companies looking for competitors or simply for information about themselves existing on the Internet. This is also a good example of the services interactive database mining can provide.

Another Autonomy agent targets the market of personal digital assistants (PDAs) and nomadic computing. One of its implementations is broadcasting and narrowcasting. Agile both in transmitting and in receiving, the agent can be instructed by its master to establish a temporary link, such as provided by a mobile telephone. This link will be dropped after the agent accomplishes its work. Alternatively, it will remain active if the agent expects it will be needed again in a short time.

- Database mining does not need to be a monolithic experience or concern only a discovery process of limited perspective.

- It should be done in a flexible and adaptable manner to face ongoing requirements, and agents can be able assistants in performing such jobs.

Flexibility is at a premium because user requirements will change over time. Therefore, the data-mining agent should be adaptable, and this is where a KDDMS can be of help. Its foremost contribution is stored experience—a process that information technologists know how to handle, having spent the last 15 years building knowledge banks for expert systems.

Let me add, in concluding this section, that what bolsters self-confidence more than anything in life is experience based on actual results. Knowledgeable physicists and engineers appreciate that, to avoid dead ends and wrong leads, they should not start a lengthy computation until:

- They know the range of values within which the answer is likely to fall as well as what constitutes outliers.

- They are able to estimate the order of magnitude and boundaries of the results being expected before engaging in the details of an investigation.

No doubt, there are some real difficulties in estimating invisible limits or barriers. Few scientists have been trained to study extremely large or extremely small systems, extraordinarily fast moving objects, or high-frequency data in time series. But that's precisely the reason that they should use knowledge artifacts.

When George Bush was in the White House, he liked to quote Woody Allen, saying that 80 percent of success is just showing up. Several companies are now showing up with their agents, but my advice is that showing up must be matched by following through. In a market economy the final test of any system is: "Does it pay?"

Agents, Network Intelligence, and Broadband

There was a widely held opinion at Comdex Fall 1996 that the year 1997 will probably see some broadband breakthroughs. Subsequently, in the 1998 to 1999 timeframe we may experience the real years of change in telecommunications. Such projections are based on the fact that in practically all telecom laboratories, current efforts focus on increasing the bandwidth either by using brute force and/or by putting intelligence in the switch and in the line.

On the surface, these two approaches seem to contradict one another, yet most likely both will be used in synergy to push forward communications technology and augment the envelope of services it can provide to users.

There was fairly widespread agreement at Comdex Fall 1996 that this envelope of services will contain a Golden Horde of agents. The more we are able to address complexity issues, the larger will be the market for computers, communications, and software, said Mike Aymar of Intel at this conference. But to do, so we need to:

- Develop new architectures
- Promote new types of software
- Start differentiating the target populations

All three bullets address important problems connected to the growth of the electronics industry. As the old markets get saturated, imaginative research must lead to new departures. This is precisely what Boelter's agents can do if used in a focused manner.

Differentiating the target populations is necessary to capitalize on the aftermaths of Moore's law: The number of transistors in a microprocessor doubles every 18 months for practically constant price. "By the year 2010, instead of 200 MHz we will have available 10-gigahertz (GHz) chips," suggested Andy Grove, Intel's CEO, in his keynote speech at the same event.

At least theoretically, there seems to be no end in sight under current technology in connection to foreseeable scientific evolution—though somewhere at a future date there is bound to be a limit set by the laws of physics. Besides this, the current rapid growth concerns processing power, but software and bandwidth are big problems that might become roadblocks:

- Data transmission does not follow Moore's law of semiconductor power, doubling every 18 months.
- Transmission capacity grows by only 2 percent a year, which is a tiny improvement in performance in view of growing requirements.

Modems do somewhat better. Rockwell's and U.S. Robotic's double-speed models are a significant step forward, and computer companies now try to speed their adoption rate. Similarly, agents are expected to bring significant improvements in software; we have already spoken of this fact.

There is another twist in the broadband's and agents' contribution, and it has to do with the fact that also with microprocessors, even if we are still far from the quantum limitations side, the market's response can validate or invalidate Andy Grove's projection. If negative, market response can slow the development process down or even bring it to a stop. Therefore, the cornerstone to Grove's vision of a relentless technological progress is the opening up of vast new markets.

Knowledgeable people today believe that, with some 200 million users, the PC industry will have a hard time keeping up with growth rate of more than 10 percent a year. Without new markets, there probably will be some years where the industry will not grow at all. It does not suffice that at this moment the trendline is very strong. Market strength has to be sustained through new openings, and agents may provide the key to new markets.

There are many reasons that I underline this particular reference—as many as the types of agents we can successfully develop and implement. One of them is return on investment (ROI). Neil Jacoby, my professor of business strategy at UCLA and dean of the Graduate School of Business Administration, was teaching his students that a banker would be happy to spend a dollar if he can make 2 dollars in return.

The same is true with all investors, with industrial companies, and with the educated men and women in the street—a fast-growing breed. ROI is an important metric, and as Grove was to suggest, the 10-GHz chip vision is doable if the critical mass of users materializes.

In practical terms to keep its growth record or even improve it, the PC industry must win users away from television. Intel's CEO rapidly reviewed recent accomplishments and innovations trying to derive out of them a lesson: From the 4004 through the Pentium Pro, he provided an overview of how the microprocessor has developed. Then he explained why, to his judgment, available evidence points to technological development continuing at a rapid pace.

Grove projected that chips available 15 years down the line will be really impressive under current standards. But at the same time, he warned that such advances cannot be taken for granted. They require a significant investment by the industry as a whole—and the new departures of which we have spoken.

"We need this [market] increase, or else the magical circle where development drives economics will break down," Andy Grove said. To acquire the needed rapid growth in user population, the computer must become significantly more interesting and more knowledgeable—bringing the issue of agents into perspective. Grove characterized this requirement as "a war of eyeballs" between the PC and the TV. Then he made the inference that entertainment supplied on the PC must be compelling enough to draw users away from the dumb tube.

His pitch was for a significantly more challenging interactive environment, suggesting that this may be attainable. Statistics are compelling. At least in the United States, sales of new PCs now slightly exceed that of TVs, but the real battle is time spent in front of the devices—and therefore content.

There are as well other business opportunities to be exploited through interactive intelligent artifacts, during the coming years. New opportunities are developing because of advances in domains such as telecommunications, which advances bring with them lots of unknowns. This is the issue addressed in the following section: the use of agents as virtual police to bend the curve of telecommunications fraud.

Using Agents to Reduce Telecommunications Fraud

Telecommunications fraud is an issue increasingly important both because of its pervasive nature and because it often costs millions of dollars before it is even detected. Additional reasons are user inconvenience and dissatisfaction, as well as bad publicity for the teleco and the public or the private network.

That a utility like telecommunications will be subject to fraud is not surprising. It is surprising, however, that despite this threat, many companies are still unaware of the issues—a key problem being that as telecom services innovate and diversify, so does the range of fraudulent activities. The most visible and publicized occurrences have been from mobile networks. But there is also considerable drain on the classical fixed-link services.

The speed with which the Internet has emerged as a major form of telecommunications sees to it that many of the security implications are not yet fully understood. Both providers and users of telecom systems also face problems with their networks being increasingly accessed by hackers.

Can agents help in bending the curve of telecom fraud? The answer is: yes! AT&T developed a methodology for detecting international calling fraud by displaying calling activity so that its people and its clients quickly see unusual patterns. GTE uses Clonedetector, which employs customer profiles to flash out cellular cloning fraud. If a particular customer suddenly starts calling in a very different way, fraud alert automatically kicks in.

Another cellular fraud detection system has been developed by NYNEX. It first mines the database to discover indicators of fraudulent use. Then it automatically generates detection procedures by feeding these indicators into intelligent detector software.

This knowledge engineering system uses the indicators to instantiate detector templates. It is also able to combine the detectors in order to improve upon its own performance.*

One of the reasons that the task of detecting and controlling fraud becomes more challenging and truly urgent is that the user population rapidly increases. Over the next 5 years, Americans are expected to at least triple their use of wireless phones.† In other parts of the world, too, there is a burgeoning *personal communications system* (PCS).

Contrary to the telecommunications carriers who use AI to curtail fraud, most user organizations have not yet adopted knowledge-enriched software solutions in connection to fraud, even if (as a recent survey by Siemens Business Communication Systems demonstrates) over three out of four respondents believed their network(s) are open to the threat of hacking.

It is generally expected that these statistics will get worse. Mobile phone IDs can now be copied from a distance, even without physical access to the phone. Given the density of networks and their usage, how can companies deal with the effects of telecommunications fraud without new technology? Few executives are ready to admit that without knowledge-enriched solutions, this is not doable or that the cost of being inactive in countering fraud far exceeds the cost of agents.

As we have seen in Part 2, the use of agents can be a major plus in connection to mobile computing. Detecting fraud is so much more important as personal communications systems spread, and, according to some projections, it is only a matter of time before this technology transforms the way we live and work.

---

*Communications of the ACM, vol. 39, no. 11, November 1996.

†*Business Week*, December 23, 1996.

To their proponents, PCS and their infrastructure, the *personal communications networks* (PCN), promise to bring the benefits of a revolution. But if the PCS/PCN solution is insecure, such revolution will not materialize. There are also applications issues to be addressed through intelligent software. The popularity of personal communications shadows the fact that PCNs are best designed to specific applications where microcell technology is more suitable. A good market, for instance, is structured around the ability to meet high demand for telephone services in relatively small geographical areas.

Standards are needed for the able use of a PCN—and they include numbering, signaling to allow for extra channels, and infrastructure sharing. Most of these activities can be served through agents. Given the massive support requirements posed by an expanding market, the way to bet is that telecoms will increasingly use agents—from network management to fraud detection and the calculation of tariffs for major individual customers.

As intelligent networks and microcellular radio infrastructures are being built, it will become increasingly more difficult for telecos to supervise and manage without sophisticated software solutions supported by new technology. Chapters 5 to 8 have demonstrated that the agents' implementation perspective in telecommunications networks is rated to grow significantly.

However, as I never tire repeating, to radically change technology, we must also change culture. Today, a lot of our images are 20 or 30 years old. As such, they do not fit the new landscape. This will change only when the majority of users come to appreciate that most of the devices they currently use must be changed—in software more than in hardware.

Boelter's Agents in a Home Area Network

Earlier the chapter presented some of the issues addressed by Andy Grove regarding conditions for the growth of the microprocessor market during the coming years. The introduction to the chapter did the same in connection to the way Bill Gates looks at agents to push forward the frontiers of software.

In discussing ways and means for making computer-based products appealing to the home market, Grove spoke of *active video*. He showed how the video capability of the PC has grown in 4 short years, exceeding original expectations. In this rapid processor evolution, we have gone from applications that were a revamp of classical chores, hence not very exciting, to new imaginative applications that are part of everyday business and increasingly encroach on the way we live.

The whole subject of home area networks, which is now attracting so much attention, is based on these two bullets.* The more intelligent are the appliances we use at home, the greater is the need to link them through a network. But networked systems have to be managed, and, even if the household has a couple of kids who are computer wizards, there is no way it will manually manage a network. This is the job of agents.

If the management of a home area network becomes transparent to the household, intelligent appliances may become a vast new industry. Consumer acceptance will help them to acquire a critical mass. In turn, this critical mass will bring up new uses and new users of computers.

Differentiation is the key. Today, there are very few industries where the lack of differentiation is so pronounced as with PCs. But a *home area network,* which is projected and implemented like an intranet, has the potential to turn this "lack of differentiation" argument on its head.

If the experience with local area networks is of any value, the way to bet is that a home area network will come by steps—following some leading-edge applications. So far, market projections are not particularly enthusiastic. To the question "When will 20 percent of U.S. households have intranets?" a learned answer is, in about 8 to 10 years, probably between 2005 to 2007.

Left on its own momentum, a critical mass will be difficult to build because currently only 35 percent of U.S. households have a PC. Many experts, however, believe the drive will probably not come from the PC but from appliances. What has this to do with agents?

■ Behind the critical-mass issue is the need to design for ease of use and user-friendliness—while providing for functionality and manageability.

■ The underlying notion is that of a home area network that should operate in a seamless manner, with the network itself and its appliances enriched through artificial intelligence.

Some people say user-friendliness is not so important because we are

---

surrounded by machines that are not easy to use but have big value; an often-quoted example is the automobile. This example is, however, wrong not only because it totally forgets the functionality of the auto but also because it pays no attention to ease of use. Automobiles became popular after Dr. Kettering, of General Motors Research Laboratories, developed the automatic starter—which enriched the functionality with ease of use.

Kettering's automatic starter more than doubled the population that was interested in buying and using autos. Prior to its advent, the large majority of women and quite a few men did not venture to jump-start the auto through muscle power. This was the job of the professional auto driver—and few households could afford one. A similar concept is valid in connection to computers and communications software, with the new automatic starter being the knowledge artifacts.

In the late 1990s, or thereafter, the Kettering of the computer industry will bring to life the new metaphor that will characterize the greatest transition of the computer industry probably for the next two decades. This is still to be seen.

The Boelter agents metaphor, whose various aspects have been examined in this chapter, is part of the basic transformation that is under way. The hardware part of it is the wired home concept, moving from an *as-is* model to a *to-be* frame of reference. Agents are the core of the new software business. Whether in the home or in the office:

■ The as-is model features a proprietary, baseband, single-use network with restrictive access and little or no intelligence.

■ By contrast, the to-be model is a multiservice platform that is user-friendly—but it is also interoperable and functional.

In the as-is model there tends to be one service per attached appliance and many different identification numbers. By all likelihood, through Boelter's agents the to-be model will be characterized by a large variety of bundled and unbundled services, many of them *personalized*. Access will be provided for any appliance, at any time, anywhere.

But this new paradigm is not for tomorrow. We are still some time away from seeing how computing and communications power will be used in the future—though we now start to realize that current computers of all types and sizes are pretty clumsy. Over the next 5 years huge changes can be expected, including a propensity to interactive visualization through handheld devices. The overriding thrust will likely be toward diversity in computing platforms, with knowledge engineering providing the seamless integration.

Machine designers also talk of the need for adjusting the computer to perceive things the way people do. Advanced work goes on in laboratories to make computers that see and hear. Here too intelligence embedded in devices makes the difference. But beware of fast-advancing technology: Computers, communications, and software are a business where a 6-month delay threatens obsolescence. Boelter's agents are not the business for the faint-hearted.

CHAPTER 10

Supporting Mission Control Functions through Intelligent Software

The goal of this chapter, as well as of the following two chapters in Part 3, is to help the reader gain the skills necessary for developing knowledge-enriched software. Most specifically, it provides guidance in choosing the parameters to be included in the design of agents. Since the best way to acquire skills is to understand the fundamentals, this chapter starts with the basics, then proceeds with selected cases of successful applications.

If one asks which has been the most significant common characteristic of communications software modules during the last 5 years, the answer would be: the wider implementation of artificial intelligence in telecommunications. *Knowledge-enriched* features enable us to develop a more thorough understanding of a network's design space. These features also:

- Lead to greater robustness of the network
- Account for functional tradeoffs
- Provide for real-time diagnostics, hence greater reliability

The second most important contribution to communications software has been done by mathematical models for *simulation*. Through simulation, users can define design variables with specific value ranges or tolerances and produce an array of permutations required for a complete implementation experiment.

The third most significant contribution is *object orientation,* both in programming and in database management. Software instances of more abstract communications objects assist in making network functions both more actual and more factual, through the concepts we will study later in the chapter.

But while all three of these contributions are technical, the precondition that applies to them all is not. It is organizational, and it underpins the three important areas of activity in Fig. 10-1 where agents serve as common frames of reference. Given the proper organization, knowledge-enriched software, simulation models, and object orientation join together to provide superior solutions in the areas of:

- Telecommunications
- Building automation
- Office automation

As we saw in Chap. 7, always under the proper organizational perspective, agents are also instrumental in supporting infrastructural issues that interest many domains, such as intelligent diagnostics and maintenance. In connection to lines, trunks, and nodes, agents perform tests, do loopbacks, analyze the contents of quality databases, and come up with quality reports. But is *our* organization ready for them?

Do we have the culture to assimilate these reports that are real time and interactive? Can we capitalize on the fact that they are proactively brought to the attention of users? End users can get so much more mileage out of knowledge artifacts if they understand how they are developed—and how they work. They also need to appreciate what the new software paradigm is all about.

Figure 10-1
Knowledge-enriched software in telecommunications, building automation, and office automation.

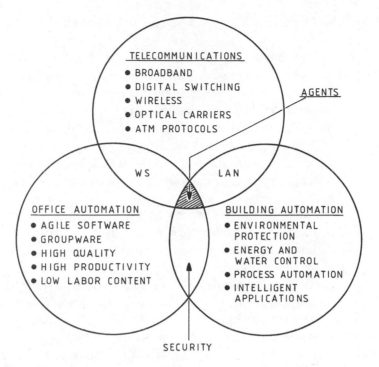

TELECOMMUNICATIONS
- BROADBAND
- DIGITAL SWITCHING
- WIRELESS
- OPTICAL CARRIERS
- ATM PROTOCOLS

AGENTS

WS

LAN

OFFICE AUTOMATION
- AGILE SOFTWARE
- GROUPWARE
- HIGH QUALITY
- HIGH PRODUCTIVITY
- LOW LABOR CONTENT

BUILDING AUTOMATION
- ENVIRONMENTAL PROTECTION
- ENERGY AND WATER CONTROL
- PROCESS AUTOMATION
- INTELLIGENT APPLICATIONS

SECURITY

Basic Concepts Underpinning Good Organization

A major part of a manager's job is getting things done through people, whether or not these people are assisted by agents. Classically, we call the process of putting things in place *organization*—but in reality it involves three issues that interact with one another: organization proper, communication, and cooperation. All three assist in efficiently allocating and coordinating productive work, particularly when they are supported by the notions of:

- Responsibility
- Accountability

Contrary to what textbooks say, organizational decisions are quite often influenced by the structure of the company, the pattern of leadership, and the assessment of capabilities and personalities in the company's human resources. Every executive is swayed by:

- His or her own attitude to management
- The degree of analytical judgment that he or she can exercise

■ The forms of control he or she uses or plans to use

Management attitudes, analytical judgment and forms of control evolve over time. In an age dominated by computers and communications, they both influence and are influenced by the new paradigms for structuring and developing software artifacts. That is why the construction and use of agents has so much to do with organization.

Whether in engineering, finance, or any other field, projects follow the same general lines as we have discussed. When we look at design from a systems viewpoint or we take an interdisciplinary approach to study and research, we have to address organizational prerequisites. For instance, anyone exposed to the process of building an airplane learns to appreciate skills such as good organization and coordination from conceptual design to final integration testing. These skills are needed to make large aggregates work. For example, a designer working in spacecraft not only needs to follow a systems approach but also to write algorithms for orbital determination, trajectory planning, and propulsive maneuvering.

Beyond hardware, this means to organize, design, and implement a software architecture able to provide a framework for coordinating several autonomous tasks. The flexible software architecture that we need would first accept high-level commands, and then decompose them into low-level operations.

Organization-wise, the designer may represent each high-level command as the root node of a task tree with the filials forming the low-level operations sequence. The implied organization enforces the rules and resource constraints needed for performing multiple tasks. The designer should simulate each task sequence with walkthroughs to assure that no rules are violated.

In projecting, studying, designing, and implementing any organizational and structural solution or architecture, we can be served by modularity and sound specifications. But what we do must also make business sense. Figure 10-2 explains what I mean in terms of an organizational approach that makes sense all the way from design to marketing.

In the mid-1960s, when the Concorde was in an advanced design state, I was invited to participate in a high-technology seminar chaired by Dr. David Rockefeller, then chairman of Chase Manhattan. One of the topics being discussed was the supersonic commercial jet, and Dr. Rockefeller asked: "Do you think the Concorde will be a commercial success?"

Having been a week prior to this meeting with British Airways, near Bristol—one of the two partners in the Concorde development—and

Figure 10-2
Flexibility is the best strategy with the design of any system.

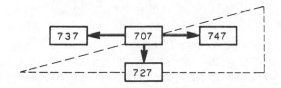

AN ADVANCED TECHNOLOGICAL PRODUCT MUST
BE DESIGNED TO:

- FIT DIFFERENT MARKETS
- DEVELOP INTO A COHERENT PRODUCT LINE
- USE STANDARD COMPONENT PARTS
- MINIMIZE MAINTENANCE REQUIREMENTS

A GOOD EXAMPLE IS THE BOEING 700 SERIES

A BAD EXAMPLE IS CONCORDE

MONOLITHIC PRODUCTS DON'T SUCCEED.
NEITHER DO THEY RECOVER THEIR DEVELOPMENT COST.
PRODUCT CONTINUITY:

- SPREADS THE R+D/M INVESTMENTS
- PERMITS A BETTER MARKET FOCUS
- PROVIDES A MASS EFFECT, AND
- PROTECTS THE FLANKS AGAINST COMPETITION

having posed exactly the same query to the British engineers, I gave verbatim the answer that I got from the technical men who knew the problem: "The Concorde will not fly commercially because it is loaded with unnecessary costs."

As an experienced banker, David Rockefeller had a smile. "This, too," he said, "is a good reason why commercially the Concorde may not fly. But it is not reason Number 1." In Dr. Rockefeller's judgment, the topmost organizational and design failure was that the Concorde was projected as a closed system, a one-shot product:

■ It could not be redesigned to become bigger, and it could not be changed to become smaller.

■ It was simply boxed in, and any advanced product that is not flexible is bound to be a commercial failure.

Thirty years passed by, and the facts of business life proved David Rockefeller's dictum. What applies to aircraft also goes hand in hand with agents. Let's never forget this basic design and marketing aspect when we talk of using a particular technology in the development of knowledge artifacts.

Object orientation, the concepts of inheritance, metalevels, ephemeral hierarchies, and inference engines are—technically speaking—very important. But if the prerequisite organization is substandard, and the marketing perspective has been skipped over, even the best technical tools will be helpless in making a product fly in a commercial sense.

Rockefeller's Concorde metaphor is valid with agents even if we talk of small autonomous artifacts rather than large supersonic airplanes. Any natural or human-made system operates within a larger environment with the qualities of flexibility and adaptability always being crucial. These are strategic organizational issues that take precedence over other, more technical subjects. Specifications must conform to organizational and marketing prerogatives, not vice versa.

Objects, Inheritance, Inference, and Metalevels in the Development of Agents

The three issues of knowledge engineering, simulation, and object orientation discussed in the introduction to the chapter are not distinct and independent from one another. They work in synergy. Knowledge engineering and simulation are greatly helped by means of object-oriented approaches; and object solution can benefit from being enriched by intelligence. As an example, a modern telephone service consists of:

- Software objects that are running on hardware devices which constitute the physical component of the network

- A knowledge orientation that provides necessary features for increasing the reliability of the system solution, as we will see in the following section with Compass

Simulation permits one to map a system into the computer, experiment with crucial variables, and optimize the system. The synergy of knowledge engineering, simulation, and object orientation makes it possible to support novel development approaches that have polyvalent perspectives. It also helps:

- In emphasizing critical system features within the chosen architectural layout

- In facilitating the task of managing a complex telecommunications system

But the definition of software-supported telecommunications functions does not come out of the blue. We spoke of this in Chap. 2 in connection to virtual engineering, as well as in Chap. 6 with reference to concurrent software-hardware codesign.

While the strategic organizational issues must be elaborated by top management, the technical specifications are studied by *domain experts*. Their description reflects the logic these experts follow in their judgments. This is the phase generally known as *knowledge acquisition*,* during which the cognizant network engineer:

- Lists the criteria he or she follows in his or her design choices and decisions

- Orders these criteria in a logical sequence, respecting priorities

- Maps the so-defined network knowledge into a program

Alternatively, the job specified by the third bullet will be done by a programmer-analyst who, as a matter of good practice, should test the rules and procedures being mapped with other domain experts. Not only is it advisable to do this form of external testing but also it is a good policy to do "negative tests": How does the knowledge artifact react to stupid questions?

There is a very good reason for this query. Usually people consider as "stupid questions" those which challenge the obvious. But without challenging the obvious, no real software testing can be done. That's how the bug that created the AT&T 9-hour time out, described in Chap. 8, was able to slip through the system unchallenged.

This said, it must as well be added that knowledge acquisition and testing is only part of the work associated with the development of agents. Other vital components are solving in an appropriate manner the interactive dialog interface between the agent and its master (or other users) as well as:

- Engineering the artifact to fit the task for which it is designed through real-time approaches

---

*See also D. N. Chorafas, *Knowledge Engineering*, Van Nostrand Reinhold, New York, 1990.

■ Addressing the crucial issue of data management where object orientation should play a leading role

While the performance of agents will up to a point depend on hardware configuration, there are other issues associated with performance that should attract plenty of attention. Functionally rich solutions are necessary and, as the introduction to the chapter outlined, these can be found in knowledge engineering and object orientation. Four concepts are particularly important:

■ Encapsulation*

■ Meta concept

■ Notion of inheritance

■ Inference engine

Encapsulation promotes a procedural separation in objects and modules, which is important in real-time environments. This separation takes place between the external specification of a class and its internal implementation. In this way, the procedure helps to limit the impact of program changes and hence the operational and maintenance costs.

We spoke of *meta* in Chap. 3 and said that it provides an automatic online constraint mechanism, which permits a large degree of automation in the handling of types and classes of objects. Metarules, for instance, are rules about rules; and metadata are data about data.

Inheritance reduces the cost of enhancing a large program by allowing changes to automatically propagate to affected parts of the system. A major contribution of object solutions is that, while they provide plenty of semantics, which is not true with relational approaches, they deal through *ephemeral hierarchies.* This contrasts to the inflexibility of hierarchical approaches that are fixed:

■ Ephemeral hierarchies are most important to real-time modeling.[†]

■ Simulation and experimentation would be nearly impossible without the ability to change the thread.

Because of inheritance, a change taking place in regard to one object's class definition (or hierarchy) automatically updates all of the more spe-

---

*See also D. N. Chorafas and H. Steinmann, *Object-Oriented Databases,* Prentice-Hall, Englewood Cliffs, N.J., 1993.

[†]See also the example given earlier in this chapter.

cialized classes that inherit behavior from the modified class. Code changes do not have to be made in each of the lower-level classes individually—as is the case with Cobol and Fortran programs.

Talking of predicates, in Chap. 3 it was stated that *inference* is both an act and a process. The goal is to use approximate reasoning strategies to arrive at an estimate of a situation, while having uncertain data and imperfect rules. To do so, we have to establish connections between facts and underlying assumptions:

- These must be of such kind that we can predict further occurrences from those already existing.
- In a sense, the successful accomplishment of this task is the real end of the scientific effort.

Table 10-1 gives a glimpse of a set of simple logical equations that helps to explain why inference is the kernel of an agent. Knowledge acquisition, object orientation, the notions of meta and inheritance are all part of the methodology that must be used, leading to a knowledge artifact. This can be an expert system, and when it is autonomous, it becomes an agent.

As a matter of principle, the simpler the logical structure is, the smaller the number of logically independent conceptual elements needed to support it. A good way to explain how the artifact works and interacts with its knowledge bank (KB) is through the process of medical diagnosis. An example system is presented in Fig. 10-3. Notice that every one of the boxes in the block diagram has:

- A vital meaning
- A role to play

The block in the diagram describing a medical diagnostic system may be compared to objects, object classes, or larger object-oriented entities. Since classes interact with one another only through their specifications, a change to the data structures used to implement one class affects only that class and no others. This greatly simplifies both data management

TABLE 10-1	**Data + inference* = smart system**
Logical Equations Leading from Inference to the Agent	**Smart system + methodology = knowledge artifact**
	Knowledge artifact + autonomous action = agent

*Through algorithms or heuristics.

Figure 10-3
Component parts of
a diagnostic system.

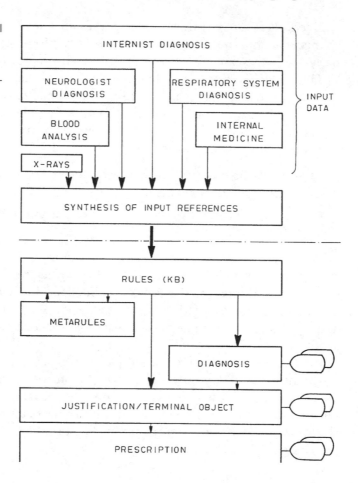

and program maintenance. It can also be a significant advantage in multimedia implementation environments.

Compass: A Case Study in Intelligent Software Functionality

A good example of the functionality expected from modern software is offered by *Compass*. This is an expert system, not an agent, but it has the incomparable asset of having been tested in practice and of having passed these tests. Besides this, at least in my opinion, agents are "next-generation" expert systems characterized by autonomy and mobility. Hence, we can learn a great deal from the experience gained with expert systems.

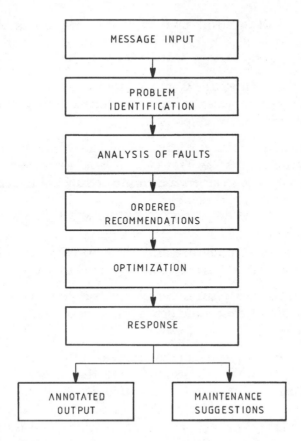

Figure 10-4
Compass function-
ality by General
Telephone and Elec-
tronics.

As we briefly saw in Chap. 8, Compass was developed in the late 1980s by the General Telephone and Electronics (GTE) Laboratories. Therefore, it has by now accumulated several years of practical experience resulting from its successful implementation. Figure 10-4 presents a step-by-step, bird's-eye view of the artifact's functionality:

1. In the *input phase*, Compass makes connection via telephone lines to the site being analyzed. An agent would work in a similar way.

The rules of the system parallel an expert's procedure in analyzing maintenance messages. Operating online, the artifact asks devices at local sites to gather desired data—for example, the last 24 hours of messages from a given switch. Then, it takes the raw messages being received and transforms the data from local format to its own knowledge structure. This is a procedure that follows most closely the way agents work. The agent will collect online information and/or mine databases. This input is the knowledge bank used by its inference engine to reach a decision, which the artifact brings to the attention of its master or uses it to do something else.

2. In the *identify phase,* Compass groups messages into clusters, or sets of messages, which expert analysts have indicated were all caused by the same switch problem.

An initial clustering is performed by identifying important commonalities between messages. This yields a large set of clusters, many of which overlap. Spurious clusters are eliminated by using expert rules for handling overlapping clusters.

The function is performed, in part, by using a precedence relation for the common situation—where the same set of messages is identified as several different problem clusters. The output of the identification phase is clusters of messages, each corresponding to one problem in the switch.

3. In the *analyze phase,* the artifact uses expert rules to examine each remaining cluster and determine a set of possible specific switch faults.

Any of these faults might have caused all the messages in the cluster. For example, the analyze phase may find that a certain cluster of messages could have been caused by a malfunction in either of two particular circuit cards or by a problem in the wiring between them.

Each fault is given an associated *likelihood.* This is the domain expert's estimate of the likelihood that this fault was the actual cause of the messages. The agent works through a quite similar procedure, except that besides the rules of the domain expert, it also has its own self-made rules—because it is a learning artifact.

As an example, in the case of a particular switch problem cluster, Compass typically finds one to five corresponding possible switch faults. Typically, the information available in the messages is such that an expert could not narrow the possibilities more than that.

4. For each possible fault, in the ordered *recommendations phase,* the agile software determines one or more possible maintenance actions that could be suggested.

Take, for instance, the case of a possible bad circuit card. The system could put forward a maintenance suggestion such as to run a diagnostic on the card while it remains in its slot in the switch. Still another suggestion might be to immediately replace the faulty card with a spare card.

Each fault has one to three corresponding possible suggestions, so the total list of alternatives for a problem cluster usually has between 3 and 10 items. Compass puts its proposals in priority terms, using expert rules to prioritize its suggestions based upon several considerations. These include:

- The a priori likelihood of the corresponding fault
- The probability that a given action will find or remedy the fault
- The ease of performing maintenance
- The potential risk resulting from lack of maintenance action

Information stored in the artifact's knowledge bank permits Compass to appreciate that certain maintenance actions should be performed only in the low telephone traffic hours of the day, usually the middle of the night. In other words, there are risks associated with the maintenance action.

Though the system knows the time of day, it does not know what time of day a network engineer will perform the maintenance action(s) for a particular problem. Therefore, Compass actually determines and eventually outputs two suggested priority lists:

- One, if the maintenance is being performed during the high-traffic part of the day
- Another, if the maintenance takes place in the low-traffic part of the day

If both lists are identical, this information is noted by the intelligent artifact, and only one list is output. Sometimes, two or more maintenance actions can be performed simultaneously. Compass has the knowhow to handle this scheduling problem.

    5. In the *output phase,* the artifact examines the suggestion lists to select those that will be communicated to the control center or the network engineer.

For some maintenance actions, the results are immediate, as, for instance, running diagnostics and loopbacks. For others, the results are delayed. The artifact does as well follow-ups on the suggestions that it makes. When a circuit card is replaced, the expert system's practice is to watch out for 24 hours to see if the problem recurs. If it does not, it is assumed that the action was successful.

Agents, Input/Output, and the Evolution of Metaphors

Some of the most awkward problems that existed and still exist with computers, dating back to the 1950s, are connected to input/output (I/O). The reasons are largely historical. During the World War II years, processing power was the king and I/O was not judged from the viewpoint of whether or not it was user-friendly; thus, the issue of human-machine communications occupied, so to speak, the backseat.

Maybe an even greater contributor to the downplaying of the needed agility and comprehensiveness for I/O chores has been the batch environment together with the fact that, in the 1950s, data processing equipment developed as an extension of accounting machines. As a result, computer science adopted accounting-type I/O approaches, from punched cards and punched tape to long printed forms.

Even in the late 1960s when the terminals attached to data processing machines started being equipped with monitors, punched-card formats and those of printed output prevailed. This sustained an awkward culture until, eventually, the input/output perspective was changed by:

- The desktop metaphor of Dr. Alan Kay[*]
- Visualization procedures introduced by Apple's Macintosh in 1984

As explained in Chap. 2, *metaphors* are conventions that people and machines can understand without any great effort, which essentially means in a manner that is fairly natural. Many metaphors are based on *protocols*; that is, rule(s), code(s), or standard(s) of conduct or behavior. Protocols may be:

- Customs or etiquette
- Formalities for a handshake
- Notes, agreements, or minutes

Any population of organisms, including agents, evolves communication protocols. In principle, however, it looks *as if* the environment is designed to favor those living species that have the ability to generate and interpret meaningful signals that they exchange between themselves and others.

---

[*]See also Chap. 1 on the contribution of Alan Kay and Chap. 2 on metaphors.

The subject of metaphors and protocols is most important not only in connection to input/output but also relative to the concepts underpinning the development and use of agents. It would be silly business to have peak technology in knowledge artifacts and maintain backward human interfaces—hence I/Os—dating to the time of a Model T Ford.

Agents should communicate with their masters and other users through virtual reality. This is the new I/O metaphor. We spoke of virtual reality in Chap. 2, and we will get into more detail in Chap. 9. Virtual-reality protocols and the code they imply are a critical issue, and the best way to look at input/output solutions is to consider their:

- Origins
- Evolution
- Status

This means we need to go back to the fundamentals. What about the origin of communications as an I/O mechanism? Is there any project that can give hints on the beginning and evolution of input/output?

Starting with random neural networks, a simulation project conducted in the 1980s at UCLA,* resulted in a progression of generations that exhibit increasingly effective mate-finding strategies. This has been achieved through metaphors that the "species" communicated through a linguistic evolution.

Eventually, the communications protocols of this experiment become a *behavioral facilitator*. But, in cases, it also proved to be a barrier to mating, thereby supporting the formation of distinct subspecies. This UCLA exercise demonstrated the *impact of language* on evolution, which is practically what it was set up to do: Metaphors are, at the bottom line, a language, and they dramatize the impact of input/output on evolution. Forgetting the importance of the language and the communications protocols could doom a project. Remember this when you build *your* agents.

Experiments with physical barriers in the environment were also performed in connection to the aforementioned project at UCLA. A partially permeable barrier allowed a separate subspecies to evolve and survive for indefinite periods of time, in spite of occasional migration and contact from members of other subspecies. This study explored the evolution of language from a simple genetically controlled signaling to

---

*By Greg Werner under the supervision of Dr. Michael G. Dyer. The object of the project was evolving neural networks.

learned patterns of communication—an important issue with agents. One of its most crucial results has been that the evolution of language and its underpinnings can support complex forms of social interaction.

The researchers have come to these conclusions by simulating environments in which the sought-out types of interaction can evolve by means of signal exchange. As the communication becomes more sophisticated, a number of formalisms, hence protocols, sets in. This is the issue the developers of agents should be addressing in order to obtain agile and friendly input/output solutions.

Metaphors Capable of Improving the Input/Output of Compass

Capitalizing on the concepts outlined in the preceding section, we return to Compass—the network expert system by GTE whose characteristics were studied earlier. We can now examine how to improve it, particularly how to modernize its input/output. Let's make the hypothesis that it will be transformed into a virtual-reality setting.

As a beginning, let's start by considering what has been learned from the UCLA project. Its findings are important to the evolution of agents because they tell how their I/O (particularly their output) should be framed. The careful reader would appreciate the following:

- The chores that have classically characterized the computer industry no longer match the needs of the evolving intelligent artifacts.

- The experimental findings that we saw are a world apart from the data processing—oriented I/O.

- Human windows are necessary to give the end user the sensation of talking to a colleague.*

Agents can be used to help in interfacing to other agents. The employment of intelligent artifacts for I/O becomes necessary because computer interfaces are today quite complex and have become fairly heterogeneous—which discourages and confuses the end user.

Human-machine interfaces cannot continue grouping a large number

---

*See also the section on the discussion of the windows of BT's Jacaranda later in this chapter.

of operations on the screen because they will be massively rejected by their users. By contrast, interfaces should be the subject of *personalization*—which can and should be done through agents who know their masters.

The interactive communication of agents with their masters is typically performed by employing graphic symbols. For instance, icons or drawings of faces whose expressions convey activity at a given moment, such as thinking, offering a suggestion, and looking pleased if a suggestion is put into effect.

As we have learned during the last dozen years through the Alan Kay metaphor—and its implementation by the Apple Macintosh—icons provide the user with feedback on the software's activities. And it has also been underlined that contrary to other forms of graphical presentations, agents are proactive:

- The now classical video presentation passively awaits a user's instructions.

- An agent-based approach tries to anticipate the user's most likely actions.

This is a quantum leap in I/Os that can be applied with existing intelligent artifacts in order to rejuvenate them. Compass did not have this level of sophistication in its input/output, though what it offered was much better than what mainframes could ever provide. For instance, for a nonexpert user, it presented only suggestions on activities that should be done that day. The output of Compass consisted of an ordered list of suggested actions for each problem, but this was still a list. Suggested actions were presented in the form and language most familiar to the maintenance personnel, but in a computer-oriented form.

This is technology of the 1980s while agents are artifacts of the 1990s and therefore should employ much more advanced I/Os, not only in communicating with humans but also in connecting to other machines, for instance, intelligent telephone lines able to fix themselves.

In terms of human-machine communication, a rejuvenated Compass could deal with end users through a virtual-reality environment. It could present a 3D color picture of the network, zoom in on the section in need of repair, and identify very precisely the malfunctioning component, including:

- Maintenance schedule

- Skills and tools

- Bill of materials

Specifically, I am suggesting the solution adopted by the University of Tokyo in 1994 in a virtual-reality project that Dr. Michitaka Hirose did for Tokyo Electric. I have described it in detail in my book on virtual-reality applications because it is pioneering.* The Tokyo Electric solution:

- Provides for walkthroughs in complex networks
- Permits through-force displays to intercept mechanical or electrical objects
- Makes possible a feeling of *being there* in the middle of the network

Even if this sounds like the stuff of science fiction, be assured that it is a practical application. Alert readers will appreciate that the way to bet is that such sophisticated input/output solutions will become more generalized within a few years.

The infrastructure for this sophisticated I/O is also being put in place. In an experiment currently being conducted in Leeds, United Kingdom, fiber connections will be made directly to business premises providing the capacity to tailor services to individual requirements. The system will include self-healing trunks and implement a method of assuring that if faults do occur, the system itself takes care of them by rechanneling the signals.

Metaphors will play a crucial role in this connection, and information scientists will be well advised to explore the evolution of intraspecies signals that are genetically hard coded into the behavior of organisms. These innate signals are commonly found in the animal kingdom, and some simulation projects are aiming to evolve animal-like communications protocols in artificial organisms.

As the environment becomes more complex, it may be possible to observe progressively more interesting communication protocols in human-made systems. The idea is that the artifacts themselves should be gaining learning ability and putting it to use.

With this, it may be possible to see the evolution of a primitive language in *artificial life* populations, along the lines of the research done at Santa Fe Institute. There are some interesting correspondences between the results of such an experiment in artificial life and what is known from the evolution of programming in connection to problem representation. The link is knowledge engineering artifacts.

---

*See Chap. 8. See also D. N. Chorafas and H. Steinmann, *Virtual Reality—Practical Applications in Business and Industry,* Prentice-Hall, Englewood Cliffs, N.J., 1995, pp. 133—136.

Developing Agents Able to Effectively Assist Network Management

Say that we have been given the mission to develop a family of agents that can effectively assist in network management. Chapter 8 has outlined what a network needs, placing emphasis on procedural characteristics. What has not yet been explained is the specific mission that should be followed in order to ascertain good network performance.

Let's start with the premise that in a large number of cases *good performance* is situational. An example is *broadband,* which is defined by several experts as a matter of offering more capacity than one needs at any specific point in time. Say, then, that in a given applications environment, acceptable channel capacity for a long haul is at the level of 50 to 150 Mbps.

In this applications environment, which concerns a bank's global network, the lines are rented from 16 different telecos in a dozen countries. This is by no means an exceptional case in connection to the operations of a money center bank. Given these specs, a very helpful group of autonomous agents can be designed, able to:

- Check continuously for the company's ongoing multimedia traffic
- Compare the prevailing bit streams against the channels allocated by the telephone companies

Other, more sophisticated agents will test the costs associated to the different providers and their channel capacity. They would analyze their fairly complex tariffs, along the line of the examples we saw in Part 2. Still another family of agents may address tariffication against basic technical characteristics such as:

- BER
- Erlang

When we talk of network usage, a basic metric is the *bit error rate* (BER). It tells about the quality of the line and is expressed in errors per so many thousand bits. Following this universal metric, an error rate at:

- 10^{-2} is a disaster. In the average, it means 1 error every 100 bits.
- 10^{-4} is bad enough, though 10^{-4} to 10^{-5} is what is known as *voice-quality lines.*

- 10^{-7} and 10^{-8} is what the telecos offer for what they call *data-quality lines.*

- 10^{-11} and 10^{-12} is what is really needed for sophisticated applications.

It is not that easy to improve systemwide the quality of transmission because big chunks of the telecommunications plant are old (lines, switches, transmitters, receivers, and interfaces). But what is possible is to check line quality continuously, and agents can effectively do that job.

- *Exploiting quality databases* in real time, agents can report on correlations between line quality, availability, and cost.

Line quality in BER is not steady. It varies in function of traffic and other factors. Some years ago, in a meeting in London, British Telecom was saying that the BER of its voice-grade lines is 10^{-5}, but for not so well known reasons, on Wednesdays it drops to 10^{-4}.

- *Filtering the data stream,* also in real time, agents can alert on BER volatility, particularly when the bit error rate goes beyond the tolerances that have been set.

If BER is the measure of quality, *Erlang* is a unit of traffic load. In terms of conversation paths in telephony, the hourly traffic volume can be expressed as the average number of calls in progress. Correspondingly, in regard to servers or other equipment, it can be expressed in number of devices in use:[*]

- The number of calls that would have been in progress if there were no blocking or delay, hence no congestion, is the *offered load.*

- When the hourly loads are averaged across days for each hour of the day, their maximum defines the *fixed busy hour.*

- If the highest load is selected for each day, without regard to the average, across days it occurs in the *bouncing busy hour.*

The mathematical description of message flow in a communications network is known as the *teletraffic* theory, and it is part of congestion theory. A. K. Erlang, a Danish communications engineer and mathematician, is the father of teletraffic theory, which he based on two assumptions:

---

[*]Bell Telephone Laboratories, *Engineering and Operations in the Bell System,* Western Electric, Indianapolis, Ind., 1977.

1. Arrivals form a Poisson process* which can be time-varying over the network.

2. The service times or holding times of the calls are independent and exponentially distributed.

Agents can effectively track the fixed hour and bouncing busy hour against the offered load. They can alert their masters to the existence of congestions. Using the services of simulators, they can also *forecast congestions*. And using schedulers and optimizers, they can *reroute traffic*.

Based on the Erlang algorithms, agents can perform evaluations that provide important feedback to the engineering and operating personnel, as well as to automated processes. In this way shortcomings can be identified in real time. They can also assign grades for central office equipment, trunks, subnetworks, and for the whole network. These are issues of great importance to effective network management. They are also examples of applications in which the development of agents can be rewarding.[†]

Using Knowledge Artifacts in Network Marketing Operations

The preceding section has explained how to develop and use agents for technical control reasons. A network, however, does not have only software and hardware issues to look after. I had at UCLA a professor of business administration, former executive vice president of TWA, who used to say: "Flying an airplane is no problem. The challenge is to fill the seats before it takes off."

A network that cannot sell its services is not worth its salt. Therefore, this section elaborates on key marketing points to be brought to the reader's attention. One of the marketing aspects of a network's implementation is data entry concerning a customer's order and its execution. This operation must be well designed to:

■ Abide by the principle of one entry, many uses of the information

---

*Dimitris N. Chorafas, *How to Understand and Use Mathematics for Derivatives*, vol. 2, Euromoney, London, 1995.

†Which helps explain why in Chap. 1, Table 1-1 placed so much emphasis on the use of agents in telecommunications and messaging.

- Permit hand-holding with the customer
- Assist the salesperson who tracks the customer order

In fact, a marketing input is not just sales; it is intended also to serve two other areas: the *engineers* and the *operating personnel*. It can assist both in interactively evaluating line availability, assigning service modules, and executing other functions.

Computers are not alien to these problems. Part of what I just said is done today through legacy programs, but, speaking from my experience, classical approaches don't do *interactive messaging*. The missing part is informing the personnel down the line of:

- The requirements that result from the most recent input
- The customer order execution, or reasons that the order has not yet been handled

Agents can search the database for relevant information, propagating it online and flashing it on the screen of the person who should take action. Such a *proactive* approach is much more preferable than waiting for the people down the line to take the initiative in looking up what has gone wrong with outstanding customer orders.

Lack of interactive feedback creates delays and also requires additional effort—hence it involves costs. This statement is as valid of customer orders as it is of another major area of marketing interest: *inventory management*. This type of application is presently missing in most traditional network marketing subsystems. Yet there should be:

- *Inventory agents* supported through mathematical models, which search online for still available telecom facilities
- *Scheduling agents* able to allocate the identified service components to the customer order automatically
- *Matching agents* that match orders against availabilities and can make the necessary evaluation for inventory replenishment

Most of the artifacts to which I refer are based on mathematical statistics and knowledge engineering. Static models are nothing extraordinary, and they been extensively used in industry for the last 20 years. Dynamic models are more sophisticated, leading to agents that automatically:

- Evaluate economic lot quantity, including that of bandwidth
- Optimize order time and order quantity in terms of cost-effectiveness

This approach is most important as telecommunications bandwidth today is being sold in the futures market, and there is a growing number of competitive access providers, as we saw in Part 2. If nothing else, keeping one's market edge calls for an ingenious use of agents.

The implementation of inventory control agents in matters concerning bandwidth, including agents able to do cost-effectiveness evaluations, will be novel. It will provide network management with foresight— hence with leadership—in the telecommunications domain. But there are as well other marketing applications that are pressing, for example, producing online answers to client requests.

We should always be keen to learn from the best applications available today, rapidly proceeding with the implementation of what works well. For instance, the General Telephone and Electronics (GTE) Laboratories have made a first-class application known as CALIDA, for California Intelligent Database Assistant, which provides seamless access to heterogeneous databases. This is one of the functions an intelligent network should support at user sites.

There used to be a time when customer queries, or even complaints, were answered with delay—perhaps never answered—by the teleco. This is no longer possible because in a highly competitive market the customer buys channel capacity from somebody else who:

- Is sensitive to his or her needs
- Cares about his or her unhappiness

The problem, however, is that telephone companies, like so many other corporations from manufacturing to banking, find themselves with a bunch of heterogeneous databases that are not easy to access online. The customer account is, for instance, under IMS, the accounting database has been converted into DB2, the service records run under Adabas, and so on.

The contribution of CALIDA is that of permitting seamless access. Figure 10-5 gives a bird's-eye view of the design underpinning this solution. Its functionality rests on four pillars that constitute a good frame of reference for the application of agents.

In the GTE case, the CALIDA solution targeted seamless access to incompatible databases. In other implementations, agents can handle very diverse functions such as memory-based reasoning and searches activated by the end user. *Efficiency* rather than inertia should guide the approach that we adopt, and agents can be instrumental in overcoming interdepartmental lines.

Figure 10-5
Conceptual approach
to the design of
CALIDA.

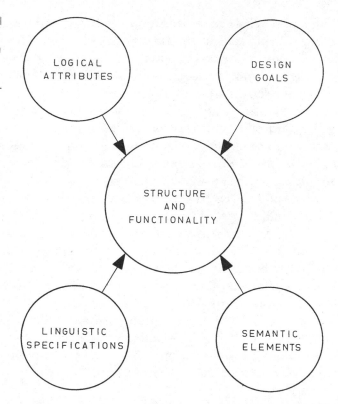

Agents and the Dynamic Modeling of Interactive Solutions

The examples that we have seen throughout this chapter illustrate that by operating online, dynamic models assist in database mining and perform opportunity searches and a number of other functions including statistical analysis.

This has not escaped the attention of tier 1 companies that use models as infrastructure for advanced applications, including the performance of specific duties. At NYNEX, for instance, this is the case of the:

- Marketing and Planning System (MAPS)
- Automated Transmission Link Analysis and Simulation (ATLAS)
- Maintenance Administration Expert (MAX)
- Dispatch of Repair and Installation Vehicle Efficiency (DRIVE)

As might be suspected, many of these applications are interdisciplinary and interdepartmental. But because they use agents, it is not necessary to change organizational boundaries. What is needed is to use technology to integrate different functions and responsibilities in the most effective way.

An integrated marketing, diagnostics, and maintenance approach will evidently pose prerequisites. These are connected to improvements that should be made in a managerial sense, as well as in technology. For instance:

- Exploiting online databases to locate values reflecting network quality and performance

- Mining quality databases in order to develop patterns of failures from trunks to nodes

- Preparing line-node maintenance orders, including needed materials and skills

- Making better market penetration feasible by matching customer requirements with network resources

MAPS of NYNEX offers an example of what this means, in matter-of-fact terms. The marketing and planning system of the New England telephone company is based on the Geographic Information System (GIS) software, targeted for use in market forecasting and outside plant engineering, as well as a range of customer services. Marketing applications supported by MAPS and GIS include:

- High and low population distribution

- High-, average-, and low-income bracketing

- A combination of the above and other demographic criteria*

- Analysis of business locations

- Zooming in on business locations within a buffer zone, for instance, a 2-mile radius

The business area analysis targets a definition of where future infrastructural investments may be needed, for instance, optical-fiber installations. It also links the marketing system to engineering and to investment projects, with both analyses and reporting assisted through agents.

British Telecom has used the Internet to develop its version of a similar structure, with an objective fairly comparable to GIS. Known as Java

---

*See also the discussion of the use of agents in merchandising.

Call Reporting and Analysis (Jacaranda) and operating on the World Wide Web, the application aims to illustrate the company's vision of future developments in online service reporting and in network management.

In the BT application, the Java language* has been used to visualize the results of database queries in a sense fairly comparable to what the preceding sections have illustrated. The end user interactively explores the underlying information elements—from services to statistics:

- The user can dynamically obtain a visualization of phone connections made from within the United Kingdom to a customer query number or product support line.

- In color graphics, the system presents the geographical source of calls by towers located at main population centers.

To learn how to work with the system, a first-time user can start with a guided tour. This will introduce him or her to what the application can provide as well as explain its mechanics. The end user will as well gain an overview of the control panels that he or she may have to manipulate in more complex applications. Alternatively, agents could provide this type of assistance.

All this is part and parcel of the *human-window perspectives* of which we spoke in a previous section in connection to the renewal of the input/output functions. The end user can, in a simple manner, select day and hour or other time of interest:

- The system will initiate animated sequences that reveal trends or identify useful patterns.

- The three-dimensional display can be zoomed, rotated, and scaled.

Jacaranda offers its user four main windows, which constitutes a good example on the evolution of input/output, without a virtual-reality setting. One of the windows is the main visualization, the other three are helpers: display control, data control, and pick information.

In an I/O sense, display control helps to select the overall mode, as well as to massage and translate the visual output. Working in normal mode permits the manipulation of the object under study. Alternatively, the so-called bounding box mode permits interactive rotation.

The job of the data control panel is to enable selection of call records to be displayed. The end user can also control an embedded animation

---

*D. N. Chorafas, *Visual Programming Technology*, McGraw-Hill, New York, 1996.

function over the timeframe that he or she chooses. The contribution of pick information is to assure that, at a selected location, the user can get more detailed multimedia information on-stream, or mine more detail from the database(s).

That Jacaranda is marketing oriented does not mean that a very similar system could be developed to address technical issues. On the one side, this dramatizes the flexibility of high technology; and, on the other, it opens broad perspectives in using agents for the personalization of the application to fit end users' needs in the most agile manner, as well as for the renewal of output operations that is so long overdue.

An example of asticius usage of knowledge technology is provided by Compaq which developed a just-in-time inventory management system shrinking stocks to just 30 days, from 69 days a year ago. This contributed $1 billion to the $4 billion cash Compaq had at the end of December 1996.

Through the new JIT models, by January 1998, Compaq expects to help in trimming more than a month off its dealers' inventories by doing more of the customization they now perform on their own. There is a golden hoard on new practical examples.

Jointly developed as a prototype system by the National Institute for Standards and Technology (NIST) and Enterprise Integration technologies, SmartProcurement employs autonomous agents over the Internet (or other networks) to facilitate and help in optimizing the purchase of goods.

- Procurement information can be located and exploited throughout the Web in heterogenenous databases.

- The agent allows a purchaser to execute knowledge-assisted procurement online, interactively.

A SmartProcurement process is initiated with either an electronic or human request for quotation (RFQ). A purchasing agent then acquires a list of agents who have been registered, for instance, with CommerceNet, as vendors for the requested item.

The RFQ is sent to those agents, who then decide whether or not to bid. Bids are returned to the purchasing agent, who accumulates them before the execution deadline. Subsequently, the buyer selects from the set of bids submitted and winning *vendor agent* is automatically notified.

CHAPTER 11

Autonomous Knowledge Artifacts That Effectively Work Online

The key to postindustrial supremacy, well into the twenty-first century, is believed to be in networked, knowledge-enriched software that works in real time. Typically, this software will be highly distributed, designed in a fine-grained fashion, reaching online databases anywhere in its operations environment, and interfacing to users through virtual reality.*

---

*See D. N. Chorafas and H. Steinmann, *Virtual Reality—Practical Applications in Business and Industry*, Prentice-Hall, Englewood Cliffs, N.J., 1995.

As Chap. 10 demonstrated, new design approaches will be sought in terms of applications development and sustenance. However, the able implementations of agents will require a deep understanding of conceptual, intuitive, and creative processes. In the background of studies associated with this goal are a number of scientific and technological advances whose synergy is actively sought:

- Projects will address problems associated with storage, transmission through *photonics* (fiber optics), and optical computing.

- A new generation of *neural networks* will be applied to a range of issues, from pattern recognition to voice recognition.

- *Fuzzy engineering* will be increasingly used for problem solution where qualitative, rather than quantitative, criteria dominate.

- *Genetic algorithms* will emulate crossovers and mutations, for the solution of optimization problems, the creation of novel situations, and experimentation.

What these references have in common is the drive for knowledge-enriched *advanced software* able to operate in a networked fashion, integrating vital components into a service-oriented environment, acting in an autonomous manner and effectively interfacing to these services.

While, as we saw in Part 1, autonomous agents will dominate the landscape, emphasis will be placed on *ultrafast,* superparallel optical information transmission, storage, and processing. This will justify the opinion originally expressed by some of the pioneers in artificial intelligence that stand-alone expert systems will not be around very long.

Part 2 has documented that one of the more compelling issues for the success of the networking of resources is the development and use of intuitive agents with the ability to monitor complex situations and compare actions against plans. Collaborative networked systems will have a major impact on how and where people work and, eventually, on how they live.

The more we develop agents and other autonomous knowledge artifacts that can successfully work online, the more emphasis will be placed on their modularity, sophistication, and integration. At the same time, information technology designers must be conscious of the fact that we cannot afford to scrap the majority of existing systems overnight. We have to build higher layers of intelligence on the existing base.

Reevaluating the Benefits of Implementing Autonomous Agents

The point has been made repeatedly since Chap. 1 that agents have similarities to expert systems in the sense that both are knowledge artifacts. But also they differ because in contrast to earlier online expert systems that usually stay put, agents operate as *autonomous vehicles*.

At this early state of the art with agents, any project developers will be well advised to keep in perspective those origins that are common to agents and expert systems. Therefore, it will be rewarding to examine the reasons that led to the evolution of goals in *knowledge engineering*, beyond the original objectives of

- Developing
- Producing
- Distributing

intelligence through human-made systems. The reader with a background in applied science and/or knowledge engineering will appreciate that, next to knowledge acquisition (of which we spoke in Chap. 10), the first major challenge we are confronted with is *knowledge representation*. The acquired knowledge must be mapped into the computer. This is done through the development of algorithms, heuristics, and scenarios. Then the artifact must be packaged to facilitate its *interactive usage*.

Knowledge representation will have little practical significance without *knowledge utilization*. Therefore, our focus must go beyond the *knowhow* and its translation into machine intelligence, all the way to how humans and machines (or machines and machines) interact.

The representation of knowhow is no longer a frontier subject because it has been achieved in many applications domains. A similar statement starts human-machine communications applications. For instance, in engineering design, knowledge artifacts have been used in interfaces for computer-aided design (CAD), for database mining, for enhancing 3D graphics, and in configuring system support.

Figure 11-1 brings to the reader's attention five milestones in the evolution of engineering design, the most recent being networked CAD—enriched through artificial intelligence (AI) constructs. The benefits obtained include higher productivity, better product quality, and a broader design to provide an integrated system solution.

Figure 11-1
The search for higher productivity and better product quality conducted by bringing agents into computer-aided design.

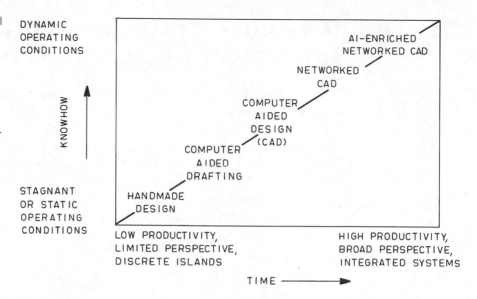

As Chap. 8 demonstrated, other important applications in engineering have taken place in online diagnostics. These are largely oriented to computers and communications, but they are also oriented to other subjects such as power production and distribution in banking and finance.

Computer-integrated manufacturing (CIM) and robotics have had significant assistance from knowledge-enriched constructs and more recently from agents. The same is true of embedded systems in areas ranging from troubleshooting to compliance control. The development and use of expert systems preceded the evolution of agents, as Chap. 1 explained. Therefore, experience gained from the implementation of expert systems can serve as a stepping stone in the implementation of autonomous agents.

Among the applications areas where expert systems proved their value, one that is of particular interest to many professionals is banking.* Implementations include investment consulting, assets management, tax advisory, information retrieval, and auditing. These are late 1980s examples.

What's the impact of this reference on agents? The answer is that, based on such experience, two different companies, a money center bank and a multinational manufacturing organization, have recently designed and implemented agents that audit online the accounts of

---

*See D. N. Chorafas and H. Steinmann, *Expert Systems in Banking*, Macmillan, London, 1991.

their subsidiaries. They are reporting to the comptroller on discrepancies that have been found, and, this permits the organizations to focus human attention and resources in greater depth, and to a higher level of detail, on only the most important situations.

In terms of forecasting, knowledge constructs have been used in the prediction of market trends as well as in sales planning. In Chap. 9 we spoke of this in connection to Geographic Information Systems. The broad area of decision support has also seen benefits—for example, in the evaluation of corporate strategy, analysis of trends, and scoring systems for loans.

While most examples come from expert systems, these and other domains are now mature for the use of agents. The same is true of learning. Knowledge artifacts have played a significant role in computer-aided instruction—for instance:

- In teaching high-technology subjects
- In supporting computer-based training

A similar statement can be made about software development in other areas: automating programming chores, providing software design support, and helping in software reuse, as well as in reengineering.

The applications examples that today exist in these domains are no minor feats, but it would be unwise to rest on our laurels. We should always improve what we have achieved because this is intellectually challenging—and, at the same time, it is the only way to remain competitive.

- Static expert systems can serve up to a point, but their contribution diminishes as requirements for online support increase.

To be sure, the expert systems of the mid- to late 1980s are not useless, in terms of functionality. They are star performers compared to the Cobol programs of the 1960s variety that continue to be written, at great cost, by a large number of backward-looking companies. But neither are static expert systems as flexible and profitable as:

- Dynamic agents able to serve in real time at the very moment the need arises, prompting their masters rather than passively waiting a demand

This ability to reside at network nodes, use the network facilities, and be proactive in problem solution make agents the best choice for a business and industrial environment. Nobody should underestimate the leading role high technology can play in terms of organizational survival.

Improving Service Quality through Rapid Deployment of Knowledge Robots

It has already been explained in Chap. 1 that some of the organizations that participated in the research project that led to this book call the dynamic intelligent artifacts which we have seen *knowledge robots,* or *knowbots.* Others prefer the agent label; still others give them no single generic name.

While terms may differ, the reasons given by the majority of user organizations regarding the development and use of agents is practically the same: They are a *more effective* means for compliance to the wishes of a client and the requirements of a project, than the type of software employed so far.

In engineering, agents also present a unique ability to integrate a number of critical design aspects that in the past constituted discrete islands, even with CAD. An example is given in Fig. 11-2 with engineer-

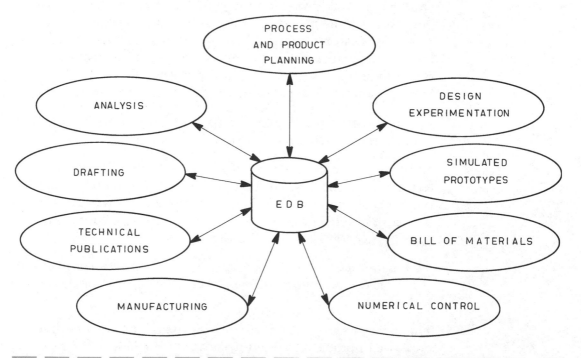

Figure 11-2 Agents helping integrate discrete island of CAD applications.

ing databases (EDBs). Notice that in this typical design problem, a number of discrete islands of conceptual activity gravitate around the engineering database. But usually it is up to the designer to integrate these islands, in an efficient manner.

The use of autonomous knowbots does away with housekeeping tasks and permits the designer to address more imaginative functions—for instance, providing a better response to client requirements for a custom-made product and improving the designer's capability to optimize design choices. We must always keep in mind that we live in a service economy, and the focal points are:

- Fast response
- Higher quality
- Lower cost

As we will see in greater detail later in this chapter, time to market is a major competitive advantage, but higher service quality has many aspects. Perhaps the easier to perceive is *zero defects*. But there are also other issues to keep in perspective. For instance, in terms of the operations of a multinational company, we can distinguish:

- A more accurate *compliance* to the law of each country of operations
- Better follow-up on *corporate decisions* and directives

In the case of a financial institution, among the characteristics of service quality are more efficient investment advice, a better screening of loans by applicants, and the ability to provide online help to less qualified bankers, including *training* them. Agents also assure an effective but low-cost and rapid way to review, prune, and restructure client portfolios on a continuous basis.

Here is what a leading bank is said to have learned through its experience in the use of knowledge artifacts: "They help to *simplify* the workflow, while the result of classical computer programs was to complicate it." And by acting as autonomous vehicles, agents run on different platforms, providing a full-service *networked* assistance.

A manufacturing company suggested that what it appreciated most with the first agents it designed and used was that it is feasible to employ them *between* other jobs, and that they also serve to promote interdisciplinary solutions. Their usage streamlined certain processes, reducing the successive steps that static routines made necessary.

What did this company learn from its experience with agents? Management said the Number 1 lesson was that it is important to develop and install the knowledge artifacts *quickly,* then enhance them while in actual operations. This is a good example of the rapid deployment policy that should be followed with software.

In a recent implementation, it took a couple of days of steady work to create a simple agent containing a couple of dozen rules. The knowledge engineer started with a list of all possible equipment a factory has available. The list is part of the program as a protocol of alternatives. The other basic input is the dynamic production schedule, a function of incoming orders. The options available for each schedule are at the center of the agent's logic trails.

The agent exploits the database that was created for an expert system developed 6 years ago, which is still in operation. To employ the older construct, the user answered a series of questions with choices based on the type of products to be made. This question-and-answer session has been replaced by the agent's action. The agent examines the logic chain of scheduling alternatives, leading to the selection of a sequence of machine tools. The agent prompts the user to take action. The latter can ask to see the rule(s) upon which the program is basing its response, but most often this is unnecessary.

A genetic algorithm (GA) has now been developed as a specialist assistant to the agent. The latter defines a feasible sequence that will be subsequently optimized by the genetic algorithm, scheduled to run on a parallel computer in order to permit rapid response.

In a worst-case scenario in terms of response time, optimization by the GA on the parallel computer takes a few minutes. Alternatively it requires an overnight run on a top-of-the-line mainframe. A couple of other agents designed with structural simplicity make it feasible for response to occur at a subsecond level on a Pentium node.

Using Agents to Shrink Time-to-Market Requirements

A study done in 1994 by industry experts in America demonstrated that locally made products are practically equal in terms of quality and costs to those made in Japan. Some other criteria important to market success were also tested, confirming the hypothesis of no significant difference. But there was one vital exception: The Japanese were found to be well ahead in terms of time to market. This gave the Japanese companies an important competitive advantage over their American counterparts.

The race toward shorter and shorter time to market is far from being over. New goals are set every day, and the time lag continuously shrinks, but a steady time shrinkage cannot be achieved without high technology, and agents play an important role in this process.

Not long ago, Toyota announced that by the end of this decade it will be able to deliver a custom-made car in $3\frac{1}{2}$ days. Such record is not achieved just by working harder. It takes a great deal of machine intelligence to get results. The use of agents can be instrumental in shrinking time to market to a bare minimum by preempting product problems:

- Providing capable, online handling of product features from customer specifications to scheduling, quality control, and delivery

- Fully automating solutions oriented to the design, manufacturing, and sale of products, including low-cost production and distribution

- Providing a cost-effective handling of a large volume of complex transactions in all their phases from order taking to analysis, inventory management, accounting, and billing

We spoke of Geographic Information Systems (GIS) in Chap. 9. Based on a recent application, Fig. 11-3 presents in a block diagram three main

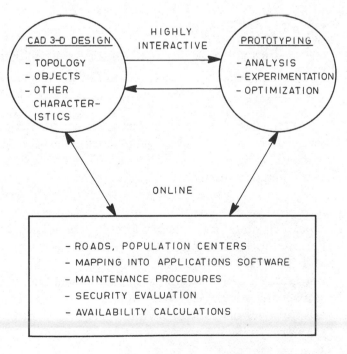

Figure 11-3
Agents assisting both the highly interactive activities and their online connection to domain knowledge.

domains where agents have been used as assistants to the analyst and the designer.

In this particular implementation, the focal area has been the highly interactive operations in the top two bullets. Benefits, however, have as well been obtained by the online connection of the CAD system to domain knowledge, with agents providing the links.

In a different project in the same frame of reference, a Japanese company recently designed a pair of agents whose goal is service differentiation by client group. Multimedia support is assured for reporting purposes. Agents were also written to sustain a steady development of the company's management reporting infrastructure.

A joint project by Hitachi and Nissan Motors developed knowledge artifacts to help garage operators working on car maintenance. Two knowledge artifacts were written because the strategy had been to distinguish between two scenarios that posed different database-mining requirements:

- Fuzzy query
- Quick query

Fuzzy engineering functions have been incorporated to permit an inexperienced person to readily retrieve part numbers from automotive inventories. *Fuzzy query* means that the exact part number is not known to the user. The number is retrieved by entering a few reference items regarding the car model:

- Classification code employed on the automobile inspection certificate
- Model type on the vehicle's manufacturing number plate
- General designation, for instance, body style

An interactive intelligent artifact does the identification work. Another proceeds with database mining either in a limited search of the local database or in a broader search requiring access to remote databases back at the manufacturing plant.

By contrast, a quick query is a crisp query. It requires part identification, and accesses nearly 1 million information elements that can be rapidly retrieved from the database. In the Hitachi/Nissan case, and similar applications, typically such information is stored on optical disks, and it is generally available locally. Figure 11-4 explains the supported procedure in this and similar projects, by a database-mining agent. The artifact investigates database contents through keywords in the case of crisp queries or through memory-based reasoning when fuzzy queries are asked. In both cases it interacts with the user.

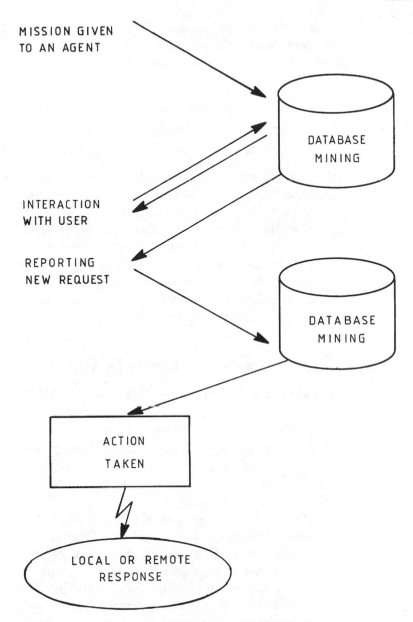

Figure 11-4
The agent as an interactive artifact at the user's disposition.

While this application has been designed primarily for car mainte-nance reasons, it holds obvious possibilities in the domain of design engineering, permitting to further shrink the lag associated in time to market. Every designer has fuzzy queries to ask, but most (currently available) CAD software does not accept them. Fuzzy engineering over-comes this handicap.

A study which I had done in the mid-1980s among leading engineering organizations[*] demonstrated that, on average, the engineering design department of these companies experienced the following statistics in the longer run:

- 34 percent of the projects were completely new designs.
- 21 percent were parameterized construction and design models.
- 45 percent were variations on existing drawings, with few changes.

The current state of the art with agents may not provide a great deal of assistance in the first 34 percent of cases though, as the agents' intelligence quotient grows, eventually it might. But agents can contribute a great deal in the other 66 percent of design projects.

In conclusion, the assistance that knowledge artifacts can provide the engineering designer is indeed polyvalent. It ranges from database mining with fuzzy queries (the way the Hitachi/Nissan knowledge artifact works) to guiding the designer's hand in making optimal choices of components as well as in reengineering.

The Service Agents Can Offer in Connection to Bank Loans

Since 1986, the topmost financial institutions have built and used expert systems for scoring company loans. This practice has significantly improved upon past procedures that were mostly manual or batch based. As we will see in this section, many of these artifacts can successfully evolve into interactive agents.

While every bank followed its own policy on the type of knowledge constructs it developed and used, over the years it became possible to derive a common denominator by class of expert systems. In terms of company loans, for example, intelligent software analyzes balance sheets using customer account information in the bank's own database and the database of the company asking for the loan, as well as public databases.

Similar criteria are employed when an investment bank does the analysis of a given concern to evaluate the soundness of the company's stock. We will talk more of the synergy between loans and investments

---

[*]See also D. N. Chorafas, *Engineering Productivity Through CAD/CAM*, Butterworths, London and Boston, 1987.

in a later section; as a way of laying the groundwork for that discussion, let me here emphasize the need to include in a sensitivity analysis:

- The company's growth prospects
- The company's financial stability
- The relationship between assets and liabilities
- The synergy between products, market share, and profit potential

Interestingly enough, this procedure approximates the Hitachi/Nissan dual scenario of fuzzy queries and quick queries, of which we have spoken. Based on database mining, agents can put together a credit score regarding companies applying for loans. In the general case, the models being used consider:

- Profits
- Liquidity
- Cash flow
- Acid test, or CA/CL*
- Long-term assets
- Capital ratio
- Products
- Markets

Agents can be instrumental in all these evaluations, interactively bringing to the attention of their masters the results they obtain. Knowledge artifacts can as well build other scoring milestones, such as annual growth and productivity.

A different way of making this statement is that each one of the chosen functional areas may be the province of an agent. An intelligent artifact can examine in depth its area of specialization, with its output used as input by another construct to integrate the obtained results.

In fact, some of the aforementioned areas of credit investigation can be served by more than one specialized agent. This is the case, for instance, of the analysis of assets and liabilities, where a whole family of agents can be applied. Similarly, agents can be developed for the analysis of other domains that impact on company performance, hence on the organization's ability to repay the loan.

---

*Current assets over current liabilities.

Figure 11-5
A radar chart for visualization of key factors in company loans connected to risk.

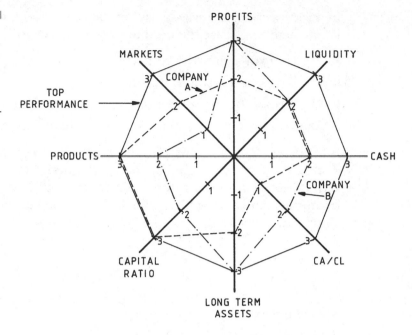

Taking a leaf out of the book of engineering, still other agents may ask their users the type of presentation and visualization they want, preparing the interactive output accordingly. In one of the financial institutions that followed this approach, the output comes in graphical form, like the radar chart shown in Fig. 11-5.*

Bank loans may be a classic product line in the financial industry, but it is as well an area of great interest to management, which would like to improve upon past performance. For many banks, particularly those of small to medium size, the loans portfolio is responsible for 65 to 85 percent of their revenue, but it is also a domain where major losses can occur:

In any financial institution, the potential earnings capacity is strongly related to lending activities governed by choosing from among risks that are measurable. Thus, major factors determining whether or not a loan is appropriate must be investigated with care.

Among the key factors to be studied outside the debtor company are the condition of the economy and the bank's own diversification and

---

*See D. N. Chorafas and H. Steinmann, *Virtual Reality—Practical Applications in Business and Industry*, Prentice-Hall, Englewood Cliffs, N.J., 1995.

hedging in its loans portfolio. In both cases, knowledge artifacts and database mining are very important because loan losses and nonperforming loans have tremendous impact on the institution's earnings and its viability.

A number of agents can be successfully built for lending purposes in a much greater level of detail than we have seen in the preceding general example. For instance, for *commercial loans,* specialized agents can operate in areas such as export credit, price financing, export financing, and government guarantees.

Other, more complex artifacts are necessary for *financial loans.* Examples include bridging loans, promissory notes, preliminary financing of securities, bonds, repurchase agreements, and collateral loans (Lombard credits). Underwriting is a major class for the use of agents. Still another case is *discount credit,* including reserves and limits.

Some agents can serve as "assistants to" and others as "analyzers" in connection with *contingent facilities:* guaranteed credit, acceptance credit, standby credit, margin credit, limits for foreign exchange, credit lines for spot transactions, taxes, compliance, and so on. The same is true about *contingent liabilities* of the company asking for credit, which may also involve private customers and public authorities.

In all these cases the knowledge artifact will act as an autonomous analytical assistant, to loan officers and financial analysts. It will perform the *skills-level work,* of which we spoke in Chap. 2, leaving it to the experts to apply a higher-up level of knowledge, provided they are qualified to do so.

Automating the Analytical Solutions Needed for Investment Advice

A professor of banking I had at UCLA some 43 years ago used to say in his seminars that at the bottom line a lending officer and an investment officer have very similar goals. The lending officer analyzes the client from the viewpoint of his or her ability to repay. The investment officer looks at the prospective company from the viewpoint of its ability to turn a profit. Both are interested in the future cash flow.*

---

*See D. N. Chorafas, *Financial Models and Simulation,* Macmillan, London, 1995.

Seen from this perspective, what was said in the preceding section about the analytics necessary to examine thoroughly whether a prospect for loans is trustworthy is true also for investments. But the agents that need to be built to answer investment queries also have other prerequisites. An example is the need to analyze the customer's profile as an investor.

If we look at a hierarchy of modules for an intelligent investment system, chances are that the customer profile analyzer will be the first agent necessary, helping its master to define client requirements in a factual and documented manner. The same agent or a variation of it can be used as a:

- *Professional advisor* to assist the account manager
- Means to *test and prune* the client's database
- A tool for *choosing investors* for new banking products, through database mining

It can also serve as a *learning module* for new account officers. Each of the references that have just been made can be the object of a separate agent or of a cluster that has been created parametrically from the same knowledge structure.

Apart the fact that it is better to have several simpler systems designed to work together than a big one that is monolithic, it is no less true that small individual agents will have to be built for *telebanking services* addressed to important clients. When this is done, provision must always be made for the integration of different agents giving the account manager one complete frame of reference.

Among the decision factors an agent designed for private investors should consider is low or high risk aversion, the client's rate of income tax, how the client evaluates the prospects for interest rates, and the client's time horizon. As an example, here are two of the rules associated to an artifact built for bond selection:

If   \<risk aversion is low\>

and   \<interest rate is impossible to predict\>

Then   \<maturity = less than time horizon\>

If   \<risk aversion is high\>

and   \<interest rate is not very likely to rise\>

Then   \<maturity = time horizon\>

Built by Nikko Securities, on the basis of similar rules, *Best Planner* is an artifact for investment advice to low- to middle-net-worth individuals. Its first module is the client profile analyzer, which has been designed along the lines described above.

Given the population to which it appeals, the investment profile is established through icon selection. Icons are presented in attractive color graphics. After the first selection has been made by the client, other queries are made: Annual income? Tax-free deposit (eligible for it, yes or no)? Own home? Loan on it? The expert artifact examines the investor's current financial assets: savings, time deposits, money market, bonds, stocks, and real estate. It reflects on:

- Short- and/or long-term investments
- Desired liquidity
- Degrees of risk (9 degrees of risk are supported)

The goal targeted by Nikko, which is a broker, is to move money out of time deposits and into securities. This is essentially a sales tool, which over the years has proved to be very effective. Therefore, it is a good example of the contribution technology can make to competitiveness.

More complex intelligent systems have to be made to answer the portfolio design requirements of high-net-worth customers. One of the artifacts built to meet this goal assesses geographical regions with their *exchanges* and different currencies, as well as possible changes in currency rates. It:

- Keeps track of *investor* requirements given by the profiling module
- *Evaluates* alternative investment instruments that are available
- *Allocates* among regions, exchanges, and moneys, as well as investment instruments (gilts, bonds, equities, precious metals, and cash)

Each one of these activities can be the subject of a different agent, with all modules working together in unison. Another agent may assess the different sectors of the economy in each country an investment is contemplated. Still other agents may evaluate different companies, per industry sector, in terms of equity and liability for investment purposes to provide an input.

The Interactive Use of Agents in Merchandising

In the general case a single database is most unlikely to cater to all the needs of a user. Even if this were feasible within the company, advantage would have to be taken of the fact that there were already a vast profusion of stored information on sales coming from public databases. Hence, intelligent artifacts should be designed in principle for a networked environment. Agents can effectively mediate between the user and the great volume of information at his or her disposition. From user to agent should pass only the description of what is sought, and from agent to user should pass only the matching or nearly matching information.

All connections to remote databases, interrogation, filtering, rejection of unwanted information, and so on should be performed by the machine intelligence residing at the workstation or accessed over the network from any node. What agents can accomplish in regard to database mining has already been shown in Fig. 11-4.

As discussed in Chap. 8, inventory management is one of the most interesting examples of where intelligent artifacts play a vital role. Of the following examples, one comes from W. H. Smith, the bookseller; the other two from Marks & Spencer and Bloomingdale's, the merchandisers:

■ W. H. Smith has to keep track of about 70,000 individual stock items.

With any approach other than an online system, sales details can be weeks out of date. But database mining requires first-class organization and proper technology, including mathematical models for forecasting of demand and for the simulation of inventory levels.

Knowledgeable readers will say that this is a 30-year-old challenge, since simulators have been used in inventory management since the mid-1960s. This is true, and for this reason W. H. Smith and other retailers have increasingly used knowledge artifacts to gain a competitive advantage.

■ Marks & Spencer developed and used an intelligent behavioral scoring artifact.

Behavioral scoring acts as an online assistant to company credit officers as well as financial auditors. Its implementation demonstrated that the assistance provided by this knowledge construct has been instrumental in controlling bad risk, which has significantly enhanced the profitability of the retailer's credit card business.

Among the benefits stressed by Marks & Spencer are quicker throughput of customers' purchases at the cash register; less time lost in stores and in Chester (where the Financial Services division is located); lower staffing for credit control and debt recovery; higher level of justified declines; lower level of risk regarding delinquency; sharp reduction in write-offs; lower telephone costs; and much better quality of customer service.* Understandably, all these are key factors to a company that has to handle 1,750,000 client accounts.

■ Using point-of-sales (POS) data for accounts receivable, Bloomingdale's shortened the lead time of receivables by 3 days.

This financial benefit has come over and above savings on the costs of data entry. Whether for credit authorization, employee productivity, or the ordering of goods, retailers need information at their fingertips: What they require this week may not be the same as they needed last week or what they will need next week. Knowledge robots operate on the point-of-sales nodes. By doing so, they extend beyond what classical POS technology or traditional data processing has to offer.

This application of knowledge artifacts in working with POS and interactively exploiting databases can be extended all the way to the automation of the payments traffic. The use of agents can be seen as an online extension of the employment of expert systems in payments, which has been beneficial at three levels of application:

■ Exceptional (large) payments

■ Spontaneous payments

■ Regular payments

The process of data clearance and transaction control by functional area is shown in Fig. 11-6. This block diagram reflects a real-life implementation in which it has been necessary to distinguish between front-end and server functions because of the structure of the legacy solution already in place. To bring this application to state-of-the-art level, agents were implemented at all layers.

Finally, as Chap. 6 highlighted, autonomous knowledge artifacts can be used not only for payments clearing services but also in connection to security management. Agents help to establish and enforce security policy and services, controlling both physical access to resources and guarding logical access to programs, files, terminals, and abstract assets such as the use of commands.

Some financial institutions are currently developing agents to protect against virus attacks. Others are working on knowledge artifacts able to exploit audit trails. Still others aim to provide a single-system image of

---

*See also D. N. Chorafas and H. Steinmann, *Expert Systems in Banking*, Macmillan, London, 1991.

Figure 11-6
Data clearance and
transaction clearance
by functional area.

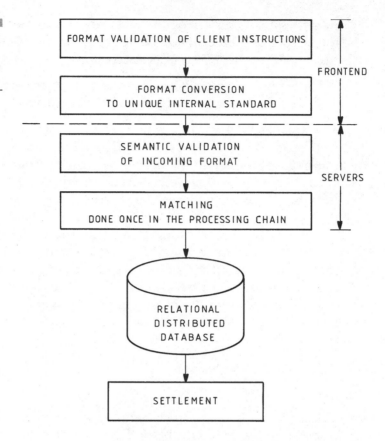

security connected to payments and settlements procedures, including one-stop log-on, log-off, and password change facilities.

Intelligent Artifacts in a Networked Environment

Agents can be very useful whether we talk of a stand-alone computer or of networked resources, but the assistance they provide increases significantly in the context of a networked environment as the examples in this section document. While these case studies come from banking, they are equally applicable in manufacturing and merchandising.

Typically in a modern financial institution all managers and professionals have their workstations attached to the corporate network. A growing number of institutions have implemented expert systems on the professionals' workstations, but more often than not these are static. Some of the goals put forward by banks developing and implementing agents are to:

■ Improve the level of client service provided by account executives and managers

■ Integrate all information sources through agent-assisted database mining

■ Effectively access the global database of in-house and public information

Other goals are technological, for instance, to achieve one logical, integrated network by using artificial intelligence. The advantages gained by this solution will be particularly appreciated if we account for the fact that today a major bank is faced with some 20 to 70 incompatible networks, none of which can be disconnected without somewhere hurting operations.* Yet, access to these different incompatible networks should be seamless to their users.

This apparent contradiction between the difficulty of replacing old networks and the need to integrate them seamlessly can be effectively solved through knowledge engineering with agents assigned to hand-holding. Network architects should see to it that a number of *physical structures* integrates into one *logical structure* whose top layer:

■ Is served by agents

■ Is universal in a corporate-wide sense

For instance, the Mitsubishi Research Institute (MRI) has developed *one logical network* that has been projected for all of Mitsubishi Bank's managers and professionals, the incorporation of client workstations, and the online handling of large distributed databases.

This and all other any-to-any solutions are aimed to integrate diverse networks functioning at different levels of the bank's operating environment. For another example, Bank of America has integrated its 67 incompatible networks into one logical superstructure, and Citibank did the same with Network 2000.

Seamless integration is the best approach because total streamlining does not make any great sense. Even if the replacement of existing net-

---

*For documentation, see D. N. Chorafas and H. Steinmann, *Implementing Networks in Banking and Financial Services,* Macmillan, London, 1988.

works inside a given financial institution had been feasible, this would have helped little, since major competitive advantages are gained by offering online access to all business partners, who cannot be made to conform to any one bank's standard. Clients should be assured of online access with full transparency of the prevailing heterogeneity. The use of agents can significantly contribute to this goal, as well as to personalized services.

A Swiss financial institution developed an agent that explains to an account manager why a given order is not being executed precisely according to a customer's wishes. The constraints may have to do with compliance to regulations, the fact that the customer delayed sending money, or for other reasons.

In terms of networking, many banks actively support clients' computer-to-computer links with current companies, which operate seamlessly: "Simply offering information does not motivate the client company to buy our financial services," said a senior executive of the Sumitomo Bank.

In parallel with the technical effort, tier 1 financial institutions have engaged in intensive marketing of the sophisticated products they now provide: "In developing new media, we first must assure good market size," suggested a senior banker who then added: "Any one of our customers is able to access our network through intelligence-enriched interfaces."

The best systems solutions are interactive. Not only banking transactions but also economic and financial information are supplied online to the clients. Mining the bank's database is accomplished in real time by authorized clients, with security and protection provided through knowledge artifacts as we saw in Chap. 6.

- The common ground characterizing the work that motivated all these projects is competitiveness.
- The emergence of an advanced communications system enriched by agents is having a deep impact on professional people and the way they work.

Part 2 has already highlighted that telecommunications is no more just telephony and data transmission, as it used to be. It is a dynamic field with any-to-any networking solutions facing steadily evolving customer requirements. These must be met in an able manner as the challenge rises.

Positioning ourselves and our companies to face the competitive issues of the coming years can no longer be relegated to classical means and worn-out tools. If agents were not available, they would have had to be invented because there is a growing requirement for their services.

In the following section, we will follow up with a specific example of this argument, when we consider the role agents play in personal communications. But whether in the special or in the general case, it is appropriate to keep in mind that the unified domain of communications, computers, and software is the largest and most potent conglomerate of services the world has ever experienced:

- Its market is huge and dynamic.
- Its products are steadily evolving.
- Its jobs increasingly shift to knowledge-enriched activities.

New applications don't cease to develop from what can be characterized as a traditional approach to new business opportunities. The very fact of their steady evolution requires knowledge robots to be designed and put into service. If we fall short of upgrading the knowledge quotient of our operations, the products and services we offer will be too costly, too unsophisticated, and too slow to be competitive.

The Assistance That Agents Offer in Personal Communications

It has been repeatedly emphasized that the currently existing applications domains need to be enriched with intelligent artifacts in order to reduce their costs and improve their competitiveness. The need for agents is, however, even greater with new products and services because without them these products or services may never have a chance to pass the market's test.

A good example is offered by the Personal Communications Network (PCN). Personal communications will ultimately allow person-to-person calling independent of location and the terminal used, the means of transmission (wired or wireless), or the choice of technology. The market potential for personal communications services is expected to be large, provided low-cost tariffs are applied. Lower and lower cost tariffs can be feasible:

- If the telecommunications industry's efficiency steadily increases
- If its management knows its goals and the best way to reach them

Starting with the network, for the foreseeable future the maximum density for fixed-wireline telephones is not expected to exceed substantially an average penetration of 50 percent of the total user population. This means approximately one connection per household, plus office use.

In contrast, the penetration of wireless personal communications has the ultimate potential to reach nearly 80 percent of the user population. This essentially means nearly one connection per adult.

A study done in 1994 by the European Union suggests that within the borders of its membership at that time, the 12 nations, total user numbers could ultimately exceed 200 million, compared to a current total subscriber base for traditional fixed telephony of 153 million. The moving gear will be the expansion of mobile communications into the:

- Personal communications market
- Mobile computing*

Leading communications companies have taken notice of these projections. Planning to reach anywhere in the world where there is a market, American Telephone & Telegraph, Motorola, and IBM are each rolling out what they are calling *intelligent messaging systems.* These are projected to make practical communications provided by cellular phones, personal digital assistants (PDAs), and other technical solutions currently in the offing.

These strategies bet on a growing income stream from the development of mobile services, including not only nodes and links but also sophisticated, agent-supported software and terminal equipment. These are practically targeted for each user, and there are reasons to believe that such plans will bear fruit.

The way service providers look at the market, intelligent software will help to identify and route the messages by the most efficient method possible—whether over wires or airwaves, or by digitized voice, fax, database connectivity, or other means. Agents will also send back confirmation that the message reached its destination.

As we saw earlier in this chapter, one of the major targets is to pass seamlessly through largely incompatible communications networks and heterogeneous computers, while making the system easy to use. Every vendor aims to offer in his or her network the services that will best attract public interest, and practically every vendor suggests that interactive messaging is best supported by agents.

AT&T's PersonaLink service is projected to browse electronic news automatically to find issues and documents of interest to the user.

---

*See also Chap. 5.

Agents will be doing the legwork, tying together incompatible systems, dialing up services, requesting information, and responding to end-user demands. They will make the information highway work for the end user, without requiring him or her to learn about all the mechanisms before getting on.

Motorola has its own notion of a universal service. Called *Mobile Networks Integration* (MNI), it includes software and hardware to mesh various wireless links, including cellular and paging systems. Its software would be installed in PDAs, portable computers, and cellular phones, as well as in the computers that run phone networks and other communications systems.

IBM's service, still in the planning stages, is code-named In-Touch. It is aimed at the corporate market, which in the longer run is expected to be the more lucrative. Whichever the vendor, the credo seems to reflect Henry Ford's philosophy on teamwork: "Coming together is a beginning; keeping together is progress; working together is success"—and agents are the catalyst, as well as at the center of attention.

CHAPTER 12

Using Agents for Analogical Reasoning, Patterning, and Productization

From science and engineering to finance and management, data analysis and patterning is one of the fertile fields in which knowledge artifacts operate. Also, as we saw through practical examples in Part 2 and in Chaps. 10 and 11, agents can be instrumental in providing their masters with assistance in analytics, and bringing attention to developing trends and patterns, which they do in real time.

While there are many generic domains of data analysis, each with its own characteristics, prerequisites, and algorithms, there exists as well a common ground among them. Common needs include statistical evidence, time series analysis, and linear and nonlinear models such as fractals, strange attractors, Laplace equations, Fourier series, heuristics, Poisson and Weibull distributions,* leptokyrtotic and platokyrtotic distributions, and chaos theory.

Interactive knowledge artifacts should be developed to handle automatically analytical requirements by level of significance, with agents designed for domain-specific studies but able to collaborate with other agents. In-depth and surface studies are important all the way from database mining to user interfaces capable of handling computer-participative applications.†

A pioneering data analysis and patterning environment, recently developed by a major organization, includes *auditing* agents that examine the accounts of subsidiaries in the United States and abroad. They develop a pattern of budget versus actual results and of realized sales plan versus actual. This analysis is done to the detail of each article in the price list, some 5000 of them. The findings are interactively reported in color, with three-dimensional visualization.

Some projects go well beyond this example. Because of high technology, both the underlying concepts and the structure of information systems are radically changing. The same is true of entertainment electronics. The epitaph has been written by Dr. Andrew Lippman, director of MIT's Media Bank, who says: "TV is already broken, and to fix it is like patching threadbare jeans." Instead of sewing awkward patches, Lippman suggests, we need to reinvent television—that "sleeping giant being stalked by the Internet. TV as we know it is going to fall, and the knockout punch is not going to be digital TV but, rather, computational media." Dr. Lippman's Media Lab provides an integrated network of smart machines that don't just tune in but also add on and modify information.

This is a merger of the World Wide Web with the content of audiovisuals and its impact goes well beyond TV, all the way to the boardroom. As we will see, patterning is the cornerstone of this process, and the same can be said of analogical reasoning.

---

*D. N. Chorafas, *How to Understand and Use Mathematics for Derivatives*, vol. 2, Euromoney, London, 1995.

†See Chap. 1.

Let me add a word of caution. While the mathematics underpinning the agent must be first class, there is much more than the math that we should care about. In a later section in this chapter, we talk of *productizing* and fielding. The serious reader will pay a significant amount of attention to what is said in that connection.

WebBots, the Internet, Virtual Agents, and Morphism*

Those of us who for the better part of the last 20 years thought that computers are not really meant to be programmed were delighted to learn about one of the World Wide Web's hottest products: Vermeer's FrontPage. Recently acquired by Microsoft, this company offers to the market:

- Interactive visual-site management tools
- A WYSIWYG editor for HyperText Markup Language (HTML)
- Templates for easy creation of Web sites and *WebBots*

WebBots are knowledge artifacts that work as search engines. They enable the creation and maintenance of discussion groups, and make feasible other applications on a given site—all without programming. Industry experts expect that Microsoft's clout could make FrontPage a standard not only for Internet but also for the intranets, a market which, in many ways, could be more lucrative than that for public Web sites.

FrontPage has pioneered the idea of a Web as means for document-type authoring. This is an interesting metaphor that can be used in interactive environments to bring together all office documents in a company. The resulting flexible structure can then be successfully served by agents both:

- For customization purposes
- In a server node type of generalization

In an application designed for merchandising, interactive knowledge robots record the complete set of transforms leading to the creation of

---

*HTML was introduced in Chap. 4 in connection to morphing expert systems into agents. See also D. N. Chorafas, *Visual Programming Technology,* McGraw-Hill, New York, 1997.

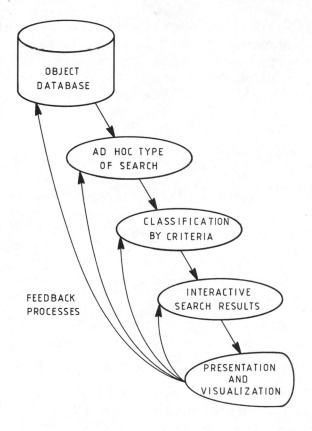

Figure 12-1
Characteristics of an effective database-mining procedure leading to visualization.

an interactive reporting system. The methodology that was followed is shown in the block diagram in Fig. 12-1. In this figure, special attention was given to the integration of:

- Interactive user interfaces
- Analytical tools at the workstation level
- Distributed database-mining procedures

Databases are mined by proprietary agents that are not too different in their design from the WebBots. Management found that the handling of compound electronic documents can be significantly simplified by using these agents.

However, other problems remain, like the mapping of analytical procedures and patterning beyond the now classical level of visualization—for instance, the link between analytical reasoning and the processes of visibilization and visistraction increasingly promoted through intelligent artifacts:

■ *Visibilization* means making visible the very big and the very small, which might otherwise escape attention.

■ *Visistraction* is the visualization of concepts and ideas, which up to a certain point can be effected through morphing.

We spoke of visibilization in Chap. 2 in connection to virtual engineering. While Chap. 2 did not make reference to visistraction, it did discuss case-based reasoning, which is instrumental in the visualization of ideas and concepts.

Virtual reality is a good example of where the advent of increasingly more sophisticated knowledge artifacts permits systems to perform feats that are both novel and powerful.

Some of the most recent constructs involve a basic intelligence that can be implemented in a practical sense, whether in communications, networking, and databases or the wide arena of advanced computer applications.

Called by some experts *virtual agents,* the new class of computer-generated artifacts are developed and controlled in real time. Their characteristic is that they can *morph,* or transform, into other objects in a live display or as background processes.

In the context of virtual-reality projects currently in development, *morphing* involves the metamorphosis of one agent into another at runtime. Such transformation is smooth and seamless. In animation, for instance, morphing provides the following possibilities:

■ A character can change into the product of a corporate sponsor and back again.

■ This character can be used for commercials, demonstrators, displays, and other marketing tools.*

In industry, these virtual agents are usually designed with specific jobs in mind. An example is real-time assembly modeling through simulation, which provides engineers with a means to design and plan concurrently most of the parts, tools, and manufacturing processes necessary to construct various products, assemblies, and systems, as discussed in Chap. 7.

Written by Simgraphics, in manufacturing the Assembly Modeler works in concert with NCAD, Northrop's production CAD system, and ICAD, a rule-based engineering system that incorporates artificial intelligence. After designing components in NCAD, engineers use the Assembly

---

*See also Chap. 9 on the use of agents in marketing.

Modeler to manipulate, test, and verify the assembly process. These components are assembled in a *virtual space*, just as if they were actual parts.

Users select parts or subassemblies, which may move according to kinematic constraints. They do so to visualize part-to-part clearances and fits and to plan tooling needs. Morphism is a way of visistraction that provides practical results. Therefore, it stands a good chance to become popular.

Virtual Reality, Agents, and Telemedicine

Basically, the contribution of virtual agents is that of providing sufficiently realistic feedback early in the design process. As a result, they facilitate the early integration of part design and manufacturing through concurrent engineering, as already discussed in Chap. 7.

The reader can employ his or her imagination to speculate on a wide range of applications. In the case of NCAD, the Assembly Modeler helps to drastically reduce the time necessary to design airframe components. It also offers the possibility of real-time walkthrough, allowing the end user to visualize and manipulate software-hardware constructs in a natural manner.

Real-life examples like these tend to provide the best references because they demonstrate that not only is the concept of intelligent agents viable but also there are instances in which it has already been put into production. In practical implementation terms, a virtual-reality environment depends on agents in order to function and give results.*

As knowledge artifacts, virtual agents can quite nicely handle visualization, visibilization, and visistraction, making that much more effective the use of networks. Networking requires this type of flexible and friendly human-machine interface to dynamically adapt to end-user needs. No longer should the end user learn from the interface. Rather, *the interface should learn from the end user.*

A similar statement can be made about access mechanisms for networks and databases and about instruments and sensory devices that feed these databases with actual, accurate, and timely multimedia data streams.

The better-known applications of high-precision instrumentation have been, so far, in space research, nuclear engineering, chemistry, and petrole-

---

*See also Chap. 2.

um. New opportunities are now being presented in other domains where things that think can make the difference. An example is *telemedicine.*

In one recent example involving telemedicine, the doctor can see some 30 patients in eight hours, while physically travelling from house to house may see only 5 or 6 patients in a day.[*] Each televisit costs $36, compared with $135 for a home visit.

- Under a managed-care system, with a fixed fee paid per person insured, telemedicine offers huge potential savings.

- But there is not yet enough evidence to demonstrate that the results being obtained are comparable to an inhouse visit.

In the late 1970s, the concept of telemedecine came under spotlight because health care became both an urgent concern and a costly practice. Two decades later we know that telecommunications is bound to play an important role. What is not clear is how far progress will be made with complex processes like *telediagnostics* and *telesurgery.*

The way to bet, in my judgment, is that current technology is better tooled to serve telediagnostics than telesurgery. One way to evaluate the two would be to ask, At which level of complexity can we bet that telemedicine may offer good results?

Teleradiology is a prime example of what is doable. This does not mean that advanced technology cannot be of assistance to surgery. In fact, it could be, an example being virtual reality.[†] As another example, optical fibers are increasingly used in deep surgery, enabling the surgeon to operate with precision through the monitor. This, however, is not telesurgery.

The University of California in Los Angeles has an imaginative project in virtual reality jointly managed by the School of Engineering and the Department of Medicine. Its objective is to improve upon the current performance of surgical operations aimed to treat aneurysms in the brain. Aneurysms are soft, pulsating tumors formed by the unnatural dilation or rupture of the wall of an artery.

The focal point of this project is the use of real-time visualization to better understand fluid-flow phenomena in an intracranial vessel with an aneurysm. An approach to mapping the aneurysm has been implemented, first using conventional computer systems and later through virtual reality.

---

[*]The Economist, January 11, 1997.

[†]See D. N. Chorafas and H. Steinmann, *Virtual Reality—Practical Applications in Business and Industry,* Prentice-Hall, Englewood Cliffs, N.J., 1995.

Virtual reality allows the surgeon to take a walk inside the aneurysm. A postprocessing graphical system helps to visualize the data produced by the numerical solver. At UCLA, data visualization has been developed with built-in tools for the investigation of fluid flow. Velocity profiles and pressure profiles are calculated at different times in the systole-diastole cycle. They are presented as contour plots, cutting planes, isosurfaces, isovolumes, arrow plots, and so on.

In terms of surgical guidance, there is interest in agents in relation to virtual reality. The Loma Linda Research Center in California employs virtual reality (VR) as a diagnostic and treatment tool. In conjunction with NASA and Stanford Medical School, the center has created a software prototype for operating on simulated patients. This project developed virtual bodies, complete with physical simulations that provide accurate representations of body parts. The VR environment enables physicians to study the limitations of muscles and tendons, the movement of fluid-filled internal organs, and so on—and agents can assist in this process.

These examples make reference to what already has been achieved. Many experts however think that there is more future in health care delivery in connection to agent-enhanced wearable items that continuously monitor the patient's health in an ambulatory nonhospitalized simulated environment.

MIT's Media Laboratory has a project along this frame of reference. Agents can support processes linked to therapy evaluation, which can induce changes in home care and care for the elderly. Telemedicine has many aspects that resemble telemetry, posing the questions:

- How could telemetry be combined with human factors?
- How intelligent could body appliances get?

In Chap. 3 we spoke of *BodyNet,* which provides intrabody linkages. Researchers suggest that among the possibilities is a sport coat that would adjust its thermal properties to different climates. Another possibility is clothing that relays a patient's vital signs to a doctor's database.

Other projects, like MIT's Things That Think, aim to develop shoes able to calculate the time it will take to walk to a given location and evaluate if this is compatible with the doctor's directives. This is one example of everyday objects that could contain artificial intelligence embedded on silicon chips. Another example is BMW's recent car models that have fuzzy chips which learn the driver's habits to optimize gas consumption.

Figure 12-2 gives a snapshot of the BMW implementation. While driving, the predicate box of the fuzzy engineering artifact receives inputs

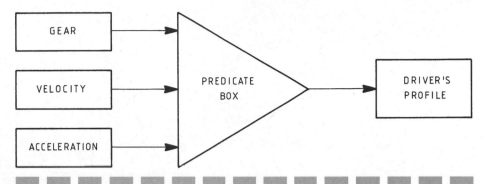

Figure 12-2 A fuzzy engineering artifact with three inputs and the driver's profile as an output.

like gear, velocity, and acceleration. These help to construct the driver's profile, which is shown in Fig. 12-3 as a fuzzy sets diagram. Notice how it contrasts to a crisp alternative:

- The fuzzy diagram is very flexible, expressed in a qualitative and quantitative manner.
- The crisp diagram is strictly quantitative and, therefore, inflexible.

Whether we talk of BodyNet or numerical control of machine tools, whether our interest focuses on computing, networking, and databasing or on agile human interfaces, there is a great deal of analogical reasoning taking place. Therefore, the process of building virtual agents is closely connected to analogical reasoning and patterning.

How Agents Work through Analogical Reasoning

The preceding chapters have provided examples on how agents can emulate the way experts think and work, albeit at a skills level rather than the higher-up layer of intelligence. The concepts underpinning analogical reasoning are not alien to the reader. In Chap. 2 we studied case-based reasoning. Prior to that, in Chap. 1, we examined how the methods of causality and teleology influence the process of thinking by analogy.

In principle, domain experts perceive events, analyze them, think about them, and make decisions by analogies. This fact suggests that we should be expanding the notions already introduced, while keeping in

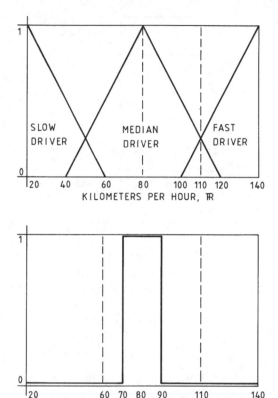

Figure 12-3
A fuzzy representation and the crisp alternative.

mind that there are several definitions of the term *analogical reasoning*. Some people consider it as being synonymous to *case-based reasoning*; others believe the two terms are distinct.

My definition of *analogical reasoning* is based on observing meaningful but possibly obscure similarities in two apparently disparate situations—which, however, have a hidden similitude. Therefore, it consists of a process of establishing apparently obvious similarities between different instances of the same type of event, then using the outcome in the context of the problem under study.

A precise definition is difficult because etymologically, one of the words is used quite loosely and in a greater variety of senses: *analogy*. The fact is that there are no hard-and-fast definitions to be given except to say that *analogy* invariably involves mapping some underlying network of relations in a comprehensive form. But often there may be many such networks in a base example, and the question arises of which one to choose for mapping.

The ability of determining the *purpose* of the analogy can be used to create, and in cases to identify, the relevant network of relations to be mapped. However, the process of selecting such a network is not self-evident, and the same is true of its representation.

In the majority of cases, though not necessarily in every single case, there exist fundamental steps in analogical reasoning beyond the retrieval of relevant cases that permit reasoning by means of similitudes. The identification of these steps is very important because each one can be served by an agent.

This step-by-step approach is fundamental in explaining how agents work, or could work, through an analogical reasoning procedure. Part and parcel of this procedure will be database mining and subsequent elaboration through creative editors. In the general case this process calls into play:

- Detailed *matching* between the observed current case and retrieved references

- Establishment of *connections* and bridges between new case and retrieval material

- *Inference* within the established domain, particularly inferential reasoning by analogy and justification

In the majority of reasoning projects, an orderly approach will involve the structural decomposition of the analogical process, keeping in mind that analogical thinking can be found in the background of most creative thinking activities.

Analogy is, however, a complex problem, and appropriate research is necessary to make use of tools that computer science and knowledge engineering make available. Agents should incorporate these tools—for instance, mapping theory. The solution that we adopt must as well be able to learn by analogy.

Learning by analogy leads to abstraction and generalization, but this is not a mission that will be necessarily given to an agent. By contrast, a knowledge artifact may be instrumental in learning when and how to provide the necessary alert regarding matching patterns—as it does in database mining.

Quite often, analogical reasoning means *approximate reasoning,* which relies on linguistic variables,* qualifiers, plausibility concepts, and a possibilistic mathematical infrastructure.† We have discussed earlier a number

---

*Which is not always accepted as a definition.

†See also D. N. Chorafas, *Knowledge Engineering,* Van Nostrand Reinhold, New York, 1990.

of examples along this frame of reference and also have spoken of the need for elaborating reasoning rules.

The establishment and observance of rules can be helpful in analogical reasoning. We reason by analogy when meaningful similarities exist between two or more domains. Any sort of knowledge held on any kind of entity—including theories, hypotheses, the interpretation of situations, and problem-solving methods—may have relevance in another. Through such analogies, by transferring, transforming, and mapping information from the one domain, which we can call the *base*, we can infer plausibly problem situations or additional information in the other domain, the *target*.

This approach is exemplified in Fig. 12-4, which shows an element-by-element analysis of computer-aided design. This case follows up on the examples provided in Part 2 on the use of CAD in telecommunications. In connection to software-hardware codesign, *logical views* and *physical*

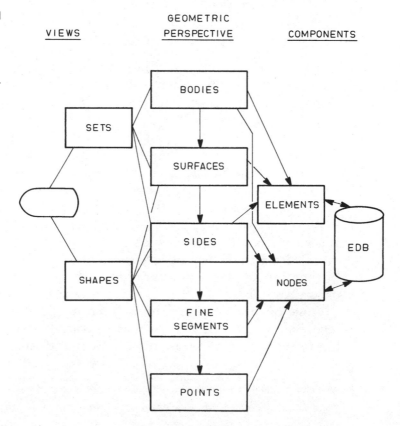

Figure 12-4
Element-by-element analysis for engineering design.

components are analogical to one another. They both integrate into the *geometric perspective*, which constitutes the target of the project.

Views are the base domain whose embedded knowledge impacts on the process of drawing by analogy. Sometimes, an initially meaningful similarity may be an illusion. But quite often it is a real event if some aspect of the base may be applicable to the target situation.

Typically, the agent would find the base information in a nearby or remote database—hence, the need for database mining. The knowledge artifact will perceive the target by analyzing a situation or by filtering new data streams. And it should have the skill to match the target to the base, and vice versa.

Object Algebras and the Role of Polyvalence in Analogical Reasoning

Let's start with the premise that we cannot build interactive knowledge artifacts without appropriate tools. At the same time, we should not use old tools, such as obsolete programming languages, because they are inefficient. We should capitalize on the rapid development of technology, the main impediment being the fact that, in too many cases, our systems personnel have fallen behind the state of the art—but humans are reprogrammable engines.

The recently emerging *object algebras* are good examples of new tools. *Object algebra* is in fact a misnomer because the new tool is mainly a relational algebra with an object orientation. These languages typically take all tuples as objects, which is a limiting approach that is nonetheless somehow able to bridge the gap between object-oriented programming and the widely used relational databases.

■ Object algebra has been used as a mapping language when the local databases use a record-oriented data model.

■ Relational algebra can be extended with new operations to give it object aspects with conflict resolution capabilities.

Within this frame of reference, the agent may be characterized by an integrated schema defined as a set of relational views derived from global schemata. In most cases, the process uses extended relational algebra operations.

Beware, however, of the fakes. SQL, for example, is considered today by many systems specialists to be a naive language. But at the same time it has been accepted by the American National Standards Institute (ANSI) and by a number of computer user organizations—hence, it will not fade away quickly:

■ There exists an object-oriented extension of SQL that reaches into object algebra.

■ It generates statements and maps them into a data manipulation language, but it is not particularly efficient.

Some people look at object algebras as linguistics for querying heterogeneous data models. Support is sought for declarative semantics permitting the study of side effects and alternative translations for view updates. In this connection, it is good to remember that database mining is an integral part of the agent's mission.

Like any other artifact, object algebras are not able to respond to all needs. For example, they will be constrained in answering the perceptual and analytical requirements for analogical reasoning, most particularly in a qualitatively oriented environment. In this case, fuzzy engineering can provide a much better support, as we saw earlier in this chapter.

For the benefit of the reader who needs to develop agents for analytical reasoning purposes, Fig. 12-5 presents a three-way classification of linguistic constructs. The axes of reference are *axiomatic, algorithmic,* and *logic-predicate.** One or more of them will be necessary depending on the case under study. The methodology is, however, quite straightforward. First, the agent must decide if the analogy is applicable in the current context. Then, it must find an analogous domain, having a similarity on which the model can capitalize.

Database mining and the descriptive approach come together because, as we saw earlier in the chapter, the agent's knowledge of the base must be richer—or more amenable to augmentation—than its knowledge of the target. Otherwise, no information flow will take place.

This is a good example of the necessary polyvalence of an agent's functionality, to which reference was made in the chapter introduction. Contrary to classical programs for data processing, which never cared for flexibility and extensibility of their features, the value of interactive agents is derived from the outlined factors.

---

*See also the discussion on predicates in Chap. 3.

■■ ■■ ■■ ■■
Figure 12-5
The development of
agents for analogical
reasoning typically
involves one or more
of three types of lan-
guages.

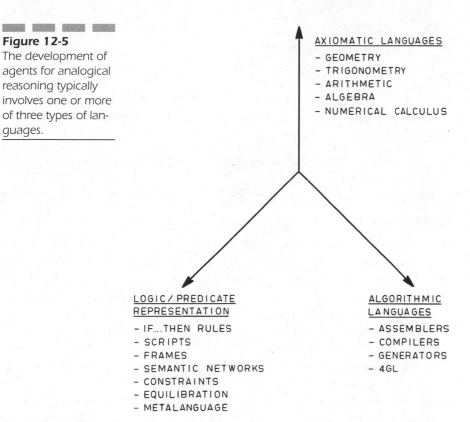

AXIOMATIC LANGUAGES
- GEOMETRY
- TRIGONOMETRY
- ARITHMETIC
- ALGEBRA
- NUMERICAL CALCULUS

LOGIC/PREDICATE
REPRESENTATION
- IF...THEN RULES
- SCRIPTS
- FRAMES
- SEMANTIC NETWORKS
- CONSTRAINTS
- EQUILIBRATION
- METALANGUAGE

ALGORITHMIC
LANGUAGES
- ASSEMBLERS
- COMPILERS
- GENERATORS
- 4GL

A similar reference can be made to the need for agile representation structures. Here again, a recurring theme among *rocket scientists** is that traditional models are not adequate to accommodate the diverse modeling needs that during the last 5 years or so have characterized interactive computational finance. The relational model is based on set theory and does not provide adequate support for entities that rely fundamentally on order for their structure. Correspondingly, object-oriented solutions assure the necessary semantic meaning and provide the basis for ephemeral hierarchies—but experience in their use is only now building up.

My advice is to do research both in new forms of modeling and in emerging technologies such as extensible databases and deductive data-

---

*Physicists, engineers, and mathematicians who gained experience with the aerospace industry, nuclear engineering, and weapons systems—and now work as financial analysts. See D. N. Chorafas, *Rocket Scientists in Banking*, Lafferty, London and Dublin, 1995.

bases;[*] and also to explore alternatives to current modeling approaches, directly supporting lists, sequences, and graphs.

In all these cases, the initially observed similarity between the base and target domains is important both in dictating which information may be mapped and in justifying the mapping itself. In scenario development, for example, such mapping is carried out by using a similarity matcher which:

- Judges the similitude between base and target by using properly chosen properties
- Brings into play classes, acts, and other relations depending on what is important

Relations and similarities are of significant interest if they take place in a causal way, creating the required connection and leading to predicates such as *intend* and *control* or, alternatively, in a teleological manner, as discussed in Chap. 1. Each approach, in its own way, helps to enrich the knowledge structure and make it more amenable to analogical reasoning.

All this is pertinent to the appropriate use of agents because of the need for conceptual models that can specify useful constructs and operators including spatial and temporal information and images. Developers should use operators that can be imbedded into languages and are able to handle in a flexible manner developing analogical situations.

In conclusion, the analyst will be well advised to focus on conceptual modeling tools that can describe the various applications in terms of objects, structures, and operators useful to the agent in performing its mission. It is not enough to have an extension to a relational model, but without an object-oriented extension, we will not gain the needed semantic support.

Capitalizing on Interdomain and Intradomain Inference by Means of Agents

While the argument remains open as to how much analogical reasoning takes place in a causal, case-based analysis, a sound way to proceed

---

[*]See D. N. Chorafas, *Intelligent Multimedia Databases*, Prentice-Hall, Englewood Cliffs, N.J., 1994.

around this point is the adoption of a policy that assures that the methodology we follow is not characterized by a limited approach or substandard tools. The agents we build should be able to improve their analytical and reasoning capabilities by learning.[*] Intelligent artifacts should learn as they act within a given domain or process, and developers should account for prevailing interdomain and intradomain syntax and structure.

The more intradomain the problem is, the more it helps to focus on analogical approaches. This supports exploitation and mapping of a larger collection of elements characterizing a given area of activity, retaining the most important specific issues relative to the problem addressed by the agent.

Only predicates that belong to a system constrained by higher-order (meta) predicates can be successfully carried from base to target.[†] This should be followed by pair-wise matches, between *predicates* and *objects*. Figure 12-6 gives a comprehensive view of an active object, which is composed of information elements and commands. A passive object consists of only data. Hence, it has extensional, rather than intentional, capabilities.

This distinction is important in the development of autonomous knowledge artifacts because agents are active objects that perform inten-

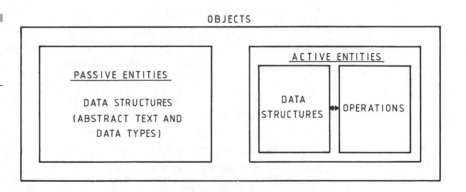

Figure 12-6
Passive and active entities in an object environment.

OBJECTS

PASSIVE ENTITIES

DATA STRUCTURES
(ABSTRACT TEXT AND
DATA TYPES)

ACTIVE ENTITIES

DATA STRUCTURES ↔ OPERATIONS

ANY OBJECT CAN INVOKE ANY OTHER OBJECT,
THUS PERFORMING OPERATIONS BY ITSELF.

---

[*] See also in Chap. 1 the discussion on analytical learning agents.
[†] See Chap. 10 on the definition of the concept of meta.

tional functions, typically supported by predicates. In an analogical reasoning application, the goal may be to:

- Build potential pairing expertise
- Bring together possible matches
- Select those best applicable among competing episodes and matches
- Assure consistency through verification

A methodology concerning the development, implementation, and use of agents as well as their contribution to analogical reasoning, should provide rules for pruning the knowledge bank. It must also lead into causal or ancestor chains or, alternatively, to teleological mapping, as explained in Chap. 1.

A relation or analogy in connection to the primary problem addressed by the agent, as well as its interdomain and intradomain relationships, may be highlighted by supplementary descriptions that can be useful in the matching process. Typically, flexible matchings are incremental. With incremental approaches the most similar parts or events are initially matched. The first matching is followed by less similar parts or events that can also play a vital role.

The agent's primary objective, and the predicates expressing it, can be used to direct this mapping process—constraining the *search space* by choosing which parts to map and match. Also, restricting the important causal relations to those somehow connected to the goal is another way to direct the mapping process.

As we have observed in some detail in Chap. 8, a good deal in this last section has to do with *inference* and, therefore, with artificial intelligence. Backward chaining for inference involves traversing links back from a goal node to its antecedents,[*] examining if analogs apply in the target, and if yes, in which way they apply.

For instance, a given relation may actually be a primary criterion in the exercise of the agent's functions. Or it may be caused by other relations in the precedent (base). If so, we try to establish the other relations in the exercise (target). But the relation in question may be absent from the exercise as well as from the precedent. If so, the agent seeks another precedent-establishing procedure, often through case-based reasoning.

Conceptually, the trial-and-error, therefore heuristic, solution is built into an agent. The approach is in conformity with the fact that when

---

[*]See also D. N. Chorafas, *Knowledge Engineering*, Van Nostrand Reinhold, New York, 1990.

encountering a new problem situation, an expert is reminded of past situations that bear a strong similarity to the present problem. Possibly this happens at different levels of abstraction—or with a twist or two in the perceived similarities.

Commonalities among previous and current situations can serve as the basis for generalization as well as for identifying a set of possible problem states, or, alternatively, a set of operators with known preconditions that transform one state into another:

- Specific applications in mapping may benefit from higher-order relations—hence the emphasis to be placed on *metareasoning.*

- *Taxonomical* approaches are methodological. Hence, they can be of significant assistance both to analogical approaches and in selections from large databases.

Implementation examples may be taken from different domains. For instance, in analyzing a financial database in terms of *customer profitability,* an agent would focus on transactions made, cost per transaction, charges to the client, fees from portfolio management, and other issues. By contrast, an agent targeting bank profitability would look into gross profit, net profit, unit costs, and ratios such as plan versus actual, in budgetary terms, and sales versus profitability. Similarly, income statistics serve to highlight relations connected to market data. Typically factors used by financial analysts include:

- Yearly earnings
- Earnings per share (EPS)
- Return on assets (ROA)
- Return on equity (ROE)
- Price-to-earnings ratio (P/E)

Other profitability agents will examine fine-grained internal information regarding the cost of doing business: production costs, sales costs, administrative costs, and the costs of staying in business (usually research and development).

In a recent application along these lines, an intradomain agent developed for management reporting by exception addressed *company safety net* issues such as the ratio of the firm's own capital to outstanding long-term and short-term loans. Another agent focused on the acid test (current assets versus current liabilities) for the company as a whole and for the accounts of its subsidiaries.

A manufacturing company built intradomain agents able to mine its own database as well as use public databases to analyze factors connected to yearly *turnover* for selected product lines and single products. Still another agent compared the number of employees prevalent in the same branch of industry. Other interactive artifacts were designed to analyze liquidity, follow up on cash flow, examine collection periods, and flash out cash-to-deposit ratios.

Generally speaking, profitability and productivity factors are good domains for agents. In a productivity *sense*, in marketing, analytical aspects concerning sales per employee and similar criteria focus sometimes on the performance of a product line and single product. Manufacturing productivity factors include production level per worker.

Statistical distributions can be fruitfully developed for comparative purposes with *alarm signals* triggered by agent(s). Prognostication will be a more complex agent development process addressing *future perspectives*, for instance, looking into the return on the company's R&D investments by way of:

- Innovation
- Time to market
- Market share

This discussion complements what we saw in Part 2 in terms of practical applications examples for agents in the telecommunications domain. It also provides an example on the differences that exist between interdomain and intradomain applications. But it should be quite clear that the best results can be obtained by internetworking the artifacts.

Agents, Applied Mathematics, Value Analysis, and Patterning

The preceding section made the point that the mathematical expression of agent functionality must match the artifact's goal. At the same time, when it is well done, it provides a dependable description of what we expect the artifacts to do.

Agent functionality can be described in mathematics (the preferable way) or by means of scenarios. Mathematics includes theories of logic, space, quantities, regularities or irregularities, arrangements, and patterns. It is a system of signs and rules that:

- Permits study through abstract symbolic structures
- Goes beyond theories and deals with test hypotheses

Data analysis is best performed through a rigorous methodology supported by mathematics. The world of mathematics is populated by signs, symbols, and abstract structures connected through relationships. Their systematic exploitation is both:

- A science
- A language

As far as the development and use of agents is concerned, it is necessary to recall that mathematical concepts deal with logical implications and contingencies. Operations can be symbolized and iteratively manipulated. But above all mathematics is a world of mental concepts that can be used to describe and model phenomena of the physical world.

Mathematical expressions act both as descriptors and as linkages. An example is given in Fig. 12-7 from a financial project. Banking services can be exploded into atomic elements, each requiring a set of resources.

Figure 12-7
A three-layered structure characterizing a financial business and its products, constituent elements, and resources.

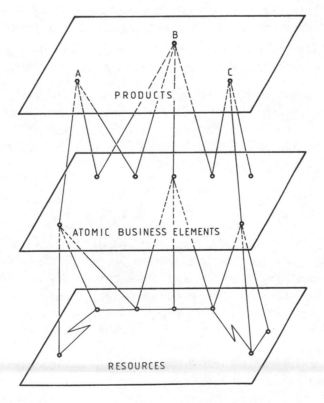

The same, incidentally, is true of manufacturing products that can be exploded into a bill of materials, with the linkages provided through mathematical rules.

Agents can be developed to search for certain criteria in this bill of materials—for instance, the criterion of lower cost. This process is known as *value analysis,* and it was developed in the 1960s but was largely performed manually for nearly three decades. The true automation of value analysis is accomplished today through agents.

Agents may look after opportunities for more rigorous analytical procedures that lead to better identification of situations and their comprehension. This particular aspect is what interests us the most in connection to how knowledge artifacts work and the kind of support they can provide to their masters.

An example is the use of mathematical signs and rules leading to the recognition of *patterns.* The real test of pattern definition and the identification of its attributes lies in the consideration of pattern relationships that must be rigorously expressed. Weak or strong, the way of identification follows the way of an evolutionary process of logical thinking:

- Expressed as a system of signs and rules, a lower-level conceptualization is represented by the creation of standard patterns.
- The higher level of generalization is that of metapattern relationships among pattern groups, which is also more sophisticated.

Microscopically, agents bring attention to detail or trigger alarms, both issues going beyond pure computation. Macroscopically, they may provide a more detailed look at information flows. They may even juxtapose and recombine information, therefore helping to analyze problems in greater:

- Depth
- Breadth

When searching for deeper knowledge, agents operate on database(s). Any new items of information or experience are used as additional information to update and check hypotheses initially made, aiming to bring their discoveries to the attention of their masters.

Sometimes, the relationships within and among patterns are uncertain, or the course of action has not been mapped into their rules. This, too, is a characteristic beyond the level of computation. The agent's ability to understand real situations and to interpret them has much to do with its embedded:

- Knowledge representation
- Inference procedures
- Explanation capabilities

Basically, the agent's reasoning is based on a semantic network involving analogical reasoning and similarity-based classification. Though these processes require computation, the high point is that they apply existing knowledge to a new problem instance, on the basis of similarities with older problems. Similarity-based classification addresses the problem of fitting an individual case within generalized cases that constitute a metapattern.

In a way, the three-layered structure in Fig. 12-7 can be seen as fitting this description. The products landscape is a metapattern of atomic business elements. The latter are elecroset-type component parts of products—and, as we saw in Chap. 1 with things that think, in the future these parts may exhibit intelligence.

Mathematical representation addresses the existing or future relationships, offering to the intelligent artifact a closer visualization of patterns and processes. In this and in many other cases, software development and computation are part and parcel of a solution, but they are not the whole solution. Yet there has been a tendency to identify the development of agents with computation:

- Computation is that part of mathematics that routinizes the processes of calculation.
- Classically, computation could not be successfully performed in the absence of human interpretation. But *agents* change that perspective.

Once accepted, the use of agents brings with it a number of practical and philosophical consequences. As intelligent artifacts, they can influence our actions and the pattern we follow, by focusing our attention on certain things that have to do with our work or daily life.

Agents and Models: Their Productization and Fielding

The preceding section brought attention to the fact that knowledge representation, inference procedures, and explanation capabilities are processes inseparable from the development and use of agents—whether these are built for value analysis or any other reason. It is, however, no less true that without user acceptance, even the best human-made intelligent artifacts will not be able to fulfill their mission.

Agents are developed for the end user. They are not made for the satisfaction of the intellectual drives of the developer or for theoretical reasons. Theoretical considerations belong in basic research—such as MIT's Things That Think project. When we talk of development:

- The basic criterion for any human-made system, and therefore its ultimate test, is: Does it pay dividends?
- A model will never pay dividends unless the user (or users) for whom it is intended appreciate it, adopt it, and implement it.

These two bullets explain the importance of *productizing* and *fielding* the artifacts we build. *Productizing* means taking the output of a project, which may be a breadboard model and turning it into a commodity. That's what Daniel Bricklin did in the late 1970s when he turned a program he had written to help himself through Harvard into a very successful product: the *spreadsheet*.

There is a very significant difference between developing an artifact—or any other product—only once or for a small series and productizing it for the wider market. Since expert systems have been the forerunners of agents, let me take one of the better-known expert systems to exemplify the problems associated with productization.

Developed by Carnegie Mellon University for Digital Equipment, XSEL (Expert Salesperson) targeted the time-consuming tasks of preparing a customer proposal. Practically all of DEC's sales engineers have been trained in XSEL, but only 25 percent have used it. Technically, there was nothing wrong with the way XSEL was built or with the knowhow it contained. Its usage, however, required a significant amount of skill at the sales engineer's level—and not everybody was willing to put in the effort.

In other words, while the interdomain and intradomain inference was first class, the analogical reasoning was ingenious, and the output patterns most commendable, the intended user population balked. Something went wrong with the way the model sold itself to its users.

Technically, the productizing of XSEL included documentation, training manuals, and methods as well as ways and means to bring the expert system to the field. Less attention was, however, paid to the equally important task of getting the artifact accepted by those it was supposed to help. This dampened its implementation prospects.

In the early 1980s I was lecturing in a symposium at the University of

Vermont, in Burlington. Another lecturer was DEC's senior vice president for marketing who conveyed the following message: "In the 1970s," he said, "DEC employed graduate engineers as salesmen. Many were brilliant, and, once they got an order, some could even develop single-handedly the technical details of the customer proposal, translating them into specs."

It sounds great, does it not? Well, not quite so because the DEC executive went on to say that these engineers had one weakness: "They could not sell." They found it difficult to hand-hold and conduct the sales meeting and bring it to conclusion. In short, they could not sign up the customer and leave with a contract.

"Therefore," the marketing executive continued, "we no longer hire engineers for sales work. We hire people who have been trained in sales. But they also have a weakness: They cannot configure the customer system and write the specifications with the same expertise the engineers did. Hence, the development and use of XSEL."

The problem, however, has been that the experts in sales were not experts in the use of a complex artifact, in spite of the training they received to that effect. The lesson to be learned and applied with agents is that even if the artifacts are first class, if their a human window is wanting or if, simply, they cannot sell themselves to their intended users, they will not become success stories. The users will not go for them. Both productization and fielding are vital in overcoming this sales problem that goes well beyond mathematical analysis, patterning, and analogical thinking.

This can be said in conclusion: We don't necessarily need to develop artifacts for the lowest common denominator in the user population, but we should surely address the majority, say, 75 to 85 percent. We also must make sure that what we develop appeals to end users. With agents, *service* is the keyword, and the same is true of *ease* of use—from the seamless access to a database to the way the agent's human window is built.

Conclusion: Notions Underpinning the Development and Use of Agents

The examples we have followed since Chap. 1 provide the reader with evidence that *agents are automata* that possess *intelligence*, operate *autonomously,* and *communicate* among themselves and with their masters. Many examples have been provided to document this statement.

In terms of physical construction, the most relevant predecessors to today's intelligent artifacts are servomechanisms and control devices, including artifacts designed for:

- Process control
- Flight control
- Fire control

Chapter 1 brought to the reader's attention Alan Turing's *eins,* which, during World War II, were hardware-implemented but which today would be agents. Another predecessor of present-day agents, Chap. 1 suggested, are expert systems which have been used by tier 1 companies in the 1980s. Expert systems constituted the first practical implementation of artificial intelligence.

But there are also differences between the earlier and the more recent artifacts, to which we should draw attention. The first major difference between agents and physical control devices is computational power; the second lies in the use of knowledge banks. The third major difference is the fact that agents interact with people in humanlike ways, with a form of natural language or animated graphics. Some agents have the potential to formulate their own goals and intentions. They are initiating actions on their own, without explicit instruction or guidance. They can also offer suggestions to knowledge workers or set up schedules.

Still, today's agents are simple in comparison to those that are being researched. These include intelligent machines programmable to one's own individual tastes and attitudes, acting on our behalf or as apprentices. They capitalize on a growing software environment that can perform complex chores, and they can anticipate the needs of their master(s) and act on them.

As we have seen through practical cases, agents can learn from examples given explicitly by the user. The master can train an agent by providing it with hypothetical events and situations, explaining what to do in each case. The agent:

- Records the notions and the actions
- Tracks relationships among objects
- Upgrades its knowledge bank by incorporating the most recent example being shown

One of the methods used by an agent to acquire competence is to ask for advice from other agents that assist other users with the same task and that may have more experience. If an agent does not know what action is appropriate in a certain case, it can present the situation to other artifacts and ask for a recommendation.

MIT's Mondrian project on intelligent human interfaces,[*] has introduced an approach to training by example. One of the applications is in the technical documentation domain, targeting the production of manuals—a process that is error-prone and impacts everyone from the designer to the reader of the manual.

The implementation is based on an expert system that interacts with a graphical simulation. As each step of the procedure is performed, the artifact sees the result and can verify that it has the intended effect. The software agent records the steps, keeping track of the procedure. In essence, it "writes the manual" by producing a description of each step. For instance, the learning agent records a picture of the state of the device at each step to serve as an illustration. But also it synthesizes a program that represents the actions taken by the user, based on the user's feedback.

Agents can learn just by observing user behavior, but to do so, they need to be interactive. There are cases in which the user instructs the agent more explicitly. Instructability is increasingly a focal point of several projects, and the same is true of productization. In terms of the ability to train the agent, the user may present examples of behavior that the agent should follow, or the user may give advice to the agent as to how the examples should be interpreted. The agent provides feedback so that the user understands what the agent knows.

Regarding productization, the developers should pay a significant amount of attention to how well the agent will be able to sell itself, and its services, to the prospective user. Like any other product—regardless of whether it is dumb, smart, or intelligent—the agent is intended for the end user.

Other things being equal, the user will be more attracted to the artifact if he or she can understand it and if he or she can appreciate its usefulness. A procedural description, if one is made, does not need to represent an exact sequence of steps, but it should be comprehensible and usable supporting:

- Automatic control of machinery that would perform the procedure
- Verification that the system really works to the knowledge worker's satisfaction

[*]See Chap. 2.

Through analogical reasoning, the agent employs a model that represents a conceptual structure. This may include the function of each aspect of a given situation as well as the effect of each action on the status of the device.

Predicates permit the artifact to infer what the operation is and what its action does in terms that are meaningful to its mission. This is communicated to the end user by means of a graphical interface.

As the examples in this book help document, by acting as an intelligent personal assistant, the agent supports a qualitatively different kind of human-machine interface than those so far known. The user can make a request, and the agent searches the database, makes inferences, and uses knowledge to determine how to satisfy the request. A knowledge artifact of this type is able to:

■ Tolerate ambiguity in its environment

■ Recover from omissions and errors in human requests

■ Deal with uncertainty in database information when confronted with *soft data*

Down to the level of nuts and bolts, agents can handle goals specified in an expressive logic subset, such as conjunction, disjunction, and negation. They can also analyze conditions inherent in a data stream. To construct a goal-oriented artifact, researchers usually instruct the knowledge robot to take a logical expression describing the user's goal as input.

Unlike standard computer programs that are committed to a rigid control flow, determined a priori by a programmer, the agent automatically synthesizes and executes plans to achieve its goals. It also operates autonomously, which in itself requires intelligence. These short sentences give in a nutshell many of the concepts underpinning the development and use of agents. In Chap. 13 we will see how these concepts integrate within a business architecture.

CHAPTER 13

A Business Architecture for Agents and Multiagents

It is not possible to build a long-term systems structure whether it is a city, a business operation, or a sales network without some master blueprint. Neither can we develop a long-term strategy for using agents without a blueprint for defining the evolution in implementation, the infrastructure, and the supported facilities. The definition of an architecture places emphasis on *structure*, and also on *rules* and on a *methodology*. An architecture not only ties a system together but also sets the pattern of how its individual components fit.

The architectural blueprint helps to set the longer-term technological perspective that underpins system functioning. It provides a common approach for the selection of hardware, operating systems, other basic software, and lower-level enabling functions. This:

- Eases the burden of application development
- Allows for coordination regarding interactive component parts

Common architectural characteristics permit components and subsystems to be purchased off the shelf or built by ourselves and by third parties according to specifications. It also makes it possible to identify and implement common utilities more easily.

In the context of the use of agents, a systems architecture is a *business architecture* that defines not only underlying issues but also current and future applications capabilities. The objective of a business architecture is to provide a master plan, just as that of a data architecture is to make data understandable, shareable, and secure.

The existence of a valid business architecture significantly impacts the development of new applications, and at the same time it provides the ability to rationalize existing application systems and their modules. This statement is true from servers to clients or, more generally, any computer on the network with a registered address:

- Information requirements are better defined within a business model.
- Interactive databases and other resources are more easily developed, from data capture to online access.
- A more credible assurance is given that technology is able to serve the business goals.

Modern architectural solutions aim to assure that both *interrelated* and *distinct* problems can be answered interactively by ad hoc interconnection of all types of computers and of software modules. The aim is one of providing a cross-network, any-to-any connectivity, capable of serving the end user.

These, it may be argued, are not new functions. We have known them since the beginning of information technology; however, we have not executed them in an appropriate manner. Now, with proactive agents, our target is to bring sophisticated systems functionality onto every executive and professional desk.

The Contribution of Agents to a Business Architecture

The chapter introduction briefly made reference to the fact that what has been so often called a "systems architecture" or an "application architecture" is essentially a *business architecture*. This is not just a new label for old functions, but a major change defining the goals to be met by:

- Architectural design rules
- The methodology to be adopted
- The infrastructure characteristics

New concepts derive from the simple observation that business considerations, rather than simply technical issues, hold the high ground. This recasts the objectives. For instance, rather than aiming at computers replacing humans, we now target the use of computers in augmenting and improving human decision-making processes. As the preceding 11 chapters of this book have explained:

- Agents and other sophisticated software artifacts would *focus* on detail and *amplify* information rather than substitute humans in their jobs.
- The new concept is to address people already possessing *expertise* and sharpen their skills, making them more effective and more productive in their work.

Agent technology can augment the capabilities of human experts to cover larger domains: developing and examining more alternatives, studying business opportunities in greater depth, executing transactions faster, and looking more rigorously at alternative plans. For instance, having applied intelligent diagnostics, the agent can then flag for its master all instances that either are trivial and can be left to computer routines or are special and require human attention for their handling.

The use of proactive agents is no free lunch. The architecture supporting them requires a concept, high-level protocols, distributed dictionary facilities, studies on delays and response time as seen by the end user, network control center software, and obviously network administration.

An agent-oriented architecture must be able to guide the proactive knowledge artifacts in what to do, when to do it, and how to do it, as

Figure 13-1
The nearly $2 trillion
(est.) communica-
tions, computers,
and software market
in 1997.

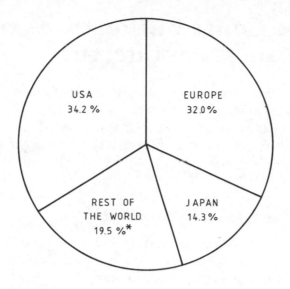

USA
34.2 %

EUROPE
32.0 %

REST OF
THE WORLD
19.5 %*

JAPAN
14.3 %

* OF WHICH A LITTLE LESS THAN A QUARTER IN
SOUTH KOREA, TAIWAN, HONG KONG AND SINGAPORE

well as in preparing how to do it, morphing if necessary,* and continuously updating the reference model to reflect changing user requirements.

The benefits to be derived from this knowledge-enriched proactive
approach to software are expected to double the estimated $2 trillion
communications and software market (of 1997) within 4 years—that is,
right after year 2000. Figure 13-1 shows how this market is distributed all
over the world. Because America was first to start with agents and moves
faster than other countries, market share may tilt in its favor.

As far as software development and usage is concerned, the difference
between legacy concepts and this new competitive environment is an
increasingly sophisticated level of functionality.

No matter where it is located in a business architecture, hardware is
dumb until it has been programmed. Programs are the expression of
how the computer should perform different tasks. It has always been
that way, but now the commanding metaphor has changed. Software
embodies knowledge of how to do various things. Therefore, the more
knowledge it contains, the better it is for the user.

---

*See also Chaps. 4 and 11.

Not only are the new, agent-oriented concepts quite different from those that characterized a legacy-type systems architecture, but also they represent the modern way of capitalizing on technology. Therefore, they provide the means for improving *return* on technology investments as well as for approaching issues characterized by increasing *complexity*, whether this is:

- Conceptual
- Descriptive
- Computational

An algorithm may be complex in terms of its expression, but it may execute very quickly. In this case, its descriptive complexity is high, but its computational complexity is low. By contrast, the need for parallel processing evolved because of problems with high computational complexity.

The Number 1 reason that business architectures increasingly require assistance from knowledge artifacts is the increasing conceptual complexity of the problems they are addressing. This is crossdisciplinary, and there exist interesting analogies between complexity issues from science and finance.

In banking, we are increasingly implementing interactive computational finance because it provides significant competitive advantages, raising the entry price of competition. Both in technology and in finance, it is becoming more and more apparent that architectural solutions focused on business are replacing the systems- and tools-oriented approaches. From a business perspective, no company is immune to the massive changes in the current technology environment. This is amplified by the fact that deregulation, globalization, and shorter windows of opportunity have caused business models to shift.

Centralized, hierarchical, tightly coupled solutions no longer fit the current competitive market environment. Therefore, they must be dispersed or outright replaced by new fully distributed paradigms, assisted by agents.

Not only is the nature of application rapidly changing but software life cycles have also collapsed—even if backward-looking companies continue using 25-year-old programs. The tools to manage the new environment should reflect the disposable nature of new software. This is, in fact, one of the major contributions agents can make to the evolving business architecture. Another is the assistance they provide in systems integration, as has been discussed in Chaps. 10 and 11.

Dynamic Business Architectures and Applications on Demand

The preceding section has explained why as business conditions are changing, architectures are being forced to follow suit. Return on investment requires that communications, computers, and software models all serve and capitalize on strategic advantages. This is what leading-edge users do.

Much of the popularity of business process reengineering and of corporate-wide globalization comes from the benefits that have been obtained by tier 1 organizations. In a similar manner, what some years ago constituted far-out missions brought up the new concepts that characterize a modern business architecture. The Gartner Group calls one of its models *Networked Dynamic Functionality* (NDF). The underlying idea is that there is no reason the location of where the code resides must be tied to the location of where the code will be executed. This is an assumption that prevailed until recently, an outgrowth of the (wrong) supposition that computers stay put.

If computers stay put, *then* they can run only code that is locally developed and resident on drum or disk. This is the concept of the 1950s. At that time, we did not have high-bandwidth networks and object-oriented software. By contrast, today we appreciate that regardless of the number of servers or clients involved in an application:

- Code can be stored at any node, at any location, by any authorized party.
- Agents are mobile and fluid, serving any master to do a better job.

Agents can propagate the code to the machines where it is required on an *as-needed* basis while the application runs. In this way, a system's functionality can also change in response to end-user requirements—and it does so in a dynamic manner. This concept underpins what is known as *applications on demand*.

A basic NDF premise is that until an application is run, the local system's code need not be resident. It will be imported as needed online. Hence, the set of things a client can do must not be determined by the user a priori as long as:

- The processing environment is fluid and dynamic.
- It changes in response to user and application needs.
- It is supported by real-time knowledge artifacts.

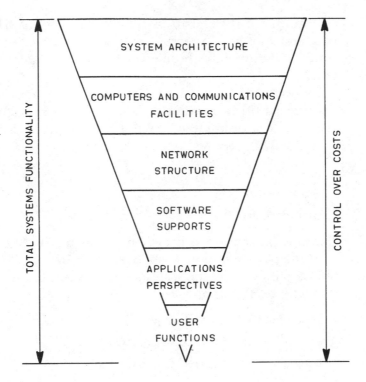

Figure 13-2
An inverted pyramid: The infrastructure as the system architecture and the visible part as the user functions.

One way of looking at the infrastructure support provided by the dynamic business architecture is through the inverted pyramid in Fig. 13-2: Like in an iceberg, in terms of system missions and cost-effectiveness, the visible part, end-user functions, is only $\frac{1}{7}$ the total mass. As a rule, the more sophisticated the total structure is, the greater the return on investment we can obtain. Agents can play a vital role at each one of the layers, both in a functional and in an optimization sense.

There are prerequisites for such solutions whose materialization presupposes intelligent systems. The described functionality of applications on demand is highly dependent on knowledge engineering, and it can be implemented only through:

■ Intelligent networks

■ Very sophisticated software

A user, for instance, may be served by an agent programmed to locate certain business references. On the Internet or in an intranet environment, the agent will use the Web, look for the information being asked for, and bring it back to its master. Or it may access private servers located throughout the global, distributed databases of the corporation. We have also spoken of special agents, the *communication facilitators.* Their function is crucial to a business architecture. It is also the object of computing.

For each server, the agent must make a connection to that remote resource, essentially acting as a mobile small personal computer. In Chap. 1 we saw the example of Alan Turing's *eins* as a precursor to this approach. The agent will

- Replicate itself
- Travel around, then
- turn back and report

The new programming paradigms promoted by KQML,* Java, ActiveX, and other agent-oriented languages can be expressed in one simple phrase: online servers of *applications on demand.* In Java jargon, executable content is referred to as *applets*

- Embedded within Web pages
- Downloaded on the network, and
- Interactively presented at the client site

In ActiveX jargon, executable content is known as *controls.* The concepts underpinning applets and controls are becoming popular because of the Internet, the externets, and the intranets. Much of their strength lies in the possibility of providing:

- Cross-platform solutions
- Multiagent implementations

Whether called "controls," "applets," or something else, these artifacts are distributed objects implemented through a mechanism that allows them to be invoked remotely. The goal is that of sustaining an integrated object environment.

Because applications on demand are based on objects, some vendors try to be compliant with Boston-based Object Management Group (OMG) standards describing *Object Request Broker* (ORB) interoperability. Java's JOE is an ORB.

Notice that interoperability is a basic characteristic of any business architecture. In OMG jargon, this is known as the *Common Object Request*

---

*See Chap. 4.

Broker Architecture (CORBA). But OMG's ORB standards are weak. Also, they currently lack testing and certification processes, which, no doubt, will be produced eventually.

What has just been stated is not a critique but the facts. It is important to make the reader aware that there presently exists a rather fragmented CORBA concept and market. As this situation will be slowly improved, applications on demand will become commonplace. Today, they are featured only by tier 1 organizations that develop their own sophisticated software and architectural solutions.

The Drive for an Order-of-Magnitude Improvement in Management Information

Corporations are increasingly storing internal documents and other data in Web format. This allows their employees to call them up using Web browser programs that run on any type of desktop machine. Another trend is to move away from massive application programs to small and simpler software to be created by languages such as Java that can be transferred over corporate networks to any type of computer. The goal is to:

- Simplify programming
- Enable intranets to handle a broader array of tasks

Instead of simply calling up and reading existing documents, a new generation of software artifacts is expected to let workers in separate offices edit documents, keep track of changes, and flash exceptions, relying on Internet-style technology that makes it easier to find or share information and to do so more effectively than ever before.

The simultaneous growth in the number of users and in advanced applications stretches the Internet (and the intranets) beyond original design specifications. Therefore, either the system must be strengthened through knowledge engineering, or the business model will become increasingly fragile.

A reason that the Internet and the intranets are extending rapidly into the corporate world is the growing awareness of nondependability of legacy approaches. As Fig. 13-3 suggests, the big market in Web server software is in the intranets—and the growth is exponential, not linear.

Figure 13-3
The market for web
server software in the
intranets.

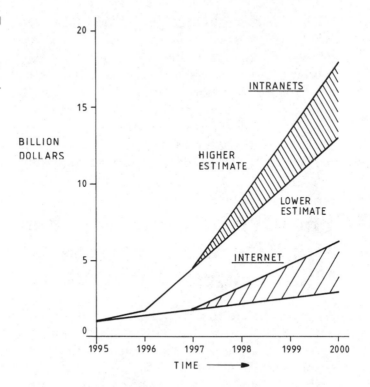

Trying to project in which domains will be the most pronounced growth in the Internet-intranets markets is tantamount to sticking out one's neck. This being said, assuming the risk that I may be awfully wrong in the projection, in Table 13-1 I show the best estimates on market growth that I have been able to obtain in my research. The market for intranets and extranets, therefore, for private networks, is much larger than that for the Internet.

The reason why intranets and interactive intelligent artifacts are becoming so popular in connection to modern business architectures is the deepening dissatisfaction with traditional *management information systems* (MISs) and *executive information systems* (EISs). As revealed by the research on information quality conducted quite recently by a known financial institution:

- Only 15.5 percent of management information used in the bank is computer based.

- In contrast, the level of user satisfaction with information resources is 67 percent for *non*-computer based and 48 percent for computer based.

This same inhouse research effort has brought into perspective the rea-

TABLE 13-1

A Projected
Change in the
Profile of
Internet/Intranets
Income Services*

	Percent of Market	
	1996	**2000—2002 (Estimated)**
Online services for Internet/ intranet access	85%	25%
Dial-up software for Internet access	11%	3%
Value differentiation channels for the Internet (broadband)	0%	25%
For-fee Web sites	0%	25%
Shopping transactions	1%	10%
Advertising on Web sites	3%	12%

*1996 revenues stand at an estimated $2.3 to $2.5 billion. In the 2000 to 2002 time frame, they will grow between $10 and $20 billion.

sons that managers are still turned off by computers. The four main reasons for dissatisfaction with computer information were found to be:

- Delays (30 percent in Number 1 position)
- Awkward presentation formats (26 percent)
- Different types of errors (24 percent)
- High billing costs (20 percent)

Long delays are due to the batch processing component still prevailing in most shops which, to the disgrace of many computer operations, is so difficult to change. Awkward formats are the result of incompatible platforms, different design teams, and parochial solutions.

Some applications have up to five versions running on different hardware and software. Bad as this may be, it is not the worst that can be found in legacy computer shops. A snapshot of worse than that is shown in Table 13-2, based on startling statistics reported by *Information and Software Technology* of London.*

The facts that "new" software usability is so low but costs are very high combine to give a dreadful image. It's information technology at its worst. Such statistics would have been ludicrous if it were not for the

*Vol. 37, no. 11, 1995.

TABLE 13-2

The Tragic State of Current Software Delivery and Usage

Software delivered but never used	47%
Software paid for but never delivered	29%
Subtotal of money down the drain	76%
Software used after extensive rework	19%
Software usable after some changes	3%
Software used as delivered	2%

Source: Reported in *Information and Software Technology,* vol. 37, no. 11, 1995.

fact that they damage the competitiveness of the enterprise. Reinventing old "electronic data processing" (EDP, for those who are nostalgic) does not provide a competitive edge. It only kills opportunities.

But getting out from under is not easy because this is a cultural challenge above all. We have to drop the habit of king-size IT projects and fat budgets, like those shown in Table 13-3. This is where KQML, Telescript, and Java can be of help, as Chap. 4 demonstrated.

Let me enrich the evidence presented in Table 13-3 with this thought. Some computer experts told me that though they may not disagree with the statistics, they wonder what level of functionality was derived from the dollars invested in these huge and slow-moving software projects. As an answer I would say: "Too little, too late."

My golden rule in software is no different than that of Admiral Chester W. Nimitz. In World War II, after the naval battle of the Coral Seas, two badly damaged American carriers made it to Hawaii. The Navy

TABLE 13-3

Project Sizes and Associated Fat Budgets as Reported in a Late 1995 Survey*

	Projects		
	Small	**Average**	**Large**
Days needed to complete the project	107	355	876
			(4 years)
Average people involved	2	6	21
Total labor-days invested	214	2.130	18.396
Cost of the project (in $1000s)	54	620	4.800—
			4.8200

*Reported in *Information and Software Technology,* vol. 37, no. 11, 1995.

engineers said that they needed *3 months* for repairs. Admiral Nimitz gave them *3 days* to do the job—and they met the challenge.

■ By decyphering Tokyo's messages, Washington, and therefore the commander in chief of the Pacific Fleet, knew that a huge armada was heading to Hawaii.

■ Nimitz also appreciated that with just the one remaining aircraft carrier, the forthcoming Battle of Midway could not be won. If restored to operational condition, the two damaged carriers could make the difference between victory and defeat.

Today, many, if not most, chief information officers (CIOs) also know that rapid development and deployment of competitive software can make the difference between profits and losses. But either they lack the tools and the methods to work fast, or they don't have the guts to face those colleagues and employees who want to work slowly. Hence the ridiculous results shown in Table 13-3.

Another systems requirement in connection to modern, more efficient solutions is to improve bandwidth for processing, databasing, and communications. As applications on demand show their weight, they impact very heavily on communications bandwidth. Any business architecture worth its salt should account for this fact.

Many experts now suggest that to alleviate network congestion problems, the Internet should implement *multicast* and *caching*. Also, telecoms should be given the chance to launch premium-rate, real-time services on the Internet to unleash additional bandwidth.

Solutions should span from local area networks (LANs) to wide area networks (WANs). Already some telephone companies in the United States and Europe are quietly rolling out an Internet infrastructure based on emerging standards such as the:

■ Realtime Transfer Protocol (RTP)

■ Resource Reservation Protocol (RRP)

Unlike TCP/IP, which handles point-to-point traffic, multicast handles one-to-many communications. Its advent in the business scene currently occupies a subset of the Internet called the *Multicast Backbone* (Mbone).

Mbone is a virtual network on top of portions of the Internet's physical backbone in the form of powerful workstations that send and receive high-speed video and audio data. Current statistics show that Mbone-compliant nodes are doubling every 7 months, which is faster than the overall growth of the Internet.

Using Agents to Solve the Year 2000 Problem

From financial analysis to auditing, many companies assign experts to perform coarse studies of data, while this work can be accomplished much more effectively through expert systems. In a properly designed and implemented business architecture, *information empowerment* will be done with:

- Agents operating stand-alone
- Fiats of agents (multiagents) cooperating with one another

Solutions along these lines can provide powerful business intelligence systems able to interpret statistics, financial time series, and historical data as well as to spot trends, unearth patterns, and measure performance against goals through plan-actual comparisons.

Agents will help to identify variances, assist in business planning activities, and allocate resources quickly and in a dynamic manner. They will also enable the organization to better adapt to unpredictable events. Agents can also address situations arising from negligence or the inability to foresee challenges still on the distant horizon, and they can do something about them. An example of an impending situation is the Year 2000 Problem, which must be solved within a short time frame either through brute force or by means of knowledge artifacts. An imaginative use of agents is by far the best approach—whether examined from the viewpoint of timetables, costs, or the able use of human resources.

The Year 2000 Problem is a major one affecting all IT applications, in any company, anywhere in the world. At its roots is the fact that virtually no software application accounts for the date change at the turn of the century. Most programs in use today are old-concept, legacy-type software that identifies the year by 2 digits—showing neither century nor millennium.

This problem comes from the punched-card era, where data processing had to be economical in terms of data entry and storage. However, 35 years down the line this shortsighted 2-digit policy creates a major problem because it is necessary to change:

- The program instructions
- The access to the database
- The database itself

The 2-digit year format has been a de facto standard since programming began, but it greatly upsets computer applications as the year 2000 approaches. In fact, current statistics indicate that it is putting some 90 percent of applications at risk of failure because they will not be able to demonstrate *compliance* to legal calendaring prerequisites.

There is a dual challenge. One is legal compliance. In a society that is increasingly oriented toward legal action, the courts are crammed with cases, and even out-of-court settlements can be very expensive. Just look at the cases of Gibson Greetings and Procter and Gamble against Bankers Trust, because of losses in derivative financial instruments.

The other challenge is algorithmic. As the algorithms fail, bank interest will be miscalculated, derivatives risk may go unnoticed, shipments will be out of date, even drug doses may be erroneous—as computer programs generate the wrong answers. In short, the guidance system will fail, which will feed into legal risk.

According to the Office of Management and Budget, the Federal government will have to spend at least $2.3 billion to reprogram its computers. But computer industry specialits dispute this figure. The Gartner Group, a Connecticut consulting firm, estimated last year that it would cost the federal government about $30 billion to fix the Y2000 problem.*

For its part, the U.S. Congress has accused some government agencies of neglecting the matter. Some Republican congressional leaders criticized the financial projections, released on Thursday February 6, 1997 by OMB, as way too low based on:

- An incomplete survey
- Inaccurate estimates of the cost of testing reprogrammed machines

They also contended that some Federal agencies had underestimated costs because the White House had not allotted them funds to fix the glitch and they did not want to trim other programs to pay for it.

Based on recent estimates on the state of the art in terms of Y2000 compliance, Table 13-4 presents some interesting statistics. These are based on inventories of 10 million lines of code, depending on the organization which contributed them. In this sample, roughly 65 percent of applications were on client server, and a little less than 50 percent was packages. Notice the significant advantage client server applications have on mainframes in terms of Y2000 compliance.

---

*International Herald Tribune, February 8/9, 1997.

TABLE 13-4

Inventory of Applications Regarding the Year 2000 Problem
(Average Percent Figures Based on a Research Sample)

	Mainframes	Client servers
In-house developments		
Compliant	33%	73%
Non-compliant	58%	7%
To be eliminated	9%	20%
Bought Software		
Compliant	0%	85%
Non-compliant	80%	7%
To be eliminated	20%	8%

In the private sector, many applications development shops at user organizations, software producers, and hardware vendors are actively engaged in year 2000 projects, or at least in project planning. These organizations say that they face a key decision for compliance purposes in connection to choosing between two alternatives:

1. *Sunset* the legacy applications that are usually on mainframes and replace them with vendor packages on client-servers that have 4-digit year identification.

Or, alternatively, restructure the databases, consider both centralized and distributed information elements as candidates for conversion, edit the programs, and, most importantly, retrain the systems personnel and change tools. In other terms:

2. Engage in *long and costly* software changes to make legacy programs compliant—but also make major changes in the files so that the corrected programs can work satisfactorily.

Year 2000 compliance will require that all applications and data be analyzed, modified, and tested. Testing, in fact, accounts for more than half the compliance effort, and it must be performed starting with the year of modification, and extending through 2001 and other years as relevant to the application. This is not a job that could or should be done through brute force. Nobody is really sure about the total cost for fixing the Year 2000 Problem—but in America alone, for all companies these costs are thought to fall between $300 and $600 billion.

The reason that so much money will be spent on fixing a problem which should not have been present in the first place is that the absence of corrections that permit distinguishing between dates such as 20*XX* or 19*XX* has even greater risks and costs.

- The risks are associated with the scope and uncertainty of addressing complex, badly documented legacy software—and the greater calamity of doing nothing about it.

- The costs are those of business damages due to the impact of the year 2000 on bills, accounts receivable, accounts payable, and business decisions on time horizons.

Time horizons include both forward and reverse directions in understanding business functions such as loans and investments and their relationship to the market environment. Both in the general accounting practice and in management reports, the fractured time horizons can have severe consequences.

For these reasons, my choice is to sunset the legacy applications. This alternative, however, is not as simple as it sounds, particularly because of the backward culture of the mainframers and the slow, ineffective way in which they work. A strategy that uses both alternatives Number 1 and Number 2 is inevitable, and for what is retained of Number 2—even if temporarily—I advise the use of enabling agents.

The Year 2000 Problem Exacerbated by the EMU Deadline

Knowledge engineering solutions, and most particularly interactive agents, can be instrumental in solving not only the year 2000 problems but also those resulting from another major event that falls in the same time frame. This is the chaos that may result because of the introduction of the European Monetary Unit (EMU) projected for 1999.

Practically all American companies operating in Europe, and many of those who don't but export to Europe, face the same challenges with the EMU as European companies do. IBM says that there will be a severe shortage of skills to cope with the transition to the single currency because it coincides with the computing overhauls needed to cope with the end of the century.* So important may be the aftermaths of these

---

Financial Times, July 18, 1996.

dual IT problems that a growing number of cognizant people argue there is a compelling case for delaying the EMU. Other experts, however, reject such gloomy conclusions, suspecting that computer vendors are simply seeking business.

Though they seem contradictory, both of these lines of thinking are right. A recent survey by the International Data Corporation (IDC) shows that only half the banks in Europe have an information technology strategy for EMU, and a mere 15 percent have allocated money to deal with the problem. This spells trouble.

- Over a 3-year period (1999-2002) conversion rates of national currencies will use 6 significant digits.

This is a concept alien to most merchants whether in America or in Europe, except in Italy where there are about 1700 lire to the dollar. The careful reader will appreciate the contribution Boelter's agents can do on this issue—along the lines of reference discussed in Chap. 9.

- The banking system of the euro countries will as well have to cope with the substitution of 12 billion coins.

The countries of the European Union are unevenly prepared for the tasks described by the above two bullets—which is another form of country risk involving many unpleasant surprises.

In a way, the EMU software conversion problem has been exacerbated because many companies are delaying their preparations for the single currency until the political climate becomes clearer. But the truth of the matter is that starting projects in software conversion 6 months or so before the changeover means that companies will not be able to meet the real deadline. Apart from the costs and delays because of software changes, the European Monetary Union will require banks to make huge investments in technology. They will also bear heavy costs of retraining staff and reprinting product literature.

Estimates filtering through the European Banking Federation in Brussels suggest that European banks could need to pay over 2 percent of their annual operating costs for 3 years to make the necessary changes in procedures and human capital. The introduction of the Euro is likely to open another front in the ongoing banking revolution. A single currency will make it easier for banks to cross borders to sell products such as loans, mutual funds, and insurance to retail customers. It will also make it easier for big corporate clients to shop around the multinational banking industry.

Until now, banks have had a strong franchise in their domestic markets. But with EMU and the introduction of the Euro, even the bigger national banks will have to face international competition without being able to hide behind national protective measures.

The year 2000 and EMU crises are good examples of where the lack of a knowledge-enriched business architecture may lead. Even if, as some major European banks think, confined strictly to itself, the change of software to cope with EMU will be relatively manageable, the process will be:

- Time-consuming
- Very expensive

This has interesting implications because many bankers and corporate finance directors sometimes argue that the reason they don't actively support a business architecture is its cost. What about the alternatives? Barclays Bank and Deutsche Bank *each* calculate the cost of the EMU conversion at about $320 million.* Taken on a global basis in Europe alone, this means costs of about $10 billion, or more, for the banking industry as a whole. Such an expenditure is huge, and this is only a tentative estimate because Europe's software expertise will be highly stretched over the next few years, and costs may boom.

Some computer vendors, IBM among them, hope to tackle the skills problem by sending work to India. But most knowledgeable people believe that it is the *new* information technology breakthroughs that could solve the EMU software problem. Agents are an example of this new technology.

We cannot hope for the best, by doing nothing truly significant in solving the two aforementioned urgent IT challenges: EMU and the year 2000. Currently few applications development and maintenance teams at:

- User organizations
- Software vendors
- Hardware manufacturers

have reached the point in their work scheduling that they set system clocks to simulate completion dates.† They also need simulation to test

---

*See also the section on more generic cost estimates for software conversion later in this chapter.

†Though many companies attempt brute force solutions through Cobol code and close down architectural groups, assigning their people to bodyshop work on the Year 2000 Problems.

code on compliance, flush out possible shortcomings, and evaluate the aftermaths of failing to reach deadlines.

For instance, in what concerns year 2000 problems, until very recently even releases of operating systems could not be initialized with dates past December 31, 1999. All this speaks volumes about preparedness by vendors and user organizations. While a rigorous business architecture and the use of agents will not make miracles, they will provide a solid basis for managing change. Without it, even those organizations that do their homework will find out the hard way how many surprises are still in store for them.

In connection to the Year 2000 Problem, for instance, because most authorization codes for system management, as well as several application products, use a date-base approach, the programs will not function if they detect a date that is past the current term of the maintenance contract. This will be difficult to bypass because, typically, software contracts do not include time frames past the year 2000.

One school of thought says that by supporting an authorization code that spans the year 2000, vendors may be forgoing protection they seek under an authorization code. From their viewpoint, however, users must re-create system dates past the year 2000 to adequately test compliance in calendaring. Similar arguments can be made in terms of EMU currency conversion codes—the use of intelligent artifacts being a more sensible approach than brute force in both cases.

The Ability of a Business Architecture and Its Knowledge Artifacts to Help in the Coming Software Crisis

While the reasons for a software crisis may be many, and the majority are specific to a user organization, two of the problems are more urgent than the others and should attract management's attention. Year 2000 and EMU are universal enough to constitute a good basis for proposing a meaningful business architecture and the use of agents.

Taken from a modern, flexible business architecture developed for a banking environment, Fig. 13-4 presents an object-oriented tree structure for relationship management. Notice that each of the 10 functional boxes in the block diagram is an object that finds itself in another ephemeral tree structure, as the application requires. While the Year 2000

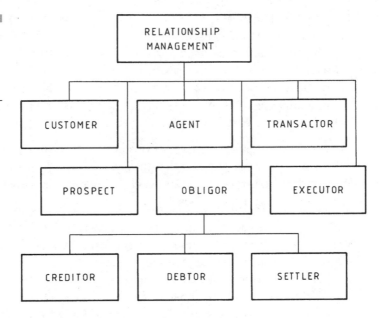

Figure 13-4
A tree structure regarding customer relationships and associated instances.

Problem and EMU will affect all boxes in the tree structure, the greater impact will be on those featured at the bottom row. Hence, a focal point in *agent* functionality should be to handle the problems connected to creditor, debtor, and settler. Had this modular design prevailed in software development, we would not be talking today of massive changes in programming libraries and databases.

I bring this contrast between an architectured modular design and the usually monolithic programming approaches to light because it reflects much of the difference in business goals between well-managed and poorly managed user organizations and vendors. This example is also helpful in defining the mission to be given to agents and multiagents in addressing the Year 2000 Problem.

1. One fiat of agents will look into the problem from the user's perspective, focusing on *compliance* and accounting for the limitations that exist for contractual reasons.

These agents should try to correct discrepancies, something that to my judgment—based on programs for the automatic conversion of Swift messages to a universal format*—would probably have an 80 percent hit

---

*Such projects were widely undertaken among tier 1 banks in the mid-1980s and were done through expert systems.

level. For the other 20 percent the agent would communicate with a human expert passing messages.

It is precisely this need for interactive exchange of queries, views, and answers that makes the proposed agent method more advisable with online systems than with batch systems. Companies with large batch programs are stuck with them. They should not have had them in their library in the first place, and now there is precious little they can do.

2. Another fiat of agents will protect the vendor's viewpoint: flashing out product trials that have passed the specific time limit or other unauthorized reuse such as copying or violating maintenance contract clauses.

Both the first and second references to the new families of agents will assist in significantly increasing the market addressed by software vendors. They also will legitimize the use of agents in organizations that today have not even heard of them.

As an example about what we are talking about in terms of market potential, in America and in Europe today about one out of every five companies is engaged in Year 2000 Problem solution and thinks that it would have brought it under control by the end of 1997. The percent of companies addressing the EMU problem is lower, but it is growing. It is estimated that by mid-1999 about 50 percent of all organizations would have solved the two problems that we are discussing. The other 50 percent will be in deep trouble, without the cultural change necessary to use high technology.

Agents specifically designed to address these problems can be of assistance to everybody: the top-tier organizations, those midrange, and the laggards. They can help, for instance, to certify for compliance with upstream and downstream interfaces, all standard and ad hoc queries, as well as calling or called parties. In principle:

■ All data field formats and calculations relying on dates and moneys passed through interfaces must be certified.

■ If filters are used to protect against noncompliant business partners, proof of the filters' effectiveness must be on hand.

A different way of making this statement is that within a flexible business architecture, agents can be effectively used to require, or even provide, proof of compliance from all processing partners to protect against transmission of faulty information, as well as erroneous calculations.

A similar statement can be made about databases in which fields must be proved to be EMU and year 2000 compliant, and/or proof must be supplied that all interfaces with the data have been modified to accept a noncompliant storage format but handle it correctly. Furthermore, system procedures and standards should be in place to assure that future maintenance accommodates noncompliant date and money fields.

As these examples help demonstrate, half-baked solutions to the EMU and year 2000 problems will not go far. The huge volume of database information and the need to randomly access stored elements will make brute force solutions:

- Costly
- Lengthy
- Ineffectual

Precisely for this reason some experts are inclined toward program manipulation—a so-called logic-only approach, eventually isolating the access points to the database. However, a logic-only approach poses higher long-term risks, which increase proportionally with the number of access points to the information elements—both at the central data warehouse and in the distributed database structure.

Furthermore, even a logic-only solution would feature very significant costs. A recent study by the Gartner Group advises that the bill for correction of the Year 2000 Problem will probably be at the level of $1.10 per line of Cobol code. For instance, a company that has 10 million lines of code in its library—which is not uncommon—will have to deal with about 100,000 function points. As a result, it will cost $11 million to correct the Year 2000 Problem at the programming end—and even this may prove to be an optimistic estimate.

Let's notice that the $1.10 per line of Cobol code is to be paid in one shot, and, as such, it is a remarkable expense. On the average the cost of maintaining the applications in the IT library stands at about $0.55 per year, or half the aforementioned conversion cost.

Besides this, there will be expenses associated to database massaging and redressal for normal processing and for ad hoc, off-platform data imports and exports. There will also be expenses associated with other data accesses, particularly those connected to end-user requirements that are in full evolution.

All this implies that a new architectural design model must be able to integrate all affected applications. It must also provide intelligent checkpoints because both program changes and data migration are high-risk tasks. This is a basic reason that the use of agents can be instrumental in solving the software conversion problems which lie ahead.

Languages, Primitives, and Facilitators for Intranet Solutions

Bad practices with database handling and the management of data processing programs resemble, in a way, third-world debt. Once relief from the crushing debt load, composed of interest and repayment, has been granted by the donors, the same donors are very quickly in selling the low-net-worth countries armaments and other hardware they don't need. This way they are piling up new debt.

In a similar manner, it can be argued, that once salient problems like the year 2000 and EMU are on their way to solution, bad practices in databases and in programming will creep in once more—to create a new emergency some years down the line. It is essentially a matter of the user organization against itself:

- A bad practice is that of building large programs that are slow to develop and monolithic, and therefore unmanageable.

- A good practice is the development of a flexible and rational business architecture with constraints able to assure that only small, intelligent, and adaptable modules are being built.

Because the distinguishing characteristic of an efficient business architecture is code movement between clients and servers on the network, agents can be of great assistance in executing tasks on the client's behalf. An example of a programming language for this type of support is Telescript, which we studied in Chap. 4. In principle, agents and executable content provide different types of functionality. But they also share the fact that the code moves from place to place for execution.

A common ground between agents and applications on demand* is interoperability and flexible functionality. Concomittant with this must be awareness of the need for small program modules in any environment, including flexibility in executing on different platforms and technologies.

Java fills the requirements for applications on demand because it creates platform-independent software solutions. A Web page can contain executable applets that can be run by any client computer with a Java-enabled browser.

---

*See the section "The Drive for an Order-of-Magnitude Improvement in Management Information" earlier in this chapter.

- This may be a Unix workstation, a Windows-based PC, or a Macintosh.

- They can all use Java applets to display real-time data feeds.

- The developers do not have to manually port applications to the various platforms employed by the user.

The other side of the coin, however, is that practically all of the new generation of Web programming languages are still incomplete. Among other shortcomings, for example, Java 1.0 lacks the features, language implementations, and mature developer tools needed to deliver a large array of business applications.

Also, the poor performance resulting from the interpretive nature of these languages may not be acceptable for mission-critical applications. It is as well wise to remember that when vendors talk of implementing Java on stripped-down PCs, the network computers (NCs), or network appliances while maintaining a fast response time, what they really mean is taking the users for a ride.*

Not everybody agrees with this statement, least of all the vendors. Sun Microsystems says that Just-in-Time (JIT) compilers improve Java's performance as compared to the interpreter. That is true, but:

- A benchmark by the Gartner Group, presented at Comdex Fall 1996, has documented that the Java interpreter reduces chip power to 3 percent of its rated cycles.

This is nothing really extraordinary. To my knowledge, the best interpreter ever written has been PRINT 1 by IBM back in the late 1950s— and it reduced machine power by an order of magnitude.

- A JIT compiler might do better than the interpreter by a factor of 4 to 5. This is not as good as it sounds because it still represents about 15 percent of machine cycles.

The Java chip is another story. When it is marketed and benchmarked, we will know what it can do. But even before that it is wise to note that the very idea of the Java chip destroys what might be the Number 1 argument in favor of applets: that they can run cross platform without any problem or any add-ons.

This is not written to discourage the use of Java, Telescript, or KQML but only to warn the reader that the most advanced tools, too, have their

---

*See also D. N. Chorafas, *Visual Programming Technology*, McGraw-Hill, New York, 1997.

shortcomings. In the case of KQML, for example, new performatives are needed for security tasks, negotiation prerogatives, and other developments demanded by the user community.

The role ActiveX, KQML, Telescript, and Java can play in connection to the information superhighway must be much better investigated and made to fit within the chosen business architecture. The same is true of applications such as digital libraries, concurrent engineering, and electronic commerce.

New performatives are necessary to meet the requirements of the expanding horizon of networking, for describing metadata to support diverse database architectures, and to eventually structure *agent-based software engineering* (ABSE) *solutions*. This will most likely involve performatives for the effective support of:

- Problem decomposition
- Declarative information distribution
- Routing agents making use of symbolic names for objects and declarations

Cognizant people in the field believe that a software wire, or information bus, will eventually evolve. It will be built on publish and subscribe primitives and the symbolic names assigned to an ephemeral hierarchy. The latter will rise over the more stable business architecture, then disappear when it is no longer needed.

While the concepts expressed in the preceding paragraphs may sound like a critique of the new, Web-based programming languages, in no way should they be interpreted as a call to look at the future through the rearview mirror. Today:

- Programming in Cobol or Fortran is an unpardonable failure.
- Writing batch processing programs is a criminal offense.

Rather than a return to the bad past practices and their huge inefficiencies, our challenge is that of developing and implementing knowledge-enriched *facilitators*. These are agents that traffic in metaknowledge about other agents. *Metaknowledge* is knowledge about knowledge. Facilitators provide services for:

- Resource discovery
- Database mining
- Network routing
- Job scheduling and other tasks

In the realm of an efficient business architecture, a communication facilitator is an agent that performs various network chores, such as forwarding messages to named services, maintaining a registry of service names, routing messages based on content, providing matchmaking between information clients and providers, and sustaining mediation and translation services at any time, anywhere.

Other facilitators enriching a business architecture may address problems with existing APIs. Nobody said that currently available APIs are complete implementations or that all their essential features are fully articulated—particularly those having to do with potential usage.

It is one of the worst-kept secrets that as we extend current technology toward newer and more complex applications, we uncover potential design flaws and gaps. These are really opportunities for the development of agents within an environment that is need driven and where solutions come both top down and bottom up.

The Crucial Role of Uniform Resource Locators in a Business Architecture*

The Uniform Resource Locator (URL) is a good example of architectural foundations. It supplies a standard nomenclature for addressing Internet services using World Wide Web browsers. Another way of looking at URLs is that they are pointers to agent information, supervisory processes (demons), and linguistic and other services. As an example, HTTP could be accessed at:

http://www.outer.net.

In a Bachus Normal Form (BNF) representation, URLs are written:

<scheme>:<scheme-specific-part>

The interpretation of the right hand of this algorithm depends on the left hand. Scheme names are characterized by a sequence of characters: lowercase letters a to z, +, ., −. Programs interpreting URLs tend to treat uppercase letters as lowercase letters of the alphabet.

---

*See also App. B, "Important Internet Addresses."

URLs involve a compact string representation for resources available through the Internet. Character-encoding sequences of the URL are an integral and necessary part of a signposting system that makes the Internet, and any intranet, accessible to end users whose sites are not enhanced through a Uniform Resource Name (URN) strategy.

The advent of a URL notation implies a standard syntax and the ability to access Internet hosts based on a URN. The strength of this solution is that while it represents an effort to uphold uniformity, it leaves open the possibility for:

- Enhancements
- Extensions

For instance, the Virtual Reality Modeling Language (VRML)[*] features a hyperlink that resembles a URL. This is a plus for interactivity, making networked graphics a rewarding experience. Through the selection of hyperlink objects, VRML browsers help in transporting users to other site(s) while scenes and images are constructed as they arrive.

URLs feature a generic syntax that constitutes a useful framework for enhancements to be provided at a later day, as well as for protocols other than those currently supported. The way this works is by featuring an abstract identification of the resource location. Thereafter, having located that resource, the system may perform a variety of operations on its facilities.

Examples of operations are add, delete, update, replace, and find attributes. The sequences of characters in different parts of a URL represent octets used in Internet protocols. Such octets comply with the ASCII code set.

Characters, however, may be unsafe for different reasons. A space character may disappear when URLs are typeset, transcribed, or subject to some sort of treatment by computer. Other reasons make characters such as #, ", <, >, and others unsafe. Therefore, all such characters must be encoded within a URL.

Some characters like =, ;, /, @, &, and ? may be reserved to be given a special meaning. In a number of cases, URLs can be used to locate resources that contain pointers or relative links to other resources. The BNF syntax definition maps existing standard and experimental protocols, like:

| file | Host-specific file names |
| ftp | File Transfer Protocol |

[*]D. N. Chorafas, *Visual Programming Technology*, McGraw-Hill, New York, 1996.

http	Hypertext Transfer Protocol
gopher	Gopher Protocol
mailto	E-mail address
news	USENET news (Net News Transfer Protocol)
telnet	Reference to interactive sessions
wais	Wide Area Information Search/Server

URLs that comprise the direct use of an IP-type protocol to a given host on the Internet or an intranet use a common syntax of the form:

//<user>:<password>@<host>:<port>/<url-path>

Though the syntax of the rest of the URL might be different, depending on the particular scheme being chosen, this uniformity is most important for real-time interactive implementation.

An example is the use of *common gateway interface* (CGI) to resolve URL addresses dynamically to locate different pages based on computation results. This permits different scenes to be built every time a page is interactively retrieved from servers. Because HTML documents and VRML documents are created on the fly, users are able to download the new scene on their browsers.

Given the popularity of URLs, a network user would be hard-pressed not to find Uniform Resource Locators to the Web sites of most major information providers. This has significant implications because instead of trying to establish individual connections between a lot of

- User communication packages
- Vendors' bulletin boards

support organizations assist users to find specific URL sites. A uniform method for resource location permits users to download files, send files directly to Internet e-mail addresses, and generally facilitate connectivity.

For this reason, URL services have been characterized as a *digital dial tone*, allowing users to reach almost any information source or other online user on the Internet. This approach works the way the telephone permits users to reach almost any person in the world.

As these points help illustrate from the perspective of a business architecture and the services it supports, URLs are quite important. They assist in site access and also in data conferencing and videoconferencing over the Web. They can also be instrumental in telepresence.

As Fig. 13-5 advises, *telepresence* not only involves meetings with people but also with agents presenting the outcome of database mining,

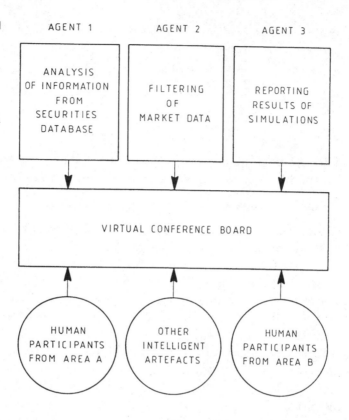

involved in activities initiated through message passing, or reporting research results. In this connection agent technology is vital in:

- Filtering information for relevance
- Establishing patterns and profiles
- Presenting applicable data sets
- Learning what a given user views and does not view

The digital dial tone is just as crucial as the ability to create platform-independent portable programming code, accelerating the move toward a global computing environment. URLs also prove to be instrumental in moving the Internet from being a relatively passive publishing medium into an interactive application deployment environment with a universal programming model that applies to both clients and servers—and it is characterized by code mobility.

Rethinking the Contribution of Agents in an Expanding Business Environment

Forty-five years ago, in 1953, addressing young students at Sherborne, his old school, Dr. Alan Turing said that people wrongly assume computers are just glorified calculating machines. "Not so," insisted Turing. "[While] it is true that computers are often used to do calculating because they can calculate very quickly, computer programs don't have to have anything to do with numbers...." And he added:

> I would go further. It is my view that a computer can perform any task that the human brain can carry out. Any task...."

"Any task" is not exactly what we can do today with current technology (hence, agents), not because of lack of want but because we don't have the tools and the experience to do so. But Alan Turing also spoke of learning programs and of chess-playing computer code, posing the question of whether or not we would credit such a machine with intelligence. The answer he gave to his own question is:

> I would say that we must. What I would very much like to do is to educate a computer, partly by direct training, partly by letting it find out things for itself....

This is something current technology permits us to do. It is quite significant that 45 years ago—at the very dawn of computing—Alan Turing felt sure that "by the year 2000 it will be considered perfectly correct to speak of an intelligent machine or to say that a computer is thinking...." He was almost right.

Being a practical man as well as a theorist, Dr. Turing tended to look for applications-oriented solutions. If he were living today, he would not have been prone to confuse, as so many people do, the fact that agents are artificial intelligence artifacts with the ability to emulate all, or even most, of the brain functions. The brain* is still one of the great unexplored frontiers of science. We don't know how to construct a better *human brain*, even a better rat brain. But we do know how to emulate a few of its functions and even improve on them.

---

*Any brain, not just the human brain, as many people think.

We know precious little about how a 3-pound mass of tissue works to coordinate not only the basic machinery of a living organism but also perception, memory, calculation, and learning—generally what constitutes natural intelligence. What we think we know is that the brain is composed by 10^{11} to 10^{12} neurons—or maybe 10^{18} elements if all cells of the body are counted as Dr. John von Neumann has suggested. 10^{11} to 10^{12}, incidentally, seems to be about the same number of stars in the Milky Way—which is another unknown entity to all of us.

From the little we know from the macroperspective of the cosmos and from the little we know from the microperspective of the brain, we try to construct an architectural solution that can serve our purposes in our daily work. In this simple sentence lies practically everything that this chapter presented to the reader.

How can we best explore the business environment in which we work? An agent called Personal Web Manager is of assistance when its user wants to venture on the Web. It runs out ahead and tests traffic conditions, routing to the user's favorite Web sites. Results are displayed in traffic-light fashion: red, yellow, or green.

This follow-me concept falls within the agent definition that we have studied since Chap. 1: Agents are proactive knowledge artifacts, job specific, and personalized. They reside on the user's workstation and/or the network nodes and are called into action. They are *not* brain substitutes. Within the domain of a business architecture, when activated through message passing, agents know the best way in which to serve their masters. Within specific, well-defined functions, the agents can do a good job.

Agents could even do a better job than humans. Quite often, humans are sloppy, particularly when under strain or in a hurry, or when they are distracted. Besides this, people are often afraid and concerned—or the opposite, they are overconfident. So far, agents don't have that sort of complex.

The confidence many people exhibit in static solutions is reminiscent of the certainty Germany had in its Enigma cryptographic code in World War II. Many people never learn. But agents can learn from examples given explicitly by the user. The evolving artifact of an instructable agent:

- Exhibits inference capability
- Is able to reason about goals

Let's recall what has been said in Chap. 1 because those lessons obviously remain valid in a business architecture. Agents are not generalized artifacts. Their power lies in achieving a high degree of *specialization.* They reside in a node and can be of great assistance to the user in:

- Addressing a problem
- Mining databases
- Routing messages and other agents
- Scheduling jobs
- Monitoring an experiment
- Playing a role in a business simulation

Also, they can be useful in the interactive visualization of results, in assisting in the construction of other agents, or in taking an active part in the implementation of virtual reality within an expanding horizon of business applications.* All these are real-life examples.

In all these cases, agents are new types of software characterized by proactive behavior, autonomous mobile action, knowhow, and intelligence. They are often visually programmed, small artifacts with an ability to enhance communications: agent to human and agent to agent. Typically they reside in networks and databases until they are awakened through message passing.

This concept is new, and it has a significant potential. As he demonstrated with the cracking of the Enigma, Alan Turing was a master in taking futuristic ideas seriously and in following them through to their logical if upsetting conclusions. This is what constitutes *true* intelligence. How are we otherwise to answer critical and unsettling questions satisfactorily?

---

*See D. N. Chorafas and H. Steinmann, *Virtual Reality—Practical Applications in Business and Industry,* Prentice-Hall, Englewood Cliffs, N.J., 1995.

APPENDIX A

GLOSSARY AND FUNCTIONAL ACRONYMS

ANSI American National Standards Institute

API Applications programming interface

APPC Advanced program-to-program communication

ARPA Advanced Research Projects Agency

ATM Asynchronous transfer mode

BER Bit error rate

BRep Boundary representations

CAD Computer-aided design

CAP Competitive access provider

CASE Computer-aided software engineering

CGI Common gateway interface

CORBA Common object request broker architecture

DBMS Database management system

DCOM Distributed Component Object Model (by Microsoft)

DDE Dynamic Data Exchange (by Microsoft)

DSP Digital signal processors

DSS Decision support system

EDI Electronic data interchange

ERep Editable representation

FDDI Fiber distributed data interface

5GL Fifth-generation language

4GL Fourth-generation language

FTP File Transfer Protocol

GUI   Graphical user interface

HDLC   High-level data link control
HTML   HyperText Markup Language
HTTP   HyperText Transport Protocol

IN   Intelligent network
I/O   Input/Output
IP   Internet Protocol
IPv6   Internet Protocol, version 6
ISO   International Standards Organization
ISP   Internet service provider

JDBC   Java database connectivity
JOE   Java objects everywhere
JPEC   Joint Photographic Expert Group

KB   Knowledge bank
Knowbots   Knowledge robots
KQML   Knowledge Query and Manipulation Language

LAN   Local area network

MAN   Metropolitan area network
MIPS   Millions of instructions per second
ML   Machine language
MPEG   Motion Picture Expert Group
MTBF   Mean time between failures
MTTR   Mean time to repair

NC   Network computer
NCSA   National Center for Supercomputing Applications
NDF   Networked dynamic functionality

NII National information infrastructure

NSF National Science Foundation

OCX OLE Controls Extension

ODBC Open database connectivity

ODBMS Object-oriented database management system

OLE Originally: object linking and embedding; now just a name

OLTP Online transaction processing

OMG Object Management Group

1 FIT One failure in 10^9 hours

ORB Object request broker

OS Operating system

OSI Open Systems Interconnection

OVAL Object View Agent Links

PBX Private branch exchange

PC Personal computer

PPP Point-to-Point Protocol

PSN Public switched network

QOS Quality of service

RDA Remote database access

RDBMS Relational database management system

RMI Remote method invocation (in JavaBeans specs)

RPC Remote procedure call

SCP Service control point

SLA Service-level agreement

TCP Transmission Control Protocol

TCP/IP Transmission Control Protocol/Internet Protocol

3D   Three dimensional

3GL   Third generation language

TQM   Total quality management

TTL   Time to live

2D   Two dimensional

URL   Uniform Resource Locator

URM   Usage reference model

VAN   Value-added network

VBX   Visual basic extension

VN   Virtual network

VOD   Video on demand

VRML   Virtual Reality Modeling Language

WAN   Wide area network

WWW   World Wide Web

APPENDIX B

IMPORTANT INTERNET ADDRESSES

This list is not intended to be complete, which would have been an impossible if not controversial task. Rather, it reflects just some of the more important Internet addresses—important, that is, in the author's judgment.

Uniform Resource Locators (URLs) use a common syntax that can be expressed in the Bachus Normal Form (BNF):

//<user>:<password>@<host>:<port>/<url-path>

An HTML service could be accessed at:

http///www.outer.net.

This is the home page of an Internet access provider.

Including email archives, a Web page on KQML is maintained at:

http://www.cs.umbc.edu/kqml/kqml95/

Listings of Java applets on the Web can be found at JARS:

http://www.jars.com

Here are some additional addresses for Java information:

http://ncc.hursley.ibm.com/javainfo

The preceding address is the IBM Center of Java Technology Development. Home pages of Java user groups include:

news:comp.lang.java: The Usenet Forum

http://www.java.de: The German Java User Group

http://www.sug.org/javasig.html

http://java.sun.com/faq2.html: The Frequently Asked Question Archive

The Online Book Store can be reached through:

http://marketplace.com/obs/top.html

Information servers for educational purposes can be found at:

www:http://www.cs.umbc.edu/kqml.html

ftp:ftp.cs.umbc.edu under pub/kqml

An up-to-date list for the National Computer Security Association is available at:

http://www.ncsa.com

Standard & Poor's Stock Reports Web site, with analyses and reports on 4600 U.S. equities along with headline summaries, is available at:

www.investools.com/cgi-bin/library/sprp.pl

The Commission des Operations de Bourse, a dual-language, French-English site with smart graphics, is accessible at:

www.cob.fr

For those who play the New York State lottery, a program that tracks lottery selections and e-mails if the numbers come up is:

www.lottotrax.com

Internet payment proposals can be accessed through the Internet Payments Roadmap at:

http://www.w3.org/pubs/www/payments/roadmap.html

BulletProof, one of few companies in the finance market using Java's functionality, has a WallStreetWeb address:

http://www.bulletproof.com/wallstreetweb

The U.S. Environmental Protection Agency outlines details of its Economy and the Environment program at:

www.e-pa.gov/docs/oppe/eaed/eedhmpg.html

Provided by Politics Now, a collaborative venture between the *Washington Post*, ABC News, and other U.S. media groups, the top 10 political sites are accessible at:

http://top10.imgis.com

INDEX

Y

Z

About the Author

Dimitris N. Chorafas is an internationally known independent consultant specializing in strategic planning and the design of information systems. He has advised many eminent clients throughout the world, including General Electric, Honeywell, Digital Equipment, the American Management Association, Nestle, the Union Bank of Switzerland, Von Tobel Bank, Commerzbank, Dresdner Bank, Bank of Scottland, Bank of Austria, First Austrian Bank, Credito Commerciale, Istituto Bancario Italiano, Banca Provinciale, Lombarda, Credit Mobiler de Monaco, Credit Agricole, and many more leading financial institutions. Dr. Chorafas is the author of 105 books, including books on management, finance, and computing topics. His seminars for banking, industrial, and government executives have been attended by over 6,000 professionals in 17 countries. A Fullbright Scholar, and graduate of the University of California, Los Angeles, Dr. Chorafas received his doctorate in mathematics and logic at the Sorbonne in Paris, France.